W0259648

MINING MEN

Mining Men

Britain's last kings of the coalface

DR EMILY P. WEBBER

Chatto & Windus

LONDON

3 5 7 9 10 8 6 4

Chatto & Windus, an imprint of Vintage, is part of the Penguin Random House group
Vintage, Penguin Random House UK, One Embassy Gardens,
8 Viaduct Gardens, London SW11 7BW

First published in the UK by Chatto & Windus in 2025

Copyright © Emily P. Webber 2025

Emily P. Webber has asserted her right to be identified as the author of this Work
in accordance with the Copyright, Designs and Patents Act 1988

Mining lamps drawn by Josh Roy, in memory of his grandfather,
Reginald Harry Burgess, who was a Bevin Boy.

No part of this book may be used or reproduced in any manner for the
purpose of training artificial intelligence technologies or systems. In accordance
with Article 4(3) of the DSM Directive 2019/790, Penguin Random House
expressly reserves this work from the text and data mining exception.

penguin.co.uk/vintage
global.penguinrandomhouse.co.uk

Typeset in 13.5 pt/16pt Garamond MT Std by Jouve (UK), Milton Keynes
Printed and bound in Great Britain by Clays Ltd, Elcograf S.p.A.

The authorised representative in the EEA is Penguin Random House Ireland,
Morrison Chambers, 32 Nassau Street, Dublin D02 YH68

A CIP catalogue record for this book is available from the British Library

ISBN 9781784745448

Penguin Random House is committed to a sustainable future for
our business, our readers and our planet. This book is made from
Forest Stewardship Council® certified paper.

For many hearts with coal are charred,
And few remember.

Wilfred Owen, 'Miners' (1918)

Contents

Acknowledgements

This book would not be possible without the generosity of the British mining community. I will forever be indebted to the men and women who have shared their stories, and to all those who opened their homes and lives to me. I only hope that I have done them justice.

Spending time at the National Union of Mineworkers (NUM) in Barnsley was a singular highlight of my research, and one which I will never forget. Paul Darlow has been incredibly gracious in sharing both his time and knowledge. Thanks also to staff and volunteers at the Aber Valley Heritage Museum, Aylesham Heritage Centre, Beamish Museum, the Big Pit National Coal Museum, the Bilsthorpe Heritage Museum, the Glamorgan Archives, the Kent Mining Museum, the Mining Art Gallery, The National Archives, the National Coal Mining Museum for England, the National Mining Museum Scotland, the Nottinghamshire Mining Museum, the Sheffield City Archives, the South Wales Miners' Library, the South Wales Miners Museum, the Woodhorn Museum, and the Working Class Movement Library.

I am very grateful to Bev Trounce, who first circulated my call for participants online, and to all those who answered my enquiries along the way: Alan Gascoyne of the Shirebrook Miners' Welfare; Ned Heywood, who told me how he made the Senghenydd memorial plaques; Graeme Hopper, who shared the story behind his sculpture in Shotton Colliery; Bernadette Hughes, who spoke to me about her work at Dream St Helens; Edith Jones Wake of the Thorne and

Moorends Colliery Monument Committee; Mike and Trish Mellor of Chase Arts for Public Spaces; Beryl Renton, who sent copies of her late husband Robert's book on the cage crash at Hatfield Main Colliery, and Kath Smith of Remembering the Past. The Reverend Canon Miranda Hayes kindly opened St Leonard's Church in Dinnington on her day off so I could see the mining memorial inside.

My heartfelt thanks to Kay Sutcliffe, who allowed me to reproduce her poem 'Coal Not Dole', and to Ed Pickford, who allowed me to use the lyrics to his song 'Ah Cud Hew'. I am grateful to Brian Morley and Barrie Ormsby, who permitted me to reproduce their artworks, and to Eric Eaton and Ann Donlan at the Nottinghamshire Mining Museum and Anne Sutherland at The Auckland Project for facilitating this. Emma Shankland of Durham Bannermakers graciously answered many queries and allowed me to use images of the Quarrington Hill Lodge banner. Thank you to Julian Harrop at the Beamish Museum and to Rebecca Hudson and Jill Clapham at the National Coal Mining Museum for allowing me to use images from their respective collections. Thank you to Fiona Matthewson and Art UK, to Graham at Out Of The Blue Artifacts.com and to Medway Urban Explorer, for allowing me to use their images also. Thank you to the staff at the Norfolk and Norwich Millennium Library who helped me source many books that were out of print.

My earlier PhD research was funded by the Arts and Humanities Research Council. During my studies, I benefitted from the expert supervision and guidance of Natalie Thomlinson at the University of Reading and Jon Lawrence at the University of Exeter. I am also grateful to my examiners Keith Gildart, Michael Roper and my convenor Matthew Worley for providing insightful comments on my thesis.

I am indebted to my incredible agent Kay Peddle, who shaped and championed my vision for the book and to Kaiya Shang, my wonderful editor at Chatto who believed in it. Thank you to the other members of the amazingly talented team at Chatto, particularly to Clara Farmer, Polly Dorner, Eoin Dunne, Susie Merry, Rosie Palmer, Binita Roy, Priya Roy and Rhiannon Roy.

I am lucky to have wonderful friends who have spent the past five years enthusiastically listening to me talk about my research and who have been my biggest cheerleaders on this journey, Kate Denereaz, Phil and Vicky Dyson, Jo Finon, Ellie Johnson, Jason and Alex Long, Louise Severinsen, and Laura de Souza. Finally, I would like to thank my family. My mother-in-law, Judy, who welcomed me into her family's history, and my father-in-law, Steve. My brother, Joe, who is one of the best historians I know, and my sister-in-law, Chloe. My mother, Lorna, who first encouraged me to write about where I came from, and whose support for me is unwavering. My father, Richard, who has been the best companion on our road trips around the coalfields – getting to spend so much time with you has been such a joy. My children, Rosie and Wilf, who have patiently accompanied me on countless visits to museums and memorials, and know more about coal mining than most of their peers. Lastly, the biggest thank you to my wonderful husband Tom, who is always in my corner. I hope that this book might be a small tribute to your namesake, David Thomas, who never returned home from his shift at the Universal Colliery in Senghenydd in 1913.

Preface

Have you ever met a coal miner? Chances are, if you were born in Britain after 1990, you are unlikely to have met any men still working in this capacity. Yet, just fifty years ago the British mining industry was a juggernaut, employing over 250,000 workers at over 250 mines, and recruitment campaigns offered young men a 'job for life' and 'money, lots of money and security'.[1] By the end of the twentieth century, coal's fiefdom as the main source of British energy had been eroded by North Sea oil and gas, though in the 1980s homeowners were still being sold the benefits of a 'real fire'.[2] Some may remember having their heart warmed by the television advert in which a bulldog, cat and mouse affectionately settle down together in the glow of a roaring fire. Fast forward three decades and the advert's soundtrack of 'Will You Love Me Tomorrow' seems more prescient than intended, while romantic winter scenes of glowing coals in the grate are little more than nostalgia.

Despite hailing from South Yorkshire, when I embarked on the research that informs this book, I possessed only a naïve understanding of miners and their communities, and little idea how I could make inroads into understanding their culture. Upon my first visit to the National Coal Mining Museum in Wakefield, I remember the laughter evinced when I asked if there were toilets underground. Similarly, I did not know what to expect when I stepped through the doors of the National Union of Mineworkers headquarters in Barnsley, a grand stone building topped with green Westmorland slate towers and turrets, which wraps the corner of the Victoria and Huddersfield Roads. Built by local architects Wade and Turner, when it first opened its doors in November 1874 it was praised as a handsome, cheerful and dignified place.[3] As well as offering men who had been sat on a lump of coal all week a better place in which to meet, it was hoped that it might signal a new era in the history of labour and raise the sights of future generations of mining men.[4]

On the day of my visit, the majesty of the building was somewhat overshadowed by the roadworks and bustling traffic outside. Other than the posters in the windows, there was little sign of life within. Fortunately, as I lingered on the steps leading up to the front doors, I was met by Paul, a former Woolley Colliery miner, who now works for the NUM, and who epitomised the spirit of generosity I would later encounter time and time again as I journeyed across the former coalfields.

Paul led me through the building's warren-like interior, and as we passed through the dark wooden doors into the hall at the heart of the building, I was dumbfounded. Sat above the entrance were effigies of two bare-chested miners, both wielding a pick in one hand, and in the other hand one held a train, the other a ship, these noble symbols of industry nothing more than children's toys in the muscular arms of these godlike men. A sky-blue barrel-vaulted ceiling stretched above, richly decorated with ornate plasterwork and gold detailing; like the heavens, it seemed intended to inspire a higher moral tone. It looked down upon rows of stout leather-studded wooden chairs, facing forwards, a sober but expectant audience. The stage at the end of the hall was empty but in place of a presenter lay a lump of shining black coal, mounted on a wooden plinth, into which two yellow flags had been wedged. As I came closer, I smiled as I read the message on one: 'Kellingley Colliery, The Last Deep Coal Mine, If The Lights Go Out Don't Blame Us.'

All along the walls there were brightly coloured banners, allegorical scenes and sombre portraits of the past looking to tomorrow. As I walked by, the words on each banner seemed to echo through the hushed hall, enlivening old battles and ideals: 'One Union For All'; 'United We Stand, Divided We Fall'; 'Comradeship, Fortitude, Courage'; 'Health, Welfare, Safety'; 'Eternal Vigilance Is The Price Of Liberty'; 'Labour Leads The Way To Prosperity'; 'From Darkness Into Light'; 'The Labourer Is Worthy Of His Reward'; 'It's Our Fight, It's Our Future'; 'We Must Heed The Lessons Of The Past To Build A Brighter Future'.

The morning sunshine streamed through the hall's leaded windows, which were punctuated with icons of the industry, their sills lined with artworks and commemorative plates for collieries long since closed. A glass cabinet near the doors housed smaller items, which were neatly if eccentrically arranged: a Bible in memory of the terrible explosion at the Oaks Colliery in 1866, what appeared to be a small rocket firework with a photograph of Margaret Thatcher affixed to its body, a miner's lamp, an old leather pit helmet, medals, badges, a snuff tin, mementos of brave deeds and lives long lost, an industrial reliquary. Upstairs in the eaves of the building, stepping around the buckets of rainwater, Paul showed me yellowing union records reaching back almost 200 years, whose survival was now threatened by the leaking roof.

Once an industry in which sons inherited a job along with their father's name, most remaining family lineages in mining were severed by the rapid pit closures at the end of the twentieth century. Yet, the more people I spoke to about my research into the late great British mining industry, the more connections I unearthed far outside of the former coalfields. Perhaps I should not have been surprised by this, given the fact that just a century ago it employed over a million workers, equivalent to around 10 per cent of the nation's male workforce.[5]

Around the family dinner table, I dug out stories closer to home. I learnt of my husband's great-great-grandfather David Thomas, a fifty-one-year-old miner, who died at the Universal Colliery, in the small mining community of Senghenydd, South Wales, on 14 October 1913. David was just one victim in an explosion that claimed the lives of 440 men and boys, including one rescuer, a mining disaster which to this day remains the worst in British history.

It took weeks to recover all the bodies. Some miners had been killed instantly, stooping to cut the coal, their tools lay beside them never to be lifted again, or kneeling as they chalked up their full tubs. Others who were spared the blast were found huddled together, overcome by carbon monoxide.[6] Fathers and sons faced death together, and the bodies of horses and their masters lay side by side in the wreckage. Many bodies were so badly burned or decomposed that victims could only be identified by their meagre personal effects: a pocket watch, a pair of new boots worn for the first time, a patch sewn onto a vest by a mother, a champagne cork in a tin water jack, given by a friend.[7] Several victims were buried known only to God.

One black and white photograph of the row of corrugated iron miners' huts in Senghenydd carried an accompanying caption that observed how there was 'a victim in every house'.[8] This did little to convey the depth of loss that occurred within individual families. One reporter, who

Film negative of a photograph by John Cornwell showing the scene at Universal Colliery, Senghenydd, following the disaster of 14 October 1913.

arrived four days after the explosion, wrote of being startled by the crowds keeping vigil: 'It is only then that a sense of the magnitude of the disaster comes to me. Each of those men, each of those women is looking toward the pitmouth with the last hope [. . .] for a brother, a husband, entombed in the mine.'[9] It was estimated that 900 people lost their breadwinners, including over 200 wives, whose husbands were dead or missing, and nearly 400 children belonging to them.[10] In the grey stone terraces of Commercial Street alone twenty men were missing from just eleven homes.

On my first visit to Senghenydd I took the steep Bwlch Carnygelli, driving slowly over a rumbling cattle grid and around errant sheep, ambling like dirty white clouds across the road. When I arrived at my destination, it was pouring with rain, a fitting backdrop to the small memorial and garden that were unveiled on the centenary of the disaster in 2013. On that day, the pit hooter sounded out across the valley once more, the same noise that alerted nearby villagers to the explosion a hundred years earlier. Adjacent is the bright new Nant Y Parc

Primary School, built on the site of the former Universal Colliery, whose cheerful logo remembers the black outline of the pit gear that once stood amidst the green hills.

Two bronze figures are frozen in time at the memorial's centre, a miner stoically leading his injured colleague forward, his lamp held aloft to light the way. On the low stone wall surrounding the pair are 440 ceramic tiles, arranged two-deep, each detailing a victim's name, age and address in neat black text, a record that they once had a home and a life nearby. Local primary school pupils helped to roll out the clay for each of these plaques before they were imprinted with the names of lost men and boys.

Tracing my fingers over the details of my husband's namesake, my eyes were drawn to the smaller wooden sculpture

Bronze statue by Les Johnson at the centre of the memorial in Senghenydd, Caerphilly, unveiled on 14 October 2013. In 2024 the memorial was formally recognised by the Welsh Government and designated the National Mining Disaster Memorial Garden of Wales.

at the rear of the garden, of a girl carrying her baby sister in the Welsh style, like a displaced Madonna and Child, waiting for news.[11] Later, in the small Aber Valley Heritage Museum, volunteers showed me David's name in the commemorative book of victims and provided us with a short summary of what he had left behind: a widow, Mary Ann, and five children: Sarah Ann (fifteen), Ceridwen (thirteen), Gwen (ten), David (seven) and Enid (five). For the loss of their husband and father, the family had been awarded £290 in compensation.

Over the next four years, I visited museums and archives, large and small, and sought out traces of the mining industry in communities across Britain. I became adept at finding markers from the more obvious ones – coal tubs that had been repurposed as flower planters, half-pit wheels sunk into roundabouts, statues and commemorative benches – to those that were easier to miss – a miner's lamp in the window of the local funeral home, murals painted on the side of public buildings, and pub names like The Colliers Arms and The Miners Sling. I searched churchyards to find obelisks in memory of children drowned underground and the graves of pitmen poets. I looked for clues in street names and discovered aged miners' homes, mines rescue stations, miners' institutes and welfare halls. I drove through new industrial centres, retail parks and housing estates built on reclaimed land and walked across nature reserves on former colliery spoil tips. I followed railway lines, looking for steel security fencing, barbed wire and 'keep out' signs guarding former colliery sites, and parted long grass to find metal discs capping lost worlds beneath. On rare occasions I came upon old colliery buildings, yet to be demolished but slowly being taken back by nature.

I met former miners in their homes and communities. One memorable encounter occurred just outside Dover, when upon walking into the pub where I had arranged to meet one former miner, it quickly became evident that my arrival had been foretold, with everyone turning around to eyeball the incomer. Just as no sitting room was the same, no interview was the same, and as everyone took me on their own journey back to the coalface, our conversations were variably punctuated by laughter, anger and grief. Too often I was reminded of a line from Alan Plater's play *Close the Coalhouse Door*, which had stuck with me: 'It might be history to some people. To us it's family, pet.'[12] All the men I spoke to were generous with both their time and memories, though after the passage of so many years some seemed defeated into silence when the occasion to tell their story arose.

My ear grew attuned to the many accents of Britain's former coalfields, an ability owed perhaps to growing up in a household with a Scouse father and a Lancastrian mother, and with grandparents from Clonmel and Dundee. Several of those I spoke to were initially suspicious of my own southern-sounding accent, but this eased as our conversations progressed. I discovered 'pit talk' or pitmatic, as it is known in the North East, and became accustomed to a whole new industrial lexicon, which shifted from place to place. In Scotland miners would eat their piece, in the North East this would be bait, but as I ventured further south it had turned to snap. Men showed me their motties, tallies and checks, once used to identify themselves underground, and spoke of their journeys in the cage or on the chair, traversing up and down the mine shaft, of travelling inbye towards the workings, or outbye when returning home. I learned of the chocks and props relied upon to hold up the roof, and the belts, manriders and paddies used to transport coal and men around the mine. I grew to fear the deadly 'damps', toxic gases that lurked unseen underground, including blackdamp or choke-damp (suffocating carbon dioxide); whitedamp (toxic carbon monoxide); or the dreaded firedamp (flammable methane). I heard of pit ponies with personality and of the monstrous mining machines that men tamed in later years. Every man spoke fondly of his marras, mates, and comrades, who could be relied upon to watch your back, no matter what.

Some men recalled the excitement of breaking into old workings underground, with shovels left behind as though their owners were soon to return, and newspapers read almost a hundred years ago, which when taken into the daylight would disintegrate into a thousand pieces.[13] Others told tales of ghostly hands felt on living shoulders, bodiless footsteps in deserted areas of the pit, flickering lights, unusual sounds and apparitions of colleagues who had met an untimely end. However, occasionally, presumed ghostly encounters disguised a more frightful reality. One man, who worked at the Beamish Mary Pit in County Durham, explained how he was talking to a colleague underground when they both noticed a strange light, wobbling in the distance. It transpired that this was not in fact a phantom, but a staggering man whose arm had been pulled off by the conveyer belt.

As COVID-19 swept across Britain and the country retreated indoors in 2020, I was forced to put all my interviews on indefinite hold. However, as the weeks rolled on, I determined to continue my research as best I could via correspondence, alongside homeschooling a strong-willed five-year-old and trying to stop an active two-year-old from destroying the house. I tentatively put a call out for mining memories, which was subsequently published online and in several local newspapers. The response I received was both entirely unexpected and incredible.[14] Some men sent a few lines summarising their experiences, while others provided poems, short stories and lengthy unpublished memoirs of their time underground. I became acutely aware of the desire many men had to share their stories, perhaps owed to the spectre of mortality brought about by the pandemic, but also as they were aware that the memory of the men who dug the coal was fast disappearing.

One letter I received came from Joseph, who, at the age of ninety-three and with the kind assistance of his neighbour, shared his memories of joining the mining industry in February 1945, as one of the Bevin Boys conscripted to spend the Second World War serving their country in Britain's coal mines. Joe narrowly escaped death after being crushed by the endless steel rope, used to shift coal tubs around the pit, and heard the announcement of VE Day from the confines of a hospital bed, where he was recovering from a broken pelvis. Once released from service, he had returned to his former role at the Post Office in Middlesbrough. Nonetheless, it was clear the few years Joe spent underground had a profound impact on him, as his letter concluded: 'The comradeship of the regular miners was unsurpassed. I went down those mines a boy, three years later I came out a man.' Joe was not the only man I heard from who had their characters forged in the crucible of the pit, and he was certainly not the only one who never forgot his time underground nor the colleagues he had worked alongside.

Other men were keen to talk, albeit at a distance, so I began conducting remote interviews over Zoom, Skype and FaceTime, a new experience for us all but one which was fast becoming the most normal way to converse in those strange contactless days. At eight o'clock in the evening, once my children had been successfully if reluctantly coaxed into their beds, I would clear a spot on the kitchen table, open my laptop and begin. Inevitably, each conversation started with the latest news on the pandemic, and on Thursdays we joined after the weekly clap for carers. It was the first time I was welcoming my interviewees into the idiosyncrasies of my own life in the background, with my kitchen clock always striking off the hour, children's artworks haphazardly arranged on the fridge and the remnants of the day piled high next to the sink. Other men preferred to speak over the phone and as our conversation began, they would pause to close the door on errant hoovers and television sets and settle down into their chair. One man spoke to me with his pet jackdaw on his shoulder, and our conversation was punctuated by disembodied 'tchacks'. Escaping into these different worlds was the greatest privilege, and I credit it with maintaining much of my sanity during that uncertain year.

Behind the doors of my mid-terraced home, I also amassed what must be the largest and most incongruous coal mining library in Norwich, if not East Anglia, acquiring as much mining-related literature as my overdraft would permit, volumes which are now stacked precariously, two-deep on the yawning bookshelves of my lounge. I poured over academic studies of miners and their communities from across the decades and disciplines.[15] I learned of miners in their own words, through the autobiographies of Jack Lawson, Bert Coombes, Abe Moffat, Will Paynter, Jim

Bullock, Joe Gormley, Malcolm Pitt and Dave Douglass, and in the words of others like Daniel Defoe, Benjamin Disraeli, George Orwell and J. B. Priestley.[16] I read fiction inspired by fact, like the writings of D. H. Lawrence, Nottinghamshire's most famous miner's son; J. C. Grant's bleak depiction of a northern mining community in *The Back-to-Backs;* Lewis Jones's mighty *Cwmardy,* set in a South Wales mining village; Totley Tom's *Tales of a Yorkshire Miner*; A. J. Cronin's heartbreaking *The Stars Look Down*, chronicling a fatal mining disaster and its aftermath, and an old family copy of Luther Thomas's *The Deep of the Earth*, based on events in Senghenydd.[17] Aided by William Maurice's beautiful anthology, I discovered mining poetry as well as prose, and with the assistance of A. L. Lloyd I hummed through the many songs of the coalfields.[18] I studied the mining banners as meticulously catalogued by William A. Moyes, John Gorman and Norman Emery, and then watched them fly past at the Durham Miners' Gala.[19] For my birthday, I received a copy of Craig Oldham's powerful visual record of the 1984–85 miners' strike.[20]

No matter how many books I read, how many coalfields I visited or how many men I have spoken to, I will never know what it felt like to labour underground for days, weeks, months or a lifetime. Nor will I ever know what it took to be a wife, mother, sister or daughter living in a community whose fate was determined by the pit wheels. Still, after five years researching the industry and speaking to over one hundred men for whom coal was their life, I feel I now know something of what it *meant* to be a British miner. Throughout my research I have been continually fascinated not by the alchemy of coal nor the spectacle of clashes between the government and the National Union of Mineworkers, but by individual miners. Men who despite decades working in all manner of other occupations, still overwhelmingly identified as miners, through their culture and principles.

In a speech published in January 1952, Sir Andrew Bryan of the National Coal Board described how there was 'no typical miner any more than there is a typical man – though I think if I wanted to find the most real man, I should go among the miners to look for him'.[21] This is the story of such real men: brothers, sons, fathers and grandfathers, uncles and nephews, who shared the common identity of being coal miners. A few were extraordinary, by virtue of the feats they accomplished: smashing through production records and creating subterranean cathedrals that would never reach the sunlight. Others went to extraordinary lengths for their colleagues, risking it all to save life and limb. Many more men were remarkable for their service in an industry that had the capacity to maim in a moment, and for returning to work after this potential had been realised.

Featuring accounts from Ayrshire to the South Wales Valleys, from the 'People's Republic of South Yorkshire', to the 'Sunshine Corner Coalfields' of East Kent, each chapter offers a different perspective of the industry, different lives with different challenges, and different stories of who men became when they could no longer return underground. As far as possible, I have supplemented these accounts with archival research and by visiting the places mentioned. I hope that the men and women who trusted me with their stories are satisfied with my rendering, but if there are errors or omissions, the fault is entirely mine. I have made the decision to use only first names in these accounts, to avoid any embarrassment my interpretation may inadvertently cause.

The two long-service certificates that hang on my study wall give no details of the lives they represent, whether these men were heroes or just good workers. I felt compelled to purchase them from eBay, after I saw that they were being sold for just £5 each and advertised as suitable adornments for a 'man cave'. If J. W. Sabin and John Beard, who each gave over fifty years of long and meritorious service to the British mining industry, were stood before me today, it is unlikely they would see anything special in their achievements. My admiration would no doubt prove an embarrassment. They would laugh and answer straightforwardly that they were simply doing their job. They were miners. This book is for them and countless others who upheld and continue to uphold this identity.

Introduction: A Brief Journey Through Coal

The centuries will burn rich loads
With which we groaned,
Whose warmth shall lull their dreaming lids,
While songs are crooned;
But they will not dream of us poor lads,
Left in the ground.[1]

For over two centuries coal formed the dark vertebrae of Britain's industrial backbone. Britain's black gold powered her factories, propelled her ships and warmed her homes. Until the early twenty-first century, most of the country's coal was produced by deep mining, with coal deposits reached vertically, via a shaft sunk deep underground, or in some instances horizontally, through a drift cut into the slope of a hill or mountain.[2] Before the Mines and Collieries Act of 1842, children as young as five and heavily pregnant women crawled like animals through the dark bowels of the earth in its pursuit, until Victorian sensibilities designated the mine an exclusively male world.[3] Thereafter, the streets of coalfield communities were punctuated by the daily march of men to the pit and the skyline was dominated by the winding gear, a postmodern totem to Fortuna, that held the life of the town in balance. Behind the doors of their homes, women of the coalfields often worked longer hours than their menfolk, as the revolving door of shiftwork demanded.

In 1913, the same year that death descended upon Senghenydd in the small Aber Valley, coal production reached its dark crescendo, when 1.1 million workers produced 287 million tons of coal.[4] Over the next four years, miners powered the country through the First World War. Across the Channel, they crawled silently beneath the fields of the Western Front. Others fought above ground, men like the Lancashire recruits in Wilfred Owen's platoon, who were 'hard-handed, hard-headed miners, dogged, loutish, ugly', but who he trusted to advance under fire and to hold their trench.[5] Miners formed the bulk of the 'Bantam battalions', made up of men who fell below the Army's minimum height requirement but were 'capable of the greatest endurance'.[6] Some forty-five miners received the Victoria Cross for exceptional bravery in the conflict, though the valour of many others, tunnelling under enemy lines, remains largely unacknowledged.[7]

The miners who stayed behind to keep the home fires burning risked a fate no less cruel than those buried beneath the devouring mud of Flanders. A work colleague sent me newspaper cuttings relating to his great-grandfather, Charles Greatbatch, a colliery fireman whose quick thinking saved forty-seven lives during an explosion at the Minnie Pit in Staffordshire on 12 January 1918.[8] The disaster claimed 155 of the 248 souls working underground that morning, and one rescuer who died as a result of faulty breathing apparatus.[9] Almost fifty of the victims were under the age of sixteen, several of whom had ventured underground for the first time that week.[10] Two of those who died had been rescued just three years prior, almost to the day, from an explosion at the same pit.[11]

After one conflict came to a bloody end, Britain's miners entered another fight, this time on home soil. The pit wheels fell silent on 1 May 1926 when over a million men were locked out of collieries across Britain, following their refusal to accept conditions and cuts in wages demanded by private mine owners. During the subsequent General Strike, workers united to cries of 'not a penny off the pay, not a minute on the day', and thronged the streets in the largest demonstration of working class solidarity ever seen in Britain.[12] Yet, just nine days later, the Trade Union Congress agreed to end their part in the dispute, leaving the miners to fight on alone for another seven months until starvation drove them back.[13] For generations to come, the minds of nascent miners would be fired with tales of 1926 and the tidal wave of suffering unleashed upon their communities.

There were no national strikes in the mining industry for over forty years after the defeat of 1926. As well as fighting for better conditions, miners' unions had long campaigned for the industry and its workers to be freed from the shackles of private ownership.[14] In 1945, the National Union of Mineworkers was established, as a reorganisation of the Mineworkers' Federation of Great Britain.[15] Two years later, miners' dreams of a new dawn under public ownership were finally realised and Britain's pits were nationalised. According to Prime Minister Clement Attlee, the 1st of January 1947 would be remembered as one of the 'great days in the industrial history of our country'.[16] In Vesting Day celebrations across the three nations, old men hoisted the new standard of the National Coal Board above their collieries, and signs announced that they were now managed 'on behalf of the people'. Though it undoubtedly boosted miners' morale, the reality of national ownership fell somewhat short of the ideal: many of the industry's old problems persisted and the same mine managers were tasked with addressing them.[17]

Over subsequent decades, the industry evolved beyond recognition. Miners were reimagined as 'skilled technicians' as technology changed the way in which coal was won and the trusted pick and shovel were tossed on the scrap heap.[18] New underground conveyor systems channelled black veins of coal to the surface and pit ponies emerged blinking into the sunlight, never to return below. New apprenticeships were offered and miners were qualified as electricians and engineers. Soon plans for so-called superpits were unveiled, high-tech colossi that represented a lifeline for men displaced as older pits were closed and the industry was 'rationalised'.

Rothes Colliery in Fife, Scotland's 'showpiece' pit, should have been the bright future of the British mining industry.[19] Its 200-foot-high twin concrete winding towers, designed by architect and Austrian émigré Egon Riss, appeared as a modernist gateway to a new era of coal, a far cry from familiar industrial landscapes of the Victorian period. At Rothes, it was claimed that no man would have to do anything a machine could do for him, while mining families were offered a good life in the adjacent Glenrothes New Town.[20] One promotional video told the story of George McKay, a third-generation miner, who was one of Rothes's optimistic new recruits.[21] It was not an easy decision for George and his wife, a miner's daughter, to leave behind the deep roots they had in their home community. However, like others, they were attracted to the promise of security at this new state-of-the-art colliery and better prospects for their family in the pleasant flower-lined cul-de-sacs of semi-detached homes nearby.

Production commenced at Rothes in 1957 and was anticipated to continue for over a century. The following year, crowds of men watched a fresh-faced Queen Elizabeth II embark upon the 1,600-foot drop to inspect the new mine, her pristine white overalls more befitting of a desert safari than her descent into the grimy underworld. Yet, within just five years, the death sentence had been passed for this £20 million pound 'wonder pit', which had suffered from flooding since it was first dug.[22] Men who had arrived with gusto just a few years earlier were now tasked with salvaging equipment and materials from a watery grave. Others looked towards the prospect of further upheaval, transferring to unfamiliar coalfields in the English Midlands and Yorkshire, which did not have an adequate housing supply to meet the demand of incomers.

As for the fate of Glenrothes, fifty years after it was hailed as Scotland's second aspirational new town, it had the dishonour of being named the most dismal in the country.[23] Today, it is home to a population of almost 50,000, and over a quarter of its children live in poverty.[24] No longer dominated by British coal, US arms manufacturer Raytheon, whose missiles litter the war-torn streets of Yemen, is now one of the town's biggest employers.[25]

Under Harold Wilson's first Labour government, between 1964 and 1970, over 200 deep pits were closed and a diminishing number of men were employed in the industry.[26] Unlike the white elephant of Rothes, most pits earmarked for closure were those designated 'uneconomic' or older 'worked out' pits. The Coal Board and the National Union of Mineworkers worked together to limit redundancies and find displaced men new jobs within the industry or equivalent work elsewhere. Nonetheless, despite being framed as 'inevitable and in the best interests' of the men, pit closures hit individual coalfield communities hard and made the front pages of local newspapers.[27] As Will Paynter, the General Secretary of the National Union of Mineworkers, observed in 1967, away from clichéd offers of redeployment and compensation, the closure of a pit represented a disaster just as poignant and harrowing as a death in the family.[28]

For the most part, escalating pit closures drew little national attention in a period of full employment. The Coal Board continued to assure prospective miners of 'permanent employment and a secure future', though the value of Britain's indigenous black gold was steadily falling. Old King Coal had long sat blithely on his throne while his attendant fog quietly suffocated British cities.[29] However, following the passage of the Clean Air Acts of 1956 and 1968, the Old King was finally usurped as Britain looked towards new energy sources to provide cheaper, cleaner power. In August 1968, after a farewell foray from Carlisle to Liverpool aboard '*The Fifteen Guinea Special*', British Rail stopped being powered by steam, and diesel engines forged ahead into the future. Contrary to the NCB tagline, it became increasingly apparent that people might *not* always need coal.

In January 1972, the miners staged their first national strike since nationalisation, in which over a quarter of a million miners fought for improved wages and conditions. As Malcolm Pitt, President of the Kent Area NUM, recalled in his later account, 'It was as if a giant asleep for half a century had come awake.'[30] Individual members of coalfield communities defended the industrial action in decidedly pragmatic terms. One miner's wife from the West Midlands wrote to the local paper to explain how her husband, a miner since the age of thirteen who was still working on the coalface at the age of sixty-three, had been earning more forty-two years earlier.[31] He continued to work despite having suffered five accidents in the last eight years, the latest requiring eighteen stitches to fix his ear back on. Another letter, from a miner's son whose father was in the 1926 strike, compared the miners' salary to that of lavatory cleaners at the Chrysler factory.[32]

During the strike, the 'Battle of Saltley Gate', in which over 20,000 other workers joined picketing miners to force the closure of a coke depot in Birmingham, became a symbolic moment, signifying the collective strength of trade unionism, and providing a panacea to the enduring grievances of 1926.[33] For thirty-four-year-old Arthur Scargill, the future leader of the NUM, who stood atop a public toilet to cheer on the mass stand at Saltley, it would be remembered as the greatest day of his life.[34]

After seven weeks, the strike was brought to a successful conclusion, with Sid Schofield, Yorkshire NUM Secretary and National Vice-President, commending the fact that 'at long last the miner has got back the dignity and the status he is entitled to'.[35] However, the wage gains the miners made were soon eroded by rising inflation. After rejecting a derisory pay offer, in November 1973, the union embarked on an overtime ban, cutting the level of coal production at a time when a global oil crisis was already in the pipeline.[36] In response, Edward Heath's Conservative Government introduced a 'three-day week', to try and eke out the nation's coal reserves. For two months, British life descended into organised chaos: television stations ceased broadcasting by 10:30

p.m., non-essential businesses were forced to limit their operations to reduce electricity consumption, families ate their dinner by candlelight and were advised to brush their teeth in the dark.[37]

In February 1974, the miners went on strike for the second time in two years. Hoping to regain control of the situation, Heath called an ill-advised General Election on 28 February, to answer the question 'Who Governs?'[38] Unfortunately for Heath, the British public determined that the answer was not to be him any longer, though it was not entirely sure who should replace him, with the election resulting in the first hung Parliament since 1929.[39] After twelve hours of negotiations with Howard Wilson's minority Labour government, the miners reached an agreement, accepting a very healthy wage increase of 35 per cent.[40] Miners had cemented their standing as the corps d'elite of the labour movement, but in mining communities most were just relieved to see their place on the wage table restored.[41]

Over the next few years, industrial relations between the NUM and the Coal Board became increasingly hostile, as Heath's successor as leader of the Conservative Party, Margaret Thatcher, was elected Prime Minister in 1979, and Arthur Scargill succeeded Lancastrian Joe Gormley as President of the NUM in 1982. The new government was determined to reduce the costs of the nationalised industries and to curtail the power of the unions.[42] In March 1983, Ian MacGregor, the 'mad axeman', who had previously overseen mass redundancies at British Steel, was appointed as the Coal Board's new Chairman.[43] One year on, on 6 March 1984, MacGregor confirmed plans for twenty pit closures and the loss of some 20,000 jobs.[44] News of the imminent closure of Cortonwood Colliery in South Yorkshire prompted a walkout, which quickly escalated until a national strike was declared by the NUM on 12 March. The industrial action was taken without a national pre-strike ballot of union members, a fact that would be a recurring source of division.[45]

During the subsequent year-long strike, over 140,000 miners came out to protest prospective pit closures in one of most bitter industrial disputes in British history.[46] The so-called Battle of Orgreave was an especially brutal confrontation that took place at a coking plant near Rotherham. Thousands of police officers were deployed there on one sunny June day in 1984, and in the resulting altercations with massed pickets, almost a hundred miners were arrested and countless men were injured.[47] Men who were at Orgreave still speak with incredulity at how events unfolded. Despite the passage of years, their voices crack as they describe the horror of seeing respected older colleagues battered by truncheons or soiling themselves in fear.

It is easy to look upon the black and white photographs of the men of 1926, a sea of flat caps and mustached faces, and see a distant past. The technicolour films of pickets colliding with truncheon-wielding police during the 1984–85 strike appear more like a dystopian nightmare than events that happened just forty years ago. Today, walking around the upmarket Waverley housing estate that has been erected on the site of the infamous Battle of Orgreave, it is hard to imagine that conflict occurred in this place now designated 'the new heart of Yorkshire'. Yet, the word Orgreave is still etched across many striking miners' arms and minds, just as scenes from the battle are still paraded on their banners, a reminder of a wound that is yet to scab.

For Member of Parliament Dennis Skinner, the 'Beast of Bolsover', the 1984–85 strike, in defence of the future of the industry, was 'the most noble' he had ever witnessed.[48] However, for many miners it had painful echoes of 1926. The strike was marred by a lack of solidarity shown by fellow trade unionists, in part due to a weakened labour force in the wake of accelerating de-industrialisation and new, tougher labour laws on picketing and secondary action. Not all miners adhered to the union directive, with most Nottinghamshire pits and around 24,000 of their men continuing to work.[49] Differences over the dispute tore some mining communities apart and caused irreparable damage to relationships between friends, fathers and sons, and even identical twins, who '*never spoke again*'. While the bonds of fraternity may have weakened, a renewed sisterhood was forged amongst coalfield women who formed support groups to provide food and domestic essentials and, in some instances, joined picket lines and political meetings.[50]

In March 1985, after twelve gruelling months on strike, the NUM called for an organised return to work. They did so without having reached an agreement with the Coal Board, fearing that the strike would otherwise disintegrate as men and their families had so few resources left to continue holding out. When Arthur Scargill emerged to face the crowds gathered outside Congress House in London, the words of one Scottish miner summed up the pain of many: 'We gave you everything . . . dead men, broken marriages, starving kids. Now you've sold us down the river. We've got nothing.'[51]

As men returned to their pits, some, like the men of Bates Colliery in Blyth, Northumberland, marched proudly behind their banners to the applause of onlookers. For others, such pageantry proved too painful. One man I spoke to became emotional as he recalled how the return to work at Thurcroft

Colliery in South Yorkshire felt like a funeral. After men had passed through the colliery gates, some found the atmosphere within had soured. Divisions during the strike reignited, with former colleagues refusing to work alongside each other. Some members of management took a new combative approach, as one man recalled the situation at Coventry Colliery: 'It became *them* and *us*, and you *will* do, not *can* you do.'

Following the strike, dozens of pits were earmarked for closure. When Grimethorpe Colliery closed in 1993, one man recalled seeing a scene that was later emulated in the film *Brassed Off*: 'Some bloke, sat there, smoking a fag, wondering where his life had gone.'[52] Men wept as they were forced to seal up the shafts their grandfathers had sunk. While some were able to move on, finding jobs in outside industry, many found the camaraderie of their new workplaces bore little comparison to the friendships they had left underground. One man, who returned to education after the closure of Blaenant Colliery in South Wales, was conscious of just how much he had been forced to leave behind: 'People don't realise you know, what else is there? You know what I've had to, the kind of culture I've had to give up.'

Deep-pit mining ended in Britain as the last miners finished their shift at Kellingley Colliery on 18 December 2015. Traces of pits elsewhere have long since been stripped away to make room for anodyne shopping centres and dry ski slopes, with little to denote the labyrinth that lay beneath, or the lives lost there. Unlike the many fallen servicemen whose names appear at home and abroad and the Unknown Tommy, whose silhouette appears throughout the land, the men who toiled beneath British soil to power the nation are often remembered by their communities alone. The rest of society has buried both the pits and the men who worked in them, in a desire to move on to clean energy and electric cars. British children struggle to recognise a lump of coal, outside of threats concerning the contents of their Christmas stockings if they are naughty. Stories of the men who once wrestled it from the ground are more likely to recall characters from Disney's *Snow White* or the *Minecraft* computer game than any real working people.

Today, a Google image search of the term 'miner' brings up photographs of dusty men, stoically looking into the camera with their arms crossed, wielding a pick or operating heavy machinery in dimly lit caverns underground. The term 'British miner' brings up many of the same images, interspersed with scenes of clashing police and pickets from 1984–85. For many people unfamiliar with the mining industry and its workers, miners are understood in these terms – as hypermasculine men labouring in the dangerous underground world of the last century, or, for those old enough to remember, as the militant trade unionists responsible for the fall of a government in the 1970s, until Margaret Thatcher decimated the industry. In popular culture since the new millennium, films like *Billy Elliot* and *Pride* have shed light on the human impact of the year-long strike in mining communities.[53] However, they often counterpose hopeful images of change against the regressive masculinity of the coalfields. Yet, such caricatures of mining men rarely reflected real life.

What follows is an account of the last generation of British coal miners: fathers and sons, brothers and comrades, big hitters and broken men, strikers and scabs, families and communities. It is a history of what was once Britain's most important industry, told through the lives of different men who left the schoolyard and carved out their identities at the coalface. Men for whom coal was all they had ever known, who reluctantly emerged into the daylight for the final time, and others who never felt at home underground, who were happier to consign the dust and darkness to the past. It explores how these men felt when their pits were closed and what happened next; from former miners who ended up policing the picket lines in the infamous strike of 1984–85, to others who became factory workers, garage forecourt attendants, property surveyors, driving instructors, counsellors, the local mayor and one who even ended up working on Fleet Street. It reflects on what the mining industry once meant to its workers and their communities, and what Britain lost when it was gone. Though no journey out of the pit was the same, almost all these men were united by the fact that over three decades later they continue to identify as miners, not just as a former occupation but as a fundamental part of *who they are*.

1. Jack the Lad

In the pecking order, you get what they call a coal hewer, the coal hewer is the guy who's actually digging the coal. And they're always known, certainly in Durham, they're always known as The Men.

Ted liked to both look and do his best. He would endeavour to excel at whatever he turned his hand to and could not understand those who failed to apply themselves in a similar fashion. By the age of just twenty, Ted had reached the top of the hierarchy at Byermoor Colliery in County Durham. Though all miners were men, they were not all '*The Men*', and once granted membership of this elite group, Ted found he did 'strut a little bit'. A decade later, he was making strides above ground as a detective with the Criminal Investigation Department of Tynemouth Borough Police. It was a role he loved as, in his own words, he 'could *relate* to the villains'. This was because Ted was not a university lad, but a Jack the Lad, who spoke with a strong Tyneside accent and ended up doing some 'good business' whilst in the drug squad.

Ted was born in 1937, a liminal time when martial masculinity, its boots brushed clean of the mud of Flanders, was once again held up as an exemplar for a new generation of men. On the day Ted made his entrance into the world, the front page of the *Newcastle Evening Chronicle* announced moves afoot to encourage men into the Army.[1] The day before, a battalion of uniformed 'Toy Soldiers' had appeared on the front page, young boys flanking their wheeled gun with bayonets ready, as they rehearsed for the South Shields Military Tattoo.[2]

The small village of Burnopfield, where Ted spent his formative years, sits 13 miles north-west of Durham, and 9 miles south-west of Newcastle upon Tyne. Its unusual name, which Ted took pains to spell out for me, is believed to derive from Old English, meaning 'open land by the valley stream'. An alternative, and decidedly more exciting, origin story was that the title harked back to a time when the English had given the order to 'burn up the fields' to thwart Scottish invaders in the mid-seventeenth century.[3] After the Second World War, the village became better known as the birthplace of Eddie Chapman, otherwise known as Agent Zigzag, a career criminal turned double agent and unconventional wartime hero. Chapman's exploits later inspired the 1966 film *Triple Cross*, starring Christopher Plummer.[4]

Despite legends of burning fields and the colourful history of its past resident, Burnopfield was the most charming and picturesque mining community I visited. Perched amongst rich green fields and deep valleys of dense woodland, which tumble down behind winding railings and dry-stone walls, the village began as an agricultural settlement before coal was discovered. The first colliery, known as the Hobson, had been sunk in 1725. Later, during the coal rush of the nineteenth century, pit wheels encircled the village, which grew to accommodate those who came to feed the mines. Ted's family had been such incomers, moving down from Norham on the River Tweed, a village similarly pulled back and forth over the centuries between Scottish and English hands. Its much-besieged

The village of Burnopfield, County Durham, *c.*1950.

castle was later immortalised in J. M. W. Turner's misty sunrise scene and Sir Walter Scott's poem *Marmion.*[5] As black gold was struck, the once agricultural family found itself industrialised and Ted's grandfather gained employment as a horse-keeper at Byermoor Colliery.

Sandstone terraces line the main road of Burnopfield, topped with dark lines of Welsh slate and set against leaden skies. Ted's childhood home was not quite so well constructed and, when he described it as a cottage he was 'being very polite', but that was 'par for the course' at the time. Many of the more ramshackle workers' dwellings of the early twentieth century disappeared many decades ago, their primary function long redundant.

Behind the aptly named Front Street, I discovered Cricket Terrace, a narrow road running between lines of neatly stacked red-brick houses. I remembered reading of the village's beloved cricketing son, the 'Burnopfield Basher', Colin 'Ollie' Milburn, who had once bowled nearby.[6] An eighteen-and-a-half-stone giant who was surprisingly light on his feet,

Milburn was one of England's biggest hitters, representing his country in nine Test matches, until his career was curtailed by a car crash in 1969, in which he lost his left eye. Afterwards, rather than being downcast by fate's cruelty, 'jolly Ollie' put on a brave face with his 'infectious good humour and indomitable spirit' lifting the morale of the whole hospital.[7] Only later was it apparent that his bonhomie had been masking inner turmoil, which would lead to alcoholism and a fatal heart attack in the carpark of his favourite pub at the age of just forty-eight.[8] On the day of Ollie's funeral, every seat of Burnopfield's Methodist church was occupied, as the large coffin of the man who was said to be terrified of being alone was carried through.[9]

At the end of Cricket Terrace, a row of Aged Miners' Homes backs onto an expansive patch of allotments. These smart single-storey dwellings are still owned by the Durham Aged Mineworkers' Homes Association, the largest almshouse charity in the country. It was founded in 1898 by miner and lay preacher Joseph Hopper of Gateshead, a benevolent soul who railed against the injustice of rewarding old miners with eviction from their tied housing when they were no longer strong enough to cut coal.[10] Between 1910 and 1957, 1,600 of these homes were built, funded by a weekly levy paid by 200,000 coal miners across 200 pits.[11] Lord Joicey, once Durham's principal coal owner and himself 'architect of his own fortunes', believed the movement was testament to the county's men, who, unlike those in other parts of the country, helped themselves.[12]

Despite being born into a man's world, Ted was different to most of the miners I spoke with, who wished to emulate their father, grandfather, war heroes, sporting stars or the trade union leader at the end of the street. Rather, when I asked

Ted who his role model had been growing up, with no hesitation he told me it was his mother, a '*very* well-read' and '*very* intelligent' church-going woman, who was 'the light' of his life. The more I peeled away the layers of Ted's personality, the more I began to see the influence of this upstanding woman upon him.

While Ted was proud of his grandfather, as a self-made man, he held his father, who was also a miner, in lesser regard, as 'one of life's unfortunates'. In 1948, when Ted was eleven, his father had suffered a serious accident when working underground, in which he broke both his spine and pelvis. He had been treated at Shotley Bridge Hospital, a specialist centre for plastic surgery during the war, which had subsequently found casualties of conflict replaced by injured miners.[13] To facilitate his recovery, Ted's father was placed in a plaster cast that extended from his neck to his midriff. When the cast was removed, after nine months, they discovered it had failed. For his next medical intervention, Ted's father had two ribs removed and fused onto his spine. He was then transferred to Durham's Dryburn Hospital, to spend a further nine months in a paraplegic ward surrounded by other men invalided out of the pit.

Slowly but surely, Ted's father had learned to walk again, using a harness and crutches, until eventually he discarded them, one by one, and he could walk with the aid of a stick alone. According to Ted, from this point forward, his father 'could manage'. He had even managed to work at the colliery again though, as Ted observed, he was only able to undertake 'a very, very *menial* task'. After the accident, Ted's father's life had been 'one of pain', a bleak admission that his son clearly did not want to dwell on, quickly following this up with the fact his old man remained a jovial character and a brilliant singer, who after half a pint would perform the music hall favourite 'Peggy O' Neil' 'in full voice'.[14]

Time and time again I heard of miners who had lost limbs and livelihoods underground, but who were praised for taking it on the chin or playing the fool. Stories of fathers buried by roof falls so severe it was assumed they had been killed outright, who had been freed only to face months confined to a hospital bed. Men who, as soon as they walked off the ward, had returned to the same job underground, with no 'whingeing' and no further discussion of the matter; stoicism which was always commended by the narrators.

Ted's account of his father's injury, his protracted recovery, and how, against all the odds and despite significant discomfort, he was able to walk and even work again, seemed particularly worthy of admiration. However, when I remarked that his father sounded like an incredible character, Ted was quick to correct me: 'I wouldn't say he was incredible [. . .] he took life's blows, he took them, and absorbed them, and carried on. And still sang "Peggy O'Neil."' Only later did I realise how it was not 'incredible' for mining men to overcome such physical hardships; rather, it was expected that they would take 'life's blows', absorb them and carry on, without remonstration.

Just like the 'cheerful stoicism' demanded from disabled veterans, Ted remembered his father as a happy go lucky figure, always singing, a man for whom 'every day was a bonus'.[15] Perhaps this was one way of restoring his father's manhood after his injuries had relegated him to the bottom of the pit's hierarchy. I wondered how many other wounded men, like Colin Milburn, had also found themselves smiling through their suffering.

Despite his father's ordeal, Ted was not put off pit work,

though as a child he aspired to more academic pursuits. He sat the eleven-plus examination, passing the first stage and taking the second exam at the grammar school he would be able to attend if he lived up to expectations. In a 'sort of big-headed way', Ted assumed he had passed, as the test had been a 'doddle'. Yet, when the results were published in the local paper a few weeks later, his mother shared the disappointing news that he had not made the grade. Ted recalled how she was '*absolutely* gutted', and so was he, because he was convinced that he had qualified. In the end, the only children Ted knew who made it to grammar school that year were two 'blue bloods', who were a 'little bit better off' than the rest.

As a result, just like most of his peers, Ted took up a place at the local secondary modern school and it was not long before he followed his forebears to Byermoor Colliery. Though he conceded to having a hint of trepidation upon his first descent underground, Ted soon found it was 'part and parcel of life, you just got in the cage, and you didn't give it a thought'. Ever quick on the uptake, he soon learned how to get ahead and that if you worked hard and fast you were accepted as part of the team because, as he explained, 'in the pit, time equals money'.

Gradually, Ted inched his way further into the pit and higher up the pecking order, working first in the frenetic shaft bottom, then on pony putting, taking the empty tubs to the coalface and bringing the full ones out: 'If you were good at it, you could make some good money, if you were bad at it, you would have a bad back.' Ted, of course, found he was pretty good at it. Eventually, he had done enough to earn his place as a hewer on the coalface, one of *The Men*.

Where others complained of the danger, dust, damp

conditions and deafening noise, the biggest downside of mining life, in Ted's mind, was the shift patterns. On a day shift, also known as back shift, he would start at ten to nine in the morning, until half past four in the afternoon; night shift would run from half past three in the afternoon until eleven o'clock in the evening, and the first shift would start at two o'clock in the morning, until half past nine. Byermoor Colliery still operated under Cavilling Rules, a practice that had existed in the Durham coalfield since the Victorian era, which meant every quarter work was distributed according to names drawn from the foreman's hat. The luck of the cavil dictated which district, or area, of the pit and which shift pattern men would be working for the next three months. At least for Ted, this system seemed fair, 'You take the rough with the smooth, you know, if you'd got a good district, you would make some money, you got a bad district, you know, you had to put up with it.' Being allocated the night shift was the most feared, as going underground at half past three on a summer's afternoon was truly punishing.

Friday morning was the highlight of the working week, as that was when the men got paid. It was always a pleasant day, with plenty of opportunities to 'create a little bit of mayhem somewhere' in the evening. Ted was part of a clique of six lads, all around the same age, who went 'virtually everywhere together'. Most were colleagues from Byermoor, but two worked at the nearby Hobson Colliery. Though shift patterns varied, at the weekend everybody was off and just like the protagonists of Sid Chaplin's 'Saturday Saga', after five days' hard labour they craved nothing more than to go 'on the bust', in a pub where the beer and the music ran unimpeded.[16]

Freed from the privations of wartime, by the 1950s the

trappings of your success at the coalface could be worn about town, and for Ted and his friends, fashion played a 'vital part' in their lives. The group frequented Jackson the Tailor, on Clayton Street in Newcastle, to ensure they 'always looked the business'. Founded by the Lithuanian immigrant Moses Jacobson back in 1906, in 1953 Jackson's had merged with the Burton group, and became one of the most well-known names on the British high street.[17] Latterly, the firm had come under the stewardship of Moses' son Lionel, who understood young men's passion for the latest trends, particularly after they were emancipated from 'maternal budgetary control'.[18] For young consumers like Ted and his peers, Jackson's offered two-piece suits, made to measure 'as de luxe as you like', and overcoats with 'quiet magnificence', at prices the ordinary man could afford.[19]

The social life of Burnopfield in the early 1950s was akin to that described by burglar turned sociologist Mark Benney in his 1946 documentary novel *Charity Main*. Informed by his own wartime posting in County Durham, Benney, a Londoner, painted a vivid picture of a mining community, where the social lives of the two sexes were almost entirely bifurcated. While women's free time was passed by each other's firesides, during the week, men born into mining would spend their evenings in the club, where pit talk extended back across the generations, with some taking a bus out of village on the weekends to drink whisky in the city.[20]

Older residents of Burnopfield were content to spend their weekends within the limits of the village, revolving around the grand Cooperative store, the Women's Institute, and the Miners' Club. However, once dressed for the occasion, Ted and his clique sought diversion further afield. Friday evenings followed a regular routine that began with the 6 p.m. bus into Newcastle. Alighting in The Toon, they would call into a familiar pub on the outskirts, one where you were allowed to have music. The group would pass the hours drinking, avoiding getting embroiled in fights, and having a spirited sing-song. The evening would be drawn to a close via the last bus from Newcastle at 11:30 p.m., by which time, according to Ted's memory, they 'were *legless*'. Saturdays followed a similar pattern; despite the fact some awoke with sore heads.

As 'prolific spenders' at the weekend, Ted and his friends found their means somewhat more limited by the time Monday rolled around. Consequently, on weekdays they would resign themselves to a pub nearby, where they could enjoy a couple of halves of beer after work. A favourite local haunt was the Burton House, a pub dating back to the 1890s that still offers real ales and live music on Burnopfield's Busty Bank. In Ted's day, its clientele were overwhelmingly miners, aside from the odd milkman and the local insurance collector, who was viewed as something of a novelty. The main topic of conversation was the pit, which governed everyone's lives, though Ted and his friends ended their evenings on a transatlantic note, singing selections from *Oklahoma!*. One lad knew the lyrics to every song in the Rodgers and Hammerstein score, and on his walk home would dart into the fields loudly beseeching the farmer and the cowman to be friends.

For both the men and women of Burnopfield, young and old, the social highlight of the year was, of course, the Durham Big Meeting, the Miners' Gala which had taken place each summer since 1871. Whole villages from the surrounding countryside would make their annual pilgrimage to the old cathedral city, not to visit the shrine of Saint

Cuthbert as in days past, but for a living celebration of working-class ideals. Each lodge proudly turned out a brass band, all peaked caps and gold braid, and its own technicolour banner, proclaiming dreams of education, the emancipation of labour, of all men as brethren and strength in unity. On occasion these banners were also memento mori: when there had been an accident underground, black crepe would drape the top corners, a mark of respect and a solemn reminder of the fate that might befall anyone toiling in the darkness below.

Before the gala, the names of men willing and able to carry the banner would go into a hat, echoing the customs of the pit. One year, Ted had been lucky enough to be picked, fulfilling a dream he had held since childhood. At eight o'clock in the morning on the day of the Big Meeting, the chosen few collected the banner from the Colliery, proceeded to walk around the colliery rows, then embarked on the bus to Durham, with everybody enjoying two bottles of Newcastle Brown en route. Upon arrival, they queued up with the banner, until their time came to parade through the bustling city.

According to one reporter, by 1958 pride had been replaced by gaiety as the key note of the gala proceedings.[21] Babes were carried in their mothers' arms and small children were lifted onto old shoulders, while young men and women linked arms and danced in circles amongst the crowds. One of Ted's proudest moments was processing across the Elvet Bridge with the banner, whilst wearing a brand-new drape suit. Above the joyful chaos, the balcony of the Royal County Hotel ached under the weight of the great and good who waved to the crowds below. The final stretch saw them all walking down onto the bustling Racecourse, by which point

Byermoor Branches of Colliery Workers banner at the Durham Miners' Gala in 1954. The banner depicts The Hermitage Rehabilitation Centre for Durham miners in Chester-le-Street.

Ted was '*strutting* down nearly, I was *full of it*'. Banners were pitched on the grass, and the outdoor congregation sat under the hot sun to listen to speeches from the left-wing leaders of the day.

Each year, two banners were selected to go to Durham Cathedral, to be displayed and blessed in the annual service. Ted's mother, who knew the cathedral back to front, was also an authority on the banners, and enjoyed taking note of which ones were floating past. His father, on the other hand, had drunk six pints of lager by this point in proceedings, and would be lost to 'Peggy O'Neil'. For everyone else, four o'clock would roll around, and the chosen men would lift the banner from the Racecourse and march out.

On his return journey through the streets of Durham,

Young folk from Wheatley Hill lead their banner onto the Racecourse at the Durham Miners' Gala in July 1959.

Ted found the beer had caught up with him, and he ended up falling headlong into a privet hedge. When he eventually managed to writhe himself free, he was distraught to find that he had left behind an arm of his new suit. Worse was to come, as on his arrival back in Burnopfield, he encountered his mother, who was less than impressed by his transformation: 'There's our Ted, he went out of the house this morning looking like a new pin, look at the state of him, he's like a rag doll.'

For Ted, miners were different from other men because 'they're *bound*, they're bound by their work ethic and by their culture'. He compared it to current times when 'you hear, time after time, ad nauseam, people saying "well this is what the community thinks" and it's a clichéd response', whereas in mining villages, 'community meant community'. Yet, by the early 1960s, the coal industry in County Durham was shrinking rapidly with pits closing each year, and men leaving their communities to seek work further afield.

As the surrounding collieries faded into the past, Ted found himself working amongst interlopers, who did not respect the hierarchy and were not born into the families of Byermoor. The strangest guys came from Swalwell, an unassuming village just over 5 miles away on the banks of the Tyne, but which was, according to Ted, 'bandit-country'. Ted recalled his bewilderment at one lad who never availed himself of a towel in the pithead baths, where miners would wash after their shift, 'He just rubbed himself down with his hands, and off he went.' Another guy was always first into the baths and first out, 'I would say "get dry", he'd say "I'll get dry tomorrow, I'm in a hurry."' Aside from demonstrating a lack of personal care, these did not seem the actions of bandits, though from Ted's perspective, this was not the way to behave.

Despite his appreciation of propriety and his reputation as a hard worker, Ted still had his share of altercations with colliery management during his time at Byermoor. One particular manager, who looked like the American actor James Cagney and was 'a nasty piece of work', caused problems. This manager would stand outside the colliery office and wait for the men to come up the shaft, and used to say to Ted's father, who was working on the pit top: 'Your Ted, he's like a rag bag, he's the scruffiest guy who comes out of the pit.' I could see how for Ted, who was always such a sharp dresser around town, this criticism would be particularly affecting. More iniquitous was the fact this same manager would pull Ted aside and coerce him into silence: 'You need to keep your mouth shut, I gave your Dad a job.'

There was little love lost when in October 1960 Ted left Byermoor and transferred to Steetley Colliery on the border of Derbyshire and Nottinghamshire, over 100 miles away. Ted was recently married and the reasons for his departure were entirely practical: he had been working in a team of twelve men in a seam called the Tilley, the conditions were *atrocious*, and they simply could not 'make it pay'. Ted already knew of a couple of guys who had successfully made the southerly transition, and so he thought he would give it a spin, and 'quite frankly I never looked back'.

Though the work at Steetley was the same, adapting to the vernacular underground was like trying to learn a foreign language. In Durham, the waste material thrown from the coal cutter was known by the marvellous word 'scufflings', whereas in Nottinghamshire they used the less poetic 'gubbins'. At Byermoor, if miners were walking in a convoy and the guy at the front came across an obstruction, he would automatically say 'look up', and everybody would understand there was something in the way. When Ted was leading from the front in Steetley, and advised the team to 'look up', they all physically looked up and bumped their heads. It later transpired that in Nottinghamshire they preferred to say, 'Watch this, bad work.' Unsurprisingly, Ted found himself permanently relegated to the back.

Despite some heads being lost in translation, Ted was readily accepted by the men at Steetley. Underground, they would run a system called 'the market', where those who did not have a regular job were selected to replace absent men. As Ted recalled, 'It was always, "I'll have that Geordie lad there."' Ted was far from being the only foreigner amongst the team of twelve he was assigned to, as there were two Italians, four Poles, a Frenchman as well as two locals, and 'you can imagine what the language was like'. However, not long after acclimatising to his new surrounds, Ted was being stripped of his boots, knee pads and tools by thrifty colleagues, as he prepared to leave the pit for the final time. Once again, the reasons for Ted's departure were bitterly pragmatic, as the consequence of an accident underground.

Ted had been working alongside another lad from Burnopfield, who had started out as a bricklayer underground but pressed for a role working on the coalface at Steetley, after seeing Ted making some good money there. According to Ted's assessment, his friend was a good collier and a hard worker, but he was noisy, always shouting. Underground, the pair had been working alongside a 7-ton machine, which was *brutal*, and 'when it was going, the whole place was *shaking*'. They had already experienced some issues with the roof collapsing, and one day Ted's colleague's hand had fallen between two bollards, where a tension chain was running: 'It pulled his fingers off, and I pulled him out, and I pulled his glove off, and two fingers came out with his glove.' The wounded man had just paid £2,500 for a new home, and as he was stretchered out of the pit, all Ted could remember him saying was, 'What's going to happen to me bungalow? What's going to happen to me bungalow?'

I had heard some truly awful accounts of injury underground, of men decapitated, limbs hewn off and torsos impaled, some of which are recounted in the later pages of this book. Yet, there was something particularly mournful about Ted's colleague's enquiries. This man's industry had carried him miles from his village and enabled him to buy a new home of his own, a place where he could lay down roots and spend his twilight years, just like Hopper had envisaged all those years ago. And yet, in an instant of taut metal meeting malleable flesh, all of this had been jeopardised. I could imagine him, the morphia temporarily elevating him from the searing pain in his hand, watching the image of his new bungalow hovering above him then distorting and fading into the empty darkness of the tunnels he was being carried through.

Afterwards, Ted reached the conclusion that it was only a matter of time before he would meet the same fate on these new mechanised faces. Though safety in the industry had improved significantly following nationalisation, by the 1960s the accident rate was creeping upwards. Seeing an advert in the newspaper for roles in the police force, which offered a salary of £800 a year to men over the age of twenty-two, Ted thought, 'I'm going to have a go at that' and he did. Preferring to be a policeman in his own area, Ted returned to the more familiar lands of the North East, joining the Tynemouth Borough Police in 1965.

For Ted, who was conscious of the need to keep up appearances, the prospect of working in a pressed uniform and mirror-polished boots would undoubtedly have appealed, particularly when compared to the pit rags he was used to wearing. Likewise, the Tynemouth Borough Police badge spoke to his mining roots as it was taken from the area's coat of arms, with figures of a pitman and a seaman, above the motto 'messis ab altis', or 'harvest from the deep', celebrating the area's hidden bounties of coal and fish. Yet, by the time Ted joined its ranks, Tynemouth Police was, in his words, a 'hard-up' force, with only around 140 officers.

What the force lacked in manpower, it seemed they made up for in other ways, as public opinion of Tynemouth Police appeared high, at least in as much as it was reflected in the local press. Day to day, officers protected members of the public and their property, tracking down stolen goods from cigarettes to cars; catching deviants ranging from the local Peeping Tom to suspected murderers and even saving people from burning buildings. By virtue of their location, Tynemouth bobbies also patrolled the river at night, rescuing gum-booted fishermen who had inadvertently plunged into the Fish Quay or entering the murky waters in full uniform to save the young, the old and the drunk who had slipped into the icy waters.[22]

The force also seemed to have had a particularly cooperative spirit, which may have reminded Ted a little of what he had left underground. In their spare time, the Z-car men ran free advanced driving courses to help local motorists break their bad habits, and in 1965, Chief Constable Walter Baharie permitted his officers to run their own licensed social club.[23] Forty officers had sacrificed their days off to transform a wartime police mustering post into a luxury bar and club, lowering the ceilings, rewiring the electrics, installing central heating, and upgrading the décor, with their wives helping by dyeing the curtains and making food.

Much like when he had joined the pit, in the police force Ted found himself working with Second World War veterans and older, more experienced men. He resolved that he would do his time, mentally committing himself to nothing more than walking the beat for twenty-five, thirty years, whatever it may be. However, he soon found himself unimpressed by the 'quality' of some of the officers he was amongst, who it appeared spent their time trying to keep out of the way, a concept alien to Ted. Considering his lack of competition, he decided to take the detective exam and subsequently found himself promoted to the Criminal Investigation Department.

Ted spent three enjoyable years in the drug squad, did the rounds, and in his words 'saw a little bit of life at the front line, too much at the front line'. However, by 1969, the winds of change were stirring once again, and after 119 years of community policing, The County Borough of Tynemouth Police retired from the front lines, and Ted and his colleagues became part of the amalgamated Northumberland Constabulary (later Northumbria Police). In the days prior, Tynemouth's last officers gathered at the Military Road Drill Hall for their final group portraits. In one black and white photograph, I spotted Ted on the back row of Detective Constables, standing alongside his CID colleagues, all smartly dressed in suits.

I asked Ted if his parents had been proud of his work in the police, but he told me that sadly his mother had died suddenly at the age of fifty-five, before he had joined, which for him was an 'absolutely shattering blow'. His father was still alive for Ted's first two years in the force, but his pride seemed to be muted in Ted's memory, 'In a quiet sort of way he was, aye, you know, he was, aye.'

Life plodded along to a familiar beat for Ted until his two worlds collided, when he found his loyalty '*seriously* torn' during the 1984–85 miners' strike. Ted was ever the realist and although he subscribed to the belief that once you made a friend in the pit 'he's your friend for life', he reminded his officers that the name at the end of their paycheck each month was that of Northumbria Police. Nevertheless, he advised them not to disrespect the striking miners, and he 'ripped into' his fellow officers when they were 'trying to be too clever'.

On one occasion, Ted was placed on strike duty at Monkwearmouth Colliery in Sunderland, where years later the

Stadium of Light would be built. Standing there in a line of police, facing the miners on the opposite side of the road, Ted could not help noticing the difference: 'Did I look as rough as that, when I worked in the pit? You know, 'cause they *did*, they *did* look rough.' They were also a handful. Moments later, Ted came back to reality and found himself flat on his back, as he had been hit across the face with half a brick. The massed miners were moving steadily toward him, and his first thought was to get up, ''cause if you're on the ground when these boys come, you're in trouble'.

Though he did not miss the pit or the work, Ted still testified his belief that once a miner, always a miner, as 'like the coal dust in your lungs mining is engrained into your DNA'. And he 'still wouldn't have anything, *anything* said about the miners'. After joining the police, he returned to Worksop on several occasions to see his friend who had lost his hand, meeting in the Shireoaks Miners' Welfare to play dominoes. As he recalled, 'I was a policeman, but I was back amongst them.' However, after the strike, Ted had to be a little more cautious, particularly as Worksop had been overrun, and guys from the Metropolitan Police had been 'very disrespectful to the locals'.

Ted was a congenial character and, just like he assured me he would, he had spoken frankly about his experiences. I understood that despite twenty-eight years in the police, he felt he was still a miner, because he spoke their language and he conducted himself in the same way as they did. Yet, unlike others, who had opened not only their worlds but their hearts to me, I finished our interview with a sense that I had only seen as much of Ted as he had been willing to show, or his strong sense of propriety would allow. Just like Eddie Chapman, who changed the part he played when circumstances necessitated it, Ted had been able to move with the times and help himself. Ultimately, following the path of pragmatism had given him a long career that outlasted all the pits in County Durham, and from which it seemed he had emerged relatively unscathed. How many men had been as lucky and how many others, like Ted's father, had seen their dreams turn to dust but kept on singing until the final curtain fell?

2. The Miner Who Went to Fleet Street

What I think is important, is knowing what you want to do, knowing what you want to be, and if you just go ahead and want to do it, and you cast aside all the doubts, all the criticisms, and anybody who comes and says, 'You're not going to do that, you'll never get there, you'll never get that', just dismiss it, and just put your head down and run at it.

George is quite remarkable, and I was not alone in thinking so. Ted put me in touch with his old friend, who he introduced as a very eloquent and extremely literate lad, who began his working life at a pit that was little more than a hole in the ground and who had ended up on London's Fleet Street. When George first answered the phone, his accent mirrored the transition he had made, opening with a warm Tyneside lilt that gradually stiffened into a straitjacket of received pronunciation.

As Ted told me, despite preconceptions about miners, there were a lot of talented men underground; something I already knew to be true. Yet, George's story was distinct from any of the others I had come across. For a start, he was a miner turned journalist, whose later career saw him writing for the likes of the *Financial Times* and the *Daily Telegraph*. Secondly, George never really fitted in with mining life and he departed after just eighteen months.

The latter fact was not in itself unusual – many young

recruits found they could tolerate neither the conditions nor culture underground, and these men invariably left the industry and rarely looked back. However, in a small village in the Derwent Valley in the 1950s, surrounded by nothing but pits, pubs and pulpits, there were scarce alternatives for young men who had failed the eleven-plus examination. Speaking to George, I realised that underlying his success was not only talent but a deep-seated desire to prove the doubters wrong, and that was what had compelled him to run headlong towards every opportunity.

Born in November 1936, George was nine months older than Ted and had also grown up in Burnopfield, County Durham. Searching his family tree, George had discovered that his father's family were all slate miners from Cumberland, 'lovely people, quiet, nice people'. However, whilst his paternal grandfather was a 'saint', who spent his weekends batting for the local cricket team as opposed to going all out in the pub, his maternal grandfather was quite the opposite: a heavy drinker, a gambler, 'just sort of Mr Nasty'. Fortunately for George, his childhood interactions with the second character had been limited, although over seven decades later, he could still remember a particularly fraught fishing trip: 'He made me sit on the bank and never move, "Don't you move, don't you move!"'

Though he acknowledged that they were 'rough, tough days', George seemed to have few other complaints about his childhood, growing up in a council house with his parents, four sisters and brother. The village had a good mix of religion, with the Roman Catholic Church at the top of the hill, the Church of England at the other end, and the Wesleyans in between. For those not aspiring to Christian perfection, it also boasted half a dozen pubs, because, as George explained, 'miners were pretty heavy drinkers, most, a lot of them, not all of them'. As he told me, reflecting on his upbringing, to say his family were poor would not be quite right, because the coal mines brought with them a degree of money for the inhabitants of the village and, after all, they were 'all in the same boat, enduring the same'. However, the real symbol of wealth, sure to set you apart from your neighbours, was a home telephone and a car, and if you had either of those, 'you were halfway to being an aristocrat'.

George recalled happy days during the miners' annual two-week holiday, when he and his family would travel to Whitley Bay on the North East coastline. Emerging from wartime, when the iconic white dome of its Spanish City complex was camouflaged to evade German bombers, the seaside town was returning to its heyday by the time George was approaching his tenth year.[1] One sunny Sunday in August 1947, Whitley Bay welcomed over 10,000 day-trippers arriving at the station; no less than 4,000 deck chairs were hired out; long queues snaked out of its ice cream parlours, and local shops sold out of cigarettes.[2] While children spent their days swinging back and forth in shuggy boats on the beach, 'The North's Pleasure Rendezvous' offered tearooms, roof gardens, and ballroom dancing for the delectation of their parents.[3] Other mining families travelled the extra miles to Blackpool, but nobody dreamed of going abroad because flights were 'non-existent', and certainly not available to those of limited means.

Like Ted, as a child George had also failed to meet the requirements for a place at grammar school and instead had ended up at Burnopfield Secondary Modern. Despite the ambitions of the 1944 Education Act, which offered a free grammar school education to all children who passed the test, it failed to improve the chances of many children from poorer backgrounds.[4] The eleven-plus forever divided a cohort of local primary school leavers between 'the intelligent ones' and 'the others'.[5]

By the time George sat his exam, overseeing committees were doing their best to ensure a 'fair and open' competition, removing personal information from papers, including the child's name and parental income.[6] Even so, this did little to change the inbuilt biases of the test itself, which naturally favoured children with greater cultural capital and fuller vocabularies.[7] In 1948, one member of the West Hartlepool Education Committee had condemned the 'ridiculous' questions being posed to local ten-and-a-half-year-olds, like their understanding of *mutatis mutandis*.[8]

Just like many other bright working-class children who were overlooked by the system, this early judgement seemed to be something both Ted and George had carried with them for the rest of their lives.[9] However, though it purported to measure a child's academic potential, the exam could not weigh their strength of character or their aptitude for playing whatever hand life saw fit to deal them. At least in George's case, perhaps this early failure had been a blessing in disguise, sharpening his desire to prove himself. Visiting Burnopfield some thirty years later, he met some of the grammar school lads he used to know at the working men's club. At the time George lightheartedly observed: '"The difference between you, when you had a grammar school education, and me, who failed my eleven-plus", I said, "I wasn't terribly brainy, but I was very ambitious", and I said, "you're terribly brainy", but I said, "you've got no ambition", and they agreed.'

Failing to gain admission to grammar school was not the only hardship George had experienced before he ever set foot underground. When he was fifteen, one of his cousins put a pen up to his head and remarked: 'George, you've got a bald spot on the back of your head.' At the time, assuming his cousin was taking the mickey, George denied the allegation; however, when he returned home, he looked in the mirror and to his dismay he realised his cousin was telling the truth. Over the next few weeks, the patch, which started off as a dot, grew larger and larger until George no longer had any hair above the back of his neck. Later, he was diagnosed with alopecia.

The medical history of alopecia areata dates all the way back to the papyrus scrolls of ancient Egypt.[10] After thousands of years making little headway into understanding its causes, by the 1950s new research was underway and some clinics were purportedly finding success in treating those afflicted with steroid injections.[11] Meanwhile, increasing numbers of adverts placed in local newspapers by 'trichological therapists', offered to remedy falling hair at their clinics in Newcastle and Stockton-on-Tees.[12] In the end, George's mother took him to the hospital, where he was paraded around a sun lamp and, whether related or not, over the next year his hair gradually began to return.[13]

Although by the 1950s this noncontagious 'disease of the scalp' was well-known enough to appear as the answer to a crossword clue in the *Shields Daily News*, George recalled how everyone was afraid they could catch it.[14] As a consequence, he was forced to go to the local barber's just before closing because, as the proprietor confessed, 'I can't have you coming in with other people seeing you.' George was still charged the same price as customers with more hair, and without such restrictions. Nevertheless, he described the experience with good humour, as just another one of the 'trials' he had faced.

Once his schooling was complete, at the age of fifteen George found himself 'more or less signposted into the mines'. At first, he aspired to be a fitter, an engineer who would look after the machinery underground. However, in his interview George was asked if he owned a bicycle, and he answered honestly to say that sadly he did not as he could not afford one. It seemed that this was the end of the matter, as the man interviewing him replied: 'I'm sorry son, but if you can't put a bicycle together you could never be an engineer.' As George explained, 'He assumed from that, that I didn't have a bike, that I didn't have an engineering mind.'

Having had his sights readjusted, George went on to complete general mining training with the other new recruits, at an old disused mine nearby. From what he could remember, the main motivation of the training had been to make 'absolutely sure' that the incoming fifteen-year-olds were not killed or involved in a terrible accident during their first few weeks underground. The instructor taught them how to listen to the wooden pit props holding up the roof, which could give early warning of movement above: '"Listen carefully, if they just crack slightly you're fine", but he said, "if you hear a lot of it, get the hell out of there, 'cause it's coming down."' Such 'pit sense' had been transmitted from old to young long before the official training schemes of the Coal Board. It reminded me of a Durham folk song I had heard, 'Jowl and Listen Lad', in which an older narrator encouraged his younger colleague to listen and 'hear that coalface workin'', and warns: 'There's many a marrer missin, lad, Becaas he wadn't listen lad.'[15]

As the industry progressed into the twentieth century, British-made steel supports began to replace props made of foreign wood, despite concerns regarding their safety.[16] Later, owing to a shortage of steel due to the rearmament programme in the 1950s, German manufacturers were contracted to send steel pit props to the coalfields of Durham.[17] As George recalled, though strong, these new supports could also be '*fatal*, because when it went crack, it just came down on you'.

With a tuned ear and a heightened appreciation of the pit as 'a hazardous and dangerous place', George graduated from his training into the nearest colliery, Barcus Close, a drift mine, located just off Burnopfield's Busty Bank.[18] Founded at the end of the nineteenth century, by the time George joined this small pit it was reaching peak manpower, employing 235 workers by 1957.[19] George's father was well-known by many of the men there, as well as the colliery manager, who employed him as a gardener.

Brothers Thomas and George Richardson doing stonework and erecting forepoling at Barcus Close Colliery *c.*1940. Photo taken by Jack Brown of Burnopfield.

Compared to its larger neighbours, Barcus Close had generated few headlines over its lifetime, and the only stories it did produce were notably positive.[20] In 1955, Mr E. H. D. Skinner, Chairman of the Durham Divisional Coal Board, praised this 'happy pit' for its thirty-year record of no disputes or serious accidents, with a solid production rate and absenteeism on the surface earlier that year 'precisely nil'.[21] Opening the new £17,000 pithead baths, he had commended the men: 'Your output has been good and you have lost no time over trivialities.'[22] I imagine the men of Barcus Close were especially happy to finally have their own baths, something men at almost 400 other collieries had been benefitting from for almost a decade. George recalled how it was a 'revolution' when men could finish work, have a shower, and put on a clean shirt and a nice pair of trousers, which meant their wives were far happier to see them return home.

The colliery worked two shifts, day and night. Much to his dismay, George was allocated the latter shift, meaning he started work at midnight and finished at eight o'clock the next morning. He was employed as a pony driver, and at the start of work he would collect Jock, his pony, from the stables, which were a five-minute walk from the drift mouth and the entrance of the mine. Thankfully, George and Jock got along like a house on fire. The two of them would spend the dark hours bringing empty tubs to the coalface and carrying full ones out after they had been loaded by the hewers, who were paid on production.

Unfortunately for both Jock and his master, where there were ponies there were often rats, who shared in both their straw bedding and food. Rats were particularly prevalent in drift mines and men labouring in such infested places risked Weil's disease, a nasty and potentially fatal form of leptospirosis that was carried in the urine of infected rodents.[23] One of George's indelible memories from this time was of entering the dimly lit stables on a bitterly cold Monday night and being greeted by two bloated rats sitting bolt upright, in the throes of a slow and painful death, after inadvertently feasting on poison. Poor old Jock was tethered to his stable, kicking and sending sparks flying out across the floor, an unwillingly captive audience. Entering on the scene, George quickly intervened, clearing the rats with his hob-nailed boots, and leading the distressed pony away.

From his earliest days underground, George knew he would not be a miner for long. Though he could tolerate the conditions, working in the dark depths of the earth, a mile below the village where his family and friends were dreaming from the warmth of their beds, was something he found particularly difficult to accept. George's older brother was also at Barcus Close, though he worked in the daylight above ground, where he was a clerk, responsible for putting the men's weekly wages together.

At the end of each week, miners would receive their own little brown packet, which was always stuffed down at the top, with the money just visible inside. Men would count the contents by flipping the corner of the notes, which were mainly of a one-pound denomination because, as George observed, one pound was a lot of money back then.[24] Laughing, he described how some of the big money men, who could be on 'twenty, thirty, forty pounds *a week*', would push a thin pencil into the gap in the top of their packet, and gently wind it round a note until they could pull it free. When they got home, the sealed packet would be handed over to their wives, who would rip it open so quickly the contents were never checked. Apparently, some men managed to take five or ten pounds out in this fashion before the packet made it home. Unfortunately, George was unable to do the same with his pay packet, as he was earning so little his mother would certainly have noticed.

Waiting in the queue for their wages many men would have remembered the robbery two years earlier, when one Thursday night in September 1949, £12,900 had been stolen from the strongroom at the nearby Marley Hill Colliery.[25] The money was already inside the wage packets of some 1,700 miners employed at Marley Hill, Byermoor, Burnopfield and Barcus Close Collieries, due to be paid out the following day.[26] Despite the Coal Board's offer of a reward of £500 for any information relating to the crime, it remained unsolved.[27] Decades later, George had written to the *Newcastle Evening Chronicle* to ask if anyone could recall the crime, which, at least in local memory, ranked in status with the later Great Train Robbery of 1963.[28]

Whilst at Barcus Close, George was witness to a more farcical crime, which had been committed by several colleagues who were 'not quite the ticket'. One day there was a wagonload of beer being transported up the hill, past the colliery; at the time, George and some others were stood watching the coal tubs being unloaded. As the wagon passed, they saw a huge barrel of beer fall off the back and roll into the entrance of a nearby farm. Oblivious to its lost cargo, the wagon proceeded on its journey. Later that day, two of the guys who had been with George proudly explained how they had followed the barrel, rolled it to a safe spot, and watered it down to enjoy later. Apparently, the beer had lasted them a good few weeks, and though the police made several enquiries about the missing barrel, they never discovered where it went, another unsolved mystery.

Reflecting on his colleagues, George observed that there were a lot of lovely people at the colliery, and though he felt camaraderie was a word used too much nowadays, he did acknowledge its existence underground. George's own interpretation was that it all hinged on self-survival, 'Because if things get rough, you've just got to get the hell out of there as fast as you can, and take your pony with you.' It was a view distinct from that of others I had spoken to and to what I had come to understand – men certainly did not hang around in the event of an accident, but in terms of survival, the self was often readily placed at secondary importance to the life of a colleague.

A mere eighteen months later, George walked out of Barcus Close and took up a new job, as a clerk in a warehouse. As he was no longer employed in the coal industry – which along with farming and the Merchant Navy was deemed one of three essential services – he was soon called up for National Service.[29] In 1955, George entered the Royal Air Force, and after ample training and square-bashing, he was posted to Malta as a fighter plotter.

Demobbed two years later, George started working for a publishing company in Newcastle, responsible for producing *Voice of the North East*, as well as *Perspective*, an architectural magazine. The company was based in the offices of the *Evening Chronicle*, and George was keen to transfer. He secured an interview with one of the editors, but, as he recalled, it did not go as hoped: 'He said, "You were a coal miner, weren't you?", and I said "yes", and he said, "You don't know enough about newspapers, so I'm sorry son, you'll just have to stay where you are."'

After being knocked back once again by circumstance, George determined that if he could not get a job there, he would have to move because, as he sagely observed, 'quite often, to get what you want, you've got to move'. During this period, he had also been attending night classes, achieving O Levels and A Levels in English language and literature; so despite being rebuffed, he knew there was only one way he was going, 'which was to write'.

George's name first appeared in print above an article published in the *Sunday Sun*, on 3 May 1963. Under the headline 'Who Shot the Quiet Stationmaster?', in a thousand words George recounted the story of a fifty-year-old unsolved murder that had taken place in the small community of Lintz Green, 8 miles west of Newcastle, where his grandfather had worked as a miner.[30] Shortly before 11 p.m. on a dark October evening in 1911, sixty-year-old Joseph Wilson, a widower, prominent Wesleyan, and the stationmaster of Lintz Green, had been shot dead by an unknown assailant just outside his home adjoining the station, from where the last train had departed moments before.[31] This unassuming man, who had a passion for gardening, was discovered lying on the garden path by his daughter.[32] At the time, it was suspected that the murder was a botched robbery attempt, but despite a porter being taken into custody, he was later released without charge.[33]

Readers had an appetite for stories which would liven the pace of a slow Sunday, and George's efforts were well-received, earning him his first cheque of £10. In subsequent years, the unsolved murder continued to appear periodically in the local press. In 1979, the occupant of the stationmaster's house described being disturbed in slumber by the touch of icy hands, and hearing trains passing through the station at midnight, despite the fact the line had been out of use for two decades.[34] Recently, the house, which dates back to the late nineteenth century, has been brought back to life with Farrow & Ball paintwork and Morris & Co wallpaper. It is currently listed for sale for a little over half a million pounds with an agency specialising in historic properties, though understandably, its chequered past is not featured in the brochure.

After his brief foray into crime reporting, George later made the transition to financial journalism. It all happened 'a little bit by accident' because he was keen to get to Fleet Street and took the first job he was offered to achieve that. He applied for a sub-editor job at the *Financial Times*, which he got, and this marked the start of his career in newspapers. Fleet Street in the 1960s must have seemed a world away from Barcus Close. Though, just as it was reimagined on stage in James Graham's recent play *Ink*, it was still a male-dominated one and, as George reflected, he still encountered his fair share of rats, albeit of a different kind.[35]

George subsequently moved to the *Daily Telegraph*, was the diary editor for *Financial Weekly* magazine, worked on *Daily News Tonight,* and when this folded, he joined the city desk of *Today* newspaper. When Rupert Murdoch closed it nine years later, George received a good pay-off, and went to work for an American television company on Oxford Street, before his retirement in 2001. Now in his late eighties, George lives a contented life in the South of England with his wife and two grown-up children.

Reflecting on his mining past, George felt he had benefitted from having had such a start, as 'it takes you straight into the realities of life', reminding you how life is in the balance all the time, with death 'always near at hand'. After leaving the pit, George had written a parody of A. E. Housman's poem 'Blue Remembered Hills' from *A Shropshire Lad*, in which he recalled the black hills and grey slag heaps of his own childhood, 'the darkness cloaked in fear'.[36] It had made him look at the world differently forever after, particularly as in his subsequent career the only thing to be afraid of was 'making an awful mess and being sacked'.

Of all the men I had spoken to, George's time in mining had been the briefest. Not only was his career trajectory unusual, his experiences demonstrated how not all men felt at home underground, or within the mining community. Despite his short spell in the pit, with the rest of his working years spent in both a very different job and locality, it had still left its mark on George.

Towards the end of our conversation, George described how in his early life he had read one of Joseph Conrad's books, which had made a lasting impression on him, reaffirming his belief that 'independence was a great thing' because 'it all happens inside you, don't go to committees, if you want something in life you have to really do it yourself'. Having been failed by so many local committees, I could understand why George had determined to place his faith in himself. In doing so, despite humble beginnings and many doubters, George had managed to find his own way to Fleet Street. I was left to wonder how different things might have been, had he owned a bike as a child.

*

'Black Remembered Hills'
'A Durham Lad'

Into my lungs a dust that kills
From yon far coalfield blows
What are those black remembered hills?
What grey slagheaps are those?
That is the land of lost content
I see it shining clear
The groaning shafts; the constant toil
and darkness cloaked in fear.
Where are the lads who hewed the coal?
Who shook with every blast?
They are but echoes underground
Now memories of the past.[37]

3. The Dark Horse

In my time down the mines, I've been in fires, underground, I've been in floods, I've been gassed, but not, not dead gas, just knocked out gas, and I've been shot, I was shot in the leg.

There were few things that could have stopped Stephen from working. The list of incidents he had endured in his twenty-four years as a miner was dreadful and eventually, after losing the sight in one eye, he had been forced to work above ground. However, what was perhaps more shocking was the matter-of-fact way he recounted his injuries, as if being shot in the leg or gassed was just par for the course, or in his own words, 'Just another day's work, that's it.' Unlike his forebears, Stephen was never destined for life underground. Though he demonstrated an admirable work ethic from an early age, he was small in stature, standing almost a foot shorter than his father, and 'very, very weak', having suffered pneumonia five times as a child. Yet, when he found himself following in his father's footsteps, he rose to the challenge, a man who was in no way cut out for pit work, but who cut a way in, nonetheless.

Stephen came from the village of Burradon, 7 miles north of Newcastle and 5 miles from the sea. First sunk in 1820, Burradon Colliery was one of the oldest in the Great Northern Coalfield. Even in the early twentieth century, locals still remembered it as the site of the terrible explosion that occurred in March 1860, which claimed the lives of seventy-six men and boys, the youngest of whom were John Pease and Jacob Weatherley, both ten years old.[1] The evening after the disaster and all the next day the neighbourhood's joiners could be seen making coffins, leaving a large pile stacked on the pit bank, ready for the charred remains being brought up to the sound of wailing.[2] Forty-year-old John Carr also perished in the explosion, and 150 years later, his great-great-grandson Alan, better known for comedy than mining tragedy, would unveil a memorial in his honour.[3] It transpired Alan's other great-great-grandfather, on his maternal side, had died in the same explosion and, in a strange twist of fate, the two men had been discovered together.[4]

As the decades passed, both the pit and its people recovered and by the time Stephen was born in March 1937, the surrounding village epitomised a well-ordered and self-contained mining community. In May, locals celebrated the coronation of George VI with a parade of schoolchildren led by the Burradon Colliery Band, followed by games, community singing with the local chapel choir and a tea on the Welfare grounds.[5] Football tournaments, ladies' bowls competitions and dances were held to benefit the Burradon School Children and Aged People's Treat Fund, which in 1937 (a particularly successful year) paid for an excursion of almost 400 children and over 150 adults to the not so far-flung destinations of South Shields and Tynemouth.[6] As summer faded into autumn, locally grown leeks were judged in the show at the Traveller's Rest pub and the annual harvest social was held in the Co-operative Hall.[7]

Stephen recalled how growing up in the village practically 'everybody knew everybody', with most related through either birth or marriage, and all with some connection to the 'family pit'. Outside of the odd falling out between neighbours – with one miner threatening to knock another's head off and using cease and desist letters as unconventional window adornments – life in Burradon seemed fairly peaceable.[8] When war touched British shores in 1939, miners agreed to pay a levy of threepence a week in support of the newly formed Burradon Village War Comforts Fund, through which parcels were dispatched to men serving abroad.[9]

Stephen was raised in a long row of sandstone cottages, overlooked by the colliery headgear. These dwellings were archaic even by the standards of the time, with no electricity or indoor water supply. In colder months, residents would have to defrost one of the outdoor taps, shared with the rest of the street, to get water to wash and cook with. Once a week, children would be scrubbed down in a zinc bathtub on a proggy mat in front of the fire, the pungent scent of carbolic soap mingling with the warm aroma of stottie cakes baking in the oven.[10] On Mondays, laundry was pegged onto lines criss-crossing the street because, according to the old Mother Goose nursery rhyme, 'They that wash on Monday have all the week to dry.'[11] The family's only toilet, or 'netty', was in a bank of four across the street and Stephen would take a bucket of ashes with him when nature called, as it did not have a flush. Periodically, the night soil man would empty these with his long-handled shovel, driving his horse and cart through the village under the respectable shroud of darkness.

Stephen's family, like most of the community, had long roots underground, with his father, both grandfathers and uncles all employed by the colliery. However, Stephen's contact with the industry as a child was minimal. When not at school, he spent most of his time in the company of his mother and only saw his father at the weekends. These were the days before the industry's nationalisation, when men would work six days a week, and Stephen's father spent his nights underground, from four o'clock in the afternoon until midnight.

On Saturdays, Stephen would usually go with his mother to visit his aunt, who lived nearby. However, when he reached the age of ten, he rebuffed the world of women, choosing instead to get up at six o'clock in the morning to cycle 12 miles with his father, brother and some ferrets, in all weathers, to catch rabbits on a nearby farm. The rabbits were rife and were eating the vegetables, so the farmer welcomed the help. In the afternoon, the family would take some of the spoils of the hunt home for dinner, while the remainder were sold, with the proceeds split equitably. At harvest time, Stephen worked amongst prisoners of war, transported to the farm in wagons to help bring in the crops.[12] At the behest of the farmer, Stephen would collect a basket of sandwiches and a large can of cocoa made with water, not milk, to feed the labourers in the fields.

Five years later, when Stephen was preparing to leave school, his father asked him what he was going to do for work, a question that rarely needed to be posed to young boys in a place like Burradon. Fortunately, the local butcher was advertising for an errand boy, a role which seemed far better suited to Stephen's capabilities than a life underground. Stephen walked to the shop and the butcher gave him a bicycle, a basketful of meat orders, a list of addresses and sent him on his way. Not long after, Stephen was lying on the ground surrounded by stray dogs, with a woman, who had been sweeping the path, now engaged in fighting them off with her broom. Rousing himself, Stephen managed to gather up his cargo and get back on the bike to complete his assignment. Fortunately, though half of the brown paper packages, tied up with string, 'had been on the bloody road', nobody complained; perhaps they had taken pity on the beleaguered delivery boy who had apparently met the same fate.

Despite a shaky start, Stephen persevered in his new role, working six days a week. One Saturday morning, his mother asked him to bring half a dozen pies home for tea when he received his wages later that day. Stephen did as instructed, but after buying the pies he was left with just £1.25, '*bloody hells bells*'. Returning home, he put the change down on the kitchen table and his mother gave him back a pound, which he refused, but she benevolently told him: 'You're not going out with your pals, with no money.' Chatting to his friends at the local cinema that evening, Stephen learned they were earning three quid a week in the mines, a veritable fortune compared to what he was bringing home in pies and pay.

The next day Stephen got up, found his father, who asked him how the job was going, to which his son replied that he would not be returning. 'He says, "Where are you going?", I says, "Up the mine", he says, "You're *bloody not.*"' Following a 'big tiff', Stephen's father instructed him to get his coat and hat and come with him. The mines were open seven days a week back then, so they went to see the manager. '"I've got the boy here", he says, "he's hoping for a job", and the manager said "Well", he says, "if he's half as good as you, he can start on Monday"', and that was the end of the interview.

Stephen began working at Burradon Colliery in the spring of 1952. Too young to go underground, his first year was spent on the surface, working on the screens, removing stones from the coal and grading it into sizes. When he reached the required age, Stephen was asked to bring his documents to the office, so they could confirm his eligibility for underground training. The following morning, Stephen got his birth certificate from his mother and dutifully handed it in. When he returned to collect it that afternoon, 'The office was *chock a block full*, it was like a bloody cinema', and as he opened the door, the audience inside erupted into hysterics. 'I says, "What's up?" and the guy, the manager's clerk, gives us me birth certificate, and he says, "Here you are," he says, "You're sacked!", I says "Why?", he says, "We don't employ females here."' Unbeknownst to him, Stephen had been living as a female 'for *fifteen year* and I didn't even know, my mother didn't know, no one had looked at it!' As a result, instead of going for training, later that week Stephen was standing in the births, deaths and marriages office in Newcastle, paying for a new birth certificate.

Eventually, after legally changing his sex and completing his training, Stephen was given his first job underground, which saw him working alongside a pit pony, just as George had at Barcus Close. British collieries had long made use of horsepower. In the days before steam was harnessed, these magnificent beasts would walk in strong, slow circles at the pit top, turning a gin which raised coal up the shaft. Later, ponies had been introduced in large numbers underground, taking over the haulage work previously done by women and children.[13] From Shetland to Shire, and Welsh Cobs whose 'pluck, hardiness and endurance' reportedly had no equal, horses of several different breeds were employed in pits across Britain.[14] However, just as with the human population underground, it was rare to find a mare, with most of them geldings.

Each pony was fitted out with a heavy leather harness and bonnet, with guards to shield their large eyes from falling debris underground. Unlike the men, who could ascend into the light at the end of a hard shift, the ponies were stabled in the pit, each in its own whitewashed stall, with straw bedding and a sign mounted to the wall denoting the name of its occupant. The pungent farmyard smells emanating from these spaces were a stark contrast to the lifeless scent elsewhere in the pit. The ponies only rose to the surface once a year, in August, when the miners took their annual fortnight holiday, or in the instance of a prolonged stoppage, as had happened in 1926. Emerging dazzled by the unfamiliar daylight and released into a nearby field, their timid trot turned into a canter, until they were galloping like they had seldom had the chance to do in the confines of the mines.

Like their human companions, the ponies of Burradon had also suffered their own tragedies across the colliery's history. A particularly awful incident occurred in 1883, when a serious fire had engulfed the stables killing nine of the fifteen resident ponies. Witnesses described the unbearable stench of burning flesh. One poor pony was found 'standing on all fours, completely charred', and when touched it disintegrated into dust.[15]

The mutual hardships of man and beast underground were immortalised on the banner of the Quarrington Hill Lodge from County Durham, that was first paraded in 1873.[16] One side shows a gaunt pony, slumped forward as it struggles to pull a coal-laden wagon, with its miner companion taking the weight from behind. Beneath the sorry scene runs the line: 'Come up, Bobby, ten hours a day!' The image on the other side depicts a healthy pony, pulling the same tub, walking alongside his smiling master, both benefitting from

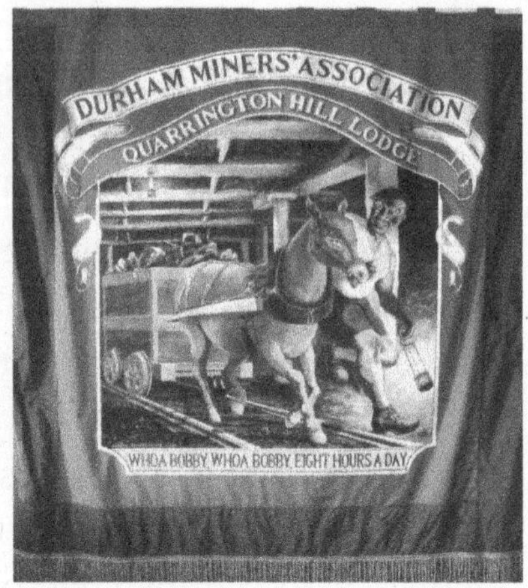

Quarrington Hill Lodge banner, first unfurled in 2013. Designed by Durham Bannermakers based on a description of the original banner paraded at the Durham Miners' Gala in 1873.

a shorter shift, above the line: 'Whoa Bobby, whoa Bobby, eight hours a day.'[17]

In response to mounting pressure from animal welfare bodies, including the newly formed National Equine Defence League, the so-called Pit Ponies Charter of 1911 protected the welfare of such animals in law, stipulating the hours they could work and how they should be kept.[18] Nonetheless, as the *Falkirk Herald* lamented, of all animals on the earth, the life of the pit pony was 'surely the most miserable'.[19] Their plight was not the result of maltreatment, as they were often favoured beyond their kin above ground, but due to an existence spent in interminable darkness and dust. It reminded me of the ill-fated Trompette of Émile Zola's *Germinal*, a pony 'still yearning for the sunshine', who eventually emerged from the pit 'a great pile of dead flesh'.[20] As Stephen conceded, it was a life that often ended at the tanyard.

Despite continuing appeals for their liberation, when the

industry was nationalised in 1947, there were still over 20,000 ponies working underground. Individual miners became very attached to their equine assistants and before leaving home for work they would fill their pockets with treats, like apples, mints and sugar lumps, to be shared underground. Apparently, some ponies even acquired a taste for tobacco, seeking out a twist from their two-legged friends. Cruelty to the ponies was not tolerated in any form. Another man I spoke to, who worked at the nearby Choppington Colliery, recalled an incident where a miner really 'had a go' at one of the ponies and the resident gentle giant, a man seldom inclined to violence, was quick to intervene, grabbing the culprit by the lapels, lifting him off the floor, and threatening to kill him if he dared to touch the pony again.

At Burradon, Stephen was teamed with Colin, a feisty Shetland, small in height and jet black in colour, with warm brown eyes. According to Stephen, you could tell just from looking at Colin that he was a proud pony, from good stock, 'a leader perhaps of his own kind'. The pair were tasked with hauling material to and from the coalface. Together, they walked through roadways that were only 4 feet high, where holes had been dug between the sleepers of the underground railway, to enable the ponies to pass through without grazing their shoulders on the roof. Like many new recruits, Colin appeared quietly terrified of his tomb-like surroundings and Stephen recalled how the pony's whole body would tremble at the slightest noise, but 'neither one of us could change a thing'.

Though he feared the pit, Colin was unafraid of the men he worked amongst, and as Stephen observed, his spirit would not be easily broken. During one shift, two older miners walked past and one of them spat out a chew of tobacco in Colin's direction. In response, the pony promptly turned around and chased the men back through the tunnel, screaming his head off. Running as fast as they could, the men sought shelter beneath an upturned tub. Undeterred Colin began to kick the tub with all his might, the pit walls reverberating with the sound of clanging metal. Eventually Stephen managed to calm the little Shetland down and lead him away from his captives, who emerged Quasimodo-like, complaining of 'the bells, the bells!'

On other occasions, Colin had proven an invaluable companion. One day, when Stephen was working deep in the pit, miles away from the shaft bottom and nearing the end of his shift, he had stumbled and fallen badly, smashing his cap lamp. It is hard to imagine the blackness that rushed in once the last light died out, almost suffocating in its denseness. Stephen was bereft; he knew he could not find his way out nor navigate the treacherous roadways blind.

Luckily, Stephen was not entirely alone in the dark. He called out to Colin, who replied with his usual snort. Stephen grabbed hold of the pony's tail and beseeched him to lead them back. After almost an entire year underground, the pony's eyes were far better accustomed to the darkness than his master's, and he negotiated the narrow corridors and low roofs towards the light. When Stephen came out into the pit bottom, after what seemed like an eternity in the dark, he flung his arms around his hooved companion and planted a grateful kiss on his brow.

This was not the only time Colin had been Stephen's salvation. Later, the duo was working together in a disused part of the mine, tasked with retrieving broken machinery. After successfully shifting three heavy loads, they took a well-earned break before returning to the old workings to resume their efforts. Halfway in, Colin stopped dead and refused to move any further. Stephen could not understand what was going on or why the industrious little pony was refusing his appeals to go forward. Moments later, the overseer appeared and enquired what the problem was. Stephen told him of the pony's reluctance to proceed, so the overseer took his lamp off his belt and tested for gas. 'Out of here, there's 2 per cent gas in the air!' The party swiftly retreated to where the air was better, and as Stephen observed: 'Once again, Colin saved my life and, as long as I live, I shall never forget him.'

After a year, Stephen was offered a better job, working on the coalface, and he had to leave Colin behind, though every time he passed the stables he would look in on his old friend. Stephen's first job on the coalface required him to withdraw the supports and let the roof fall behind him. At Burradon, everything was still done by hand, using picks and shovels, without the aid of machines. Still something of a weakling, Stephen struggled to keep up. Fortunately, he was taken under the wing of an older man, a boxer, who offered to train him up, which Stephen gladly accepted.

The figure of the boxer embodied many of the ideals of mining masculinity. He was strong and tenacious; he could think on his feet and react fast; he willingly engaged in a pursuit that risked both life and limb and, perhaps most important of all, he played by the rules. In the early twentieth century, stories of bare-knuckled fights between miners in the streets after dark often appeared in the local news.[21] However, over time such hypermasculine energies were increasingly redirected to boxing clubs, and it became a popular sport in coalfield communities across Britain.

Men in the ring often appeared on the cover of *COAL,* the industry's monthly magazine, and the popular *Mining Review* films featured boxers in no less than fourteen items.[22]

Front cover of *COAL* magazine, February 1952.

The Coal Board even hosted its own Mineworkers' National Amateur Boxing contests, which in 1949 saw J. Holman of Kent's Chislet Colliery victorious over J. Gill of Washington Colliery, County Durham, in the light-heavyweight championship bout at Wembley.[23]

Maurice Cullen, who like Stephen was a man of modest stature but who became a giant of the boxing world, was born in Wheatley Hill, 30 miles from Burradon, where Stephen had been born the same year. Cullen's father was a professional pugilist who used to take on miners who fancied trying their chances in Taylor's Boxing Booth during Durham's annual Big Meeting.[24] Cullen started his own working life as a pipe fitter in the local colliery before moving down the road to Shotton Colliery, which was, as its name suggests, another mining community. Realising he had inherited his father's talent for boxing, after an unplanned skirmish with a fellow miner at the age of seventeen, Cullen went on to fight in the Coal Board championships. He won both the featherweight and lightweight titles, before embarking on a career during which he would fight at New York's Madison Square Garden.

Later life found Cullen working as the local milkman, running between his deliveries to stay fit, until he died of a heart attack at the age of sixty-three. Still, the legacy of the North East's 'one-armed bandit' has not been forgotten by his community.[25] Driving through Shotton Colliery, you cannot miss the two enormous black boxing gloves, sculpted from steel, that hang on the green in front of the concrete houses of the Ashbrooke Estate, close to where Cullen used to live.[26] The size of the gloves mirrors the spirit of 'The Pitmen's Champion', who continued to inspire younger generations despite his failing health.[27]

Steel sculpture by Graeme Hopper unveiled in Shotton Colliery, County Durham, in 2018. The gloves were modelled on those worn by Maurice Cullen when he won the Lonsdale Belt.

Not unlike Cullen, who in addition to training in the gym would run up and down the Shotton pit heap, from the age of eighteen through to twenty-one, Stephen followed a gruelling routine. He would run 5 miles before breakfast, go down the mine, work an eight-hour shift, go home for tea, take two buses, from Burradon to Newcastle, then to Gateshead, where he would box until nine o'clock at night, before returning home to sleep. Stephen maintained this schedule across five days a week for three years in order to build himself up, 'and to make me strong, which it did'.

Thanks to his training, Stephen was eventually able to undertake the work of two men underground and found himself earning more money than his father. However, the ultimate recognition of his status came on the day a group of SAS men, from the British Army, 'really hard, hard men', wanted to have a look around the pit. He recalled how once the group reached the shaft bottom, they refused to get out of the cage, as 'they were that terrified'. Stephen felt particularly proud of this fact, as he observed: 'They're supposed to be the hard men, what the hell were we?'

On other occasions, Stephen's own tolerance for risk was found to be lacking. One morning he had been waiting to go down the pit when there was a loud bang, and when the ascending cage reached the surface it was full of clumps of wood. While the incident was investigated, men were advised to go down the secondary shaft, which did not have any cages, descending instead in a bucket attached to a rope, 'one leg in the bucket and one leg out, and balance yourself to go down a thousand foot'. Not fancying his chances hanging out of a bucket over such a drop, Stephen decided he would spend his shift in the safety of the club: 'You either went down or you didn't, and if you didn't go, you didn't get paid, well that was it, I wasn't going to risk me leg for it.'

Later, Stephen's mettle had been truly tested in a situation which he could not avoid. One particularly sunny morning, Stephen had descended in the cage, feeling quite content with life, and ready for a hard day's labour. He and fifteen others had been tasked with working out a new seam where it was a little on the damp side and the coal was not of the best quality, but it was still saleable. As Burradon was such an old mine, there were few seams that had not been worked out.

Led by a deputy, the group of fifteen walked several miles uphill from the pit bottom, until they were around 100 feet from the surface. Reaching their destination, Stephen and four colleagues proceeded to the coalface. They commenced work and after about an hour or so, all was going as expected, until they heard a loud noise and water suddenly came rushing down upon them from the roof above. As Stephen later noted, until that moment, he had not ever seen so much water in one place underground. Like a cork released from a bottle, the deluge rushed out, sweeping away everything in its path.

Thinking quickly, the men found something to hang on to, with Stephen clutching one of the roadway supports 'like grim death'. No one dared put their feet onto the ground, as they were only yards away from the downward drift towards the shaft, and they knew that 'to be swept away would be sudden death'. As for their colleagues, stationed a hundred or so yards away, they could do little more than pray for their safety, as the deafening roar of the waters prevented any communication. Freezing cold and soaking wet, Stephen's group had no choice but to hang on until the inrush eased. During what seemed like an interminable wait, he found his mind wandering, 'You think of all sorts of things – am I going to die in this godforsaken place? Did I do something wrong in a past life? Is it payback for some past deeds? Was it wished on me?'

It took hours for the torrent to slow. Eventually, the men were able to release their grip and review the damage that had been done. In that peculiarly human response to a disaster being realised, the party found themselves smiling and even giggling with relief that they had survived. As Stephen told me, when accidents occurred underground, 'if you were OK, you just laughed about it'. Fortunately, the group discovered their other colleagues further down the passage safe and sound, and they managed to locate a working telephone to report the incident to the surface. Another hour or so later, the party were escorted into the hazy afternoon sunlight.

The management were apparently dumbfounded as to what had happened, and how the workings might be saved underground. They reviewed the old plans of the mine, dating back to when the pit had first been sunk and discovered a subterranean lake directly above the place where Stephen and his colleagues had been labouring. During a drought one long dry summer in days long past, the owners had pumped the water up from the lake to the surface for the villagers to use. The rescued men were sent home to rest but not for long, as they needed to return the next day, ready for hard work.

In the end, Stephen's twenty-two years underground finished as a result of a much less dramatic incident, when he was struck by a falling piece of wood, which blinded him in one eye. Stephen's injury coincided with the time when Burradon Colliery ceased production for the final time, in November 1975, over 150 years after it was first sunk. At its peak, this 'great family pit' had employed over 1,700 local men.[28] However, by the 1970s manpower was steadily falling, with miners shunning the old 'pick and shovel' pits in favour of newly mechanised operations.[29] By the time Burradon closed through exhaustion, only 300 men were left. Above ground, the colliery was already in a state of decay, paint was peeling off, and the sign declaring National Coal Board ownership 'on behalf of the people', triumphantly thrust in the ground decades ago, was tatty.

A local resident, who lived in one of the few remaining colliery cottages on Strawberry Terrace, told the paper how she mourned the familiar sounds of men on their way to work and the reässuring sight of the pit's wheel turning round.[30] Most of Burradon's miners had spent their whole working lives there. Even Betty, the cook, had been in the canteen since it first opened in 1940.[31] Thankfully, Stephen's father had retired two years earlier, at the age of sixty-five. After giving fifty years of his life to the industry, the Coal Board rewarded him with £500 and a plaque, 'Thank you very much for your services.' As Stephen recalled, 'It was an insult to men that.'

One of the greatest virtues of the Coal Board, or so I had been told by several of its former employees, was that it took back its wounded and found a job for them wherever possible. After being barred from returning underground due to his partial loss of sight, Stephen transferred to Brenkley Colliery at Seaton Burn, around 3 miles away, the smallest Coal Board-owned pit in the Northumberland coalfield. Stephen was given the role of lamp cabin attendant, checking, lighting and issuing lamps to miners about to descend underground. He also became the designated first-aid man, overseeing the ambulance room and on standby through the night for injured miners carried up during the evening shift.

Not busy enough, Stephen also got involved in the union, becoming the colliery's representative and attending monthly meetings with management, for which he was able to take the whole day off for a late afternoon meeting. Later, he took on the role of compensation secretary, visiting the offices of doctors and solicitors to fight the cases of injured men. Stephen was still fighting his own case, having rejected an offer of £10 for full and final compensation following the loss of one eye. After a battle lasting almost four years, he was eventually awarded £7,500 and a pension for life.

On the eve of the strike in 1984, Stephen attended a meeting with the union. He asked where his voting paper was, to which he recalled being told: 'Arthur Scargill says you're on strike, and that's the end of it.' For Stephen, this did not represent democracy as he understood it, and after the meeting he returned home and remained there for almost the entire year, refusing to have anything to do with the strike. Later, he received a notice from the Coal Board advising him that if the pit closed before he returned to work, he would lose any redundancy he had accrued. By that point, Stephen was entitled to £1,000 for each of his thirty-four years in the industry.

As the strike entered its penultimate month, over a hundred men were back working at Brenkley, and the pit started production for the first time in almost a year.[32] Seven pits in the area were also producing coal, with only the 'solid' Bates Colliery in Blyth still out of action. A week before the strike ended, witnessing more and more men returning to work, including his own son, Stephen decided to go back, bitterly aware that from this point forward he would be classified as a scab.

Just a few months later, notice was served by the Coal Board, meaning Brenkley Colliery would be closed by the end of 1985 due to 'persistently adverse geological conditions'.[33] The union did not oppose the closure plans, knowing as they did that the coal reserves were running out.[34] More devastating was the fact that Brenkley was just one name on a list of pits set to close in the local area, including Bates, Horden, and Sacriston, with the North East coalfield haemorrhaging over 4,500 jobs in a handful of months.[35]

The noon shift was the last to cut the coal, which came to the surface for the final time at Brenkley in October 1985. Of the workforce of more than 600 men, over half took voluntary redundancy, including Stephen, with the remainder offered alternative work with the Coal Board.[36] While other men lamented the loss of friendships underground, one miner, who had spent nine of his thirty-three years underground at Brenkley, described how he had taken the decision 'very badly', despite a sizeable redundancy pay-out, as the prospect of working at another pit was closed to him: 'I went to work during the strike and the other men would make life very difficult for me.'[37] The men who opted to transfer were found places at the so-called long-life pits of Ellington and Ashington, with a handful going to Westoe. Ashington closed in 1988, Westoe followed suit in 1993, with Ellington being the last deep mine in the Great Northern Coalfield to close in 2005. Incidentally, Ellington was also the last pit with working ponies, who had finished their final shift eleven years earlier.

Aged just forty-eight, Stephen was too young to retire and too old to start in a new occupation, and because of his eyesight he could not get any of the driving jobs that were being offered to the other men. He ended up working on a local garage forecourt, cleaning the pumps, picking up rubbish, and scrubbing the toilets, which paid £2.50 an hour. Despite feeling disheartened, he resolved: 'If it's this or nothing, I'll have to stick with it', and over time the job improved. Stephen ended up splitting his week working at three different garages to make ends meet. Still there over fifteen years later, at the age of sixty-five, he asked to work at the garage nearest to his house, where he remained employed until his eightieth year.

Now in his twilight years, people still tell Stephen he looks at least fifteen or twenty years younger. His manner seems to fit his appearance better than his years, and though he is reluctantly retired, he remains as absorbed in life as I imagine he ever was. The story he told me had few grand moments of heroism or despair and, unlike many others, his career at the pit was drawn to a close without a fight. I never discovered exactly how he came to be shot in the leg, but it was an incident that, like the others, was simply shrugged off. From that first moment when he fell off his bike, Stephen was never knocked down again, he just kept getting back into the ring. Despite his natural disadvantages and the injuries he sustained, Stephen demonstrated a tenacity that even the greatest men would struggle to match, though it seemed that in Colin he had found an equal, a fellow dark horse.

4. Last of the Big Hitters

It was my first day there, and I told you, you're working with men, you're working with the real McCoy, so the canteen's full, it's five o'clock in the morning . . . kicked the canteen door, rattle, rattle, rattle, rattle, all these men started, 'What the bloody hell you bloody-', and I stepped in, I looked round, I said, 'I'm the Daddy here!'

Stewart is a formidable character. Though the years had mellowed him, you could still understand why before he became known as the Daddy, his nickname underground had been Bluto, after the hypermasculine nemesis of *Popeye the Sailor*. Each miner I spoke to told their own tales of 'big hitters' they had encountered in the pit. Stories of legendary men with a reputation for superhuman strength and stamina; memories of giants who could hew with a pneumatic pick in each hand and throw up weighty steel girders like feathers. Until now, however, I had not spoken to one. Though our conversations took place over the phone, Stewart conjured himself as a larger-than-life presence, and shared black and white photos of his earlier days, when he had been a veritable He-Man, with a 48-inch chest and a 34-inch waist.

Unlike Stephen, Stewart was *built* to be a coal miner. This was the result of both his physique and family history, as a man whose ancestry in the industry traced a dark line all the way back to the 1640s. Stewart had lost two grandfathers underground: one whilst he was tunnelling under the blood-soaked battlefields of the Somme and the other closer to home, after he broke his spine in the Lancashire coalfield at the age of thirty-four. The latter accident left five small children not only fatherless but homeless too, as Stewart reminded me, 'Back then, when somebody was killed underground, and you were living in a colliery house, you were only in for seven days and then you were out, whether you liked it or lumped it.' Perhaps because of this personal legacy of blood on the coal, Stewart's father had assured his friends and brothers, who like him were all miners, that his own lad would *never* work in the pit. This paternal vow was oft-recited across Britain's coalfields, but far less frequently upheld. One team of sociologists observed, in their aptly titled 1956 study *Coal Is Our Life,* that although 70 per cent of the people they spoke to in one mining community 'would not encourage their sons to be miners', the young men were all miners.[1]

Stewart was born in 1953, the year of Queen Elizabeth II's coronation, when Churchill was still Prime Minister, and children across the country flocked to buy toffee apples, as sweet rationing finally came to an end in Britain. He had been raised in sight of the pit's headgear in the busy industrial town of St Helens, Lancashire. However, unlike other mining communities, in which a career at the pit was a foregone conclusion, the young men of St Helens were fortunate to have an array of alternatives on offer. School leavers could look to the area's long-established glassmaking industry and the gleaming empire built by the Pilkington Brothers. Others chose to mould their futures in local clay and joined Roughdales brickworks, which had been in the town for over a hundred years. Some found a job at Beechams to be more to their taste, whose St Helens factory had been making world-famous recuperative remedies since 1877.

Like many of the men I spoke to, Stewart had grown up in a political household. Both his parents were committed socialists, and Stewart felt these principles had stayed with him throughout his life, 'I was born a socialist, I will die a socialist [. . .] it never ever leaves you.' As a consequence, at the age of eighteen, Stewart was sacked from 'another mundane job' for starting a union, and subsequently determined to follow his forefathers underground. It was ten o'clock on a Sunday evening when he plucked up the courage to tell his father he had joined the ranks of Bold Colliery. In response to this deeply unwelcome news, the older man shouted so loudly it seemed that the slates lifted off the roof above them. As he spoke to me, Stewart could still see his father standing across the family's living room, pointing his finger, as he forcefully assured him: 'You my lad, you won't last five minutes in a coal mine, *you will not last five minutes.*' In his early days underground, when he was petrified and 'could have given that job up a million times', Stewart would hear these words ringing in his ears and they would harden his resolve to continue. It was only much later in life, after he became a father himself, that he grew to understand his father's warning was the result of his own fears for his son's safety.

It was not hard to believe Stewart when he told me he had never been a 'soft kinda kid'. He spent his formative years living on a council estate in Parr, surrounded by large mining families. With two sisters and no older brothers, Stewart had to find his feet early on. He soon grew into a 'rum lad', who played rugby league, enjoyed manual work and drank in the *roughest* pubs. No one had the nerve to bother him, because 'if you crack me, I'm going to crack you back'. He was, in his own words, 'like any sixteen-year-old now', walking the streets, thinking 'they're all gangsters'. Yet, when Stewart started work at Bold Colliery, he soon realised he was not who he thought he was. Underground, there were bigger and stronger men, *the real McCoy*, who Stewart credited with making him into a man.

At Bold, Stewart found himself in a particularly well-seasoned gang. He worked alongside Hungarians who were there when the Soviet tanks rolled through the streets of Budapest, crushing the uprising of 1956. At the time, the National Coal Board had hoped to welcome 10,000 refugees fleeing the country, in order to quell labour shortages in British pits.[2] Sadly, the scheme had limited success, owing to local fears of competition, language barriers and an undoubted element of racial bias.[3] Stewart also met Germans, who had given themselves up in the deserts of North Africa during the Second World War but who, as he was keen to stress, were *not* Nazis. For young men of the postwar generation, working amongst real veterans underground was quite a boon. Stewart loved to listen to their stories and recalled how brilliant it was to be in the company of such hard men.

Like many others, Stewart felt it was a different world underground, where you could kill somebody and get away with it, because 'nobody would know', or be killed in a moment by the restless weight of thousands of tons of earth above you. Although adverts in the 1970s assured men they could get 'more out of life' in mining, with catchy soundtracks promising 'money, lots of money and security', a career underground still remained one of the most dangerous in Britain.[4] In 1972, Lord Wilberforce had reported to Parliament on the unique hardships faced by miners, and how 'other occupations have their dangers and inconveniences, but we know of none in which there is such a combination of dangers, health hazard, discomfort in working conditions'.[5] The year after his report was published, fatal accidents occurred at Lofthouse Colliery in Yorkshire, Markham Colliery in Derbyshire and Seafield Colliery in Scotland.[6] The opening words of the 1975 documentary *The Miners' Film* were quite right, a 'man's life' was still at stake for each piece of coal.[7]

The men willing to navigate such risks had long been framed as heroic, otherworldly figures. Union banners carried technicolour scenes of working-class champions battling against the snake of capitalism or other mythical beasts, alongside instructive mottos like 'only the strong survive' and 'victory through strength'. Outsiders like Daniel Defoe, Benjamin Disraeli and Richard H. Horne found the miners they encountered 'frightful' in appearance, 'stalwart men, broad-chested and muscular', who smiled at the dangers of their work.[8] A more favourable portrayal, which several men were able to quote, sprang from the pen of George Orwell, for whom the miner was a 'sort of grimy caryatid', performing 'an almost superhuman job by the standards of an ordinary person'.[9] Once a friend had asked Stewart what it was like working underground with all those men. He responded by describing how when he stepped out of the cage at the end of his shift, he turned back into a human being.

In 1947, the Coal Board had commissioned its own mining giant, as a figurehead for the newly nationalised industry. The *Ideal Miner*, by sculptor A. Barney Seale, stood at 10 feet 6 inches and was modelled on the strong-jawed Welsh coal miner Thomas Idris Lewis.[10] The figure debuted at the

Industrial Wales Exhibition in London's Olympia but continued to be deployed around the coalfields decades later, as a promotional tool for the industry and an aspirational figure for future generations of young men.[11] Two of these giant miners now man the gates to the National Coal Mining Museum in Wakefield.

Although the industry was modernising as the decades rolled on, the mythical mining superman maintained his stronghold in mining culture. In 1961, when Stewart was eight years old, the folk singers Ewan MacColl, Charles Parker and Peggy Seeger released *The Big Hewer*, a ballad inspired by colliers' tales from throughout the British coalfields.[12] Over the BBC airwaves they sang of a mining giant born into a cradle of darkness, who cut his teeth on 5-foot timber and could hold up the pit roof with his little finger. Across the Atlantic, the very same year, the Texas-born country singer Jimmy Dean had his first big hit with 'Big Bad John'. The song told the story of a miner built like a giant oak tree, who rescued his colleagues from a roof fall but ended up entombed, as the imagined memorial read: 'At the bottom of this mine lies a big, big man.'[13]

Closer to home, the parish of Bold, St Helens, had its own ancient myth to inspire local boys like Stewart, which predated the sinking of its colliery by hundreds of years. According to legend, the founding father of the Bold family, who gave the settlement its name, had single-handedly slayed a griffin that had been tormenting the local population.[14] Following news of his triumph, the man, a blacksmith by the name of Robert Byrch, was rewarded not only with land, but also a new title, 'Robert the Bold'. The eighteenth-century Griffin Inn still stands on Bold Heath, where the creature's dismembered remains were said to have been scattered.

Amongst Britain's miners, there were many men who might have been suitable candidates for griffin slaying, but in industrial times had instead found themselves cast as 'soldiers in the battle for coal'.[15] The 'Pit Profiles' produced by portrait draughtsman and former war artist H. A. Freeth, which appeared in each edition of *COAL* magazine, showcased real-life supermen of the coalfields. In 1949, there was the 'piratical-looking giant' John Jones, better known as 'Long Jack', a Welsh miner of 'ox-like strength' and stature, weighing over sixteen stone.[16] Later came Scotsman Archie Henderson, a born fighter who in his younger years could lift a man of ten stone above his head with just one hand, and Morgan Morgans or 'Moc the Pugy', an eighteen-stone former boxing champion who worked with a towel wrapped around 'his bull-like neck'.[17] Another feature in 1959 showcased the talents of Derbyshire's Harold Cope, a deputy at Ripley Colliery and decade-long holder of the title Britain's Strongest Man, whose prodigious strength had saved men's lives.[18]

In later years, the newspaper *Coal News* continued to celebrate similar characters, such as all-England weightlifter Dave Hancock, a 6-foot sixteen-stone pit giant, and twenty-three-stone warrior Peter Gee, a heavyweight wrestler and a pipefitter at Nottinghamshire's Cotgrave Colliery, where he was known as 'Goliath'.[19] Like Stewart, young miners never forgot the incredible feats of strength they saw performed underground by such bigger, stronger men, nor witnessing their naked muscularity on show in the pithead baths. One man remembered seeing a school friend's father in the showers, his description echoing the giants of mining folklore, as he told me: 'He was a mountain, a mountain of a man', 'He must have been a monster when he was younger.'

Of course, even in the early decades of public ownership, mechanisation was threatening to dethrone these kings of the coalface. Aspirational films, produced by the Coal Board's own film unit, sought to reimagine the miner as no longer a 'sweat and blood worker', but someone whose contribution to the industry would now be 'brains not brawn'.[20] Bold Colliery's Moses Heyes, newly returned to mining after a spell in an aircraft factory, was the spokesman for the Coal Board's 1948 recruitment campaign. Heyes's cheerful portrait appeared across national newspapers alongside his personal assurance that mechanisation was making the miner's job a far better one than he ever thought possible.[21]

After a seven-year transformation, costing £6.5 million, in 1957 Bold Colliery was heralded as the 'bright star of a new age in mining', producing coal at a rate of 760,000 tons a

National Coal Board recruitment advert from 1948 featuring Moses Heyes from Bold Colliery.

year, and turning over a profit of £750,000.[22] According to the *Western Mail,* the new-look colliery resembled a biscuit factory in a garden suburb and was as clean as 'a nurse's fingernails'.[23] At Bold, they no longer called a spade a spade, as it was now referred to 'with shame' as a defunct implement, abolished through the introduction of metal monsters underground.[24] Particularly revolutionary was the British-built Anderton Shearer Loader, described as a machine that 'thinks for itself'.[25] Invented by quiet Lancashire family man James Anderton, the Coal Board's Area Production Manager for St Helens, this steel-toothed crocodile would devour the coalface, then toss the broken rock onto a moving belt.[26] First launched in St Helens, within twenty years it was responsible for the lion's share of coal produced in Britain.

During an interview with the American talk show host Dick Cavett in 1980, actor and Welsh mining son Richard Burton explained how, according to miners like his father, who had worked the Great Atlantic fault by hand, those who won the coal with machinery had lost the right to call themselves miners.[27] Older miners often recalled a time when they had been the ones working like machines and heckled younger colleagues with stories of how props were once wooden and the men were steel, but now the reverse was true. One cartoon published on the back cover of *COAL* in 1959 illustrated the concerns of some miners, as it depicted a bent miner, sweating profusely with a coal cutter machine strapped to his back, little more than a packhorse.[28]

A far more equitable fusion of the power of man and machine was offered in the bronze sculpture commissioned by the Coal Board in 1964 and created by Arthur Fleischmann. A miner's naked torso emerges from the upturned steel cutting drum of the Anderton Shearer Loader, the teeth in each of its revolving blades shining and sharp. This appears to be no threat to the miner, whose muscular arms heave a lump of coal upwards onto his broad shoulder, his strong fingers tensed to support the load. Lord Robens, Chairman of the Coal Board, had originally unveiled the sculpture on the driveway of Anderton House in Lowton, the new seven-storey 'nerve centre' of the North Western Division.[29] When this was demolished just over two decades later, Fleischmann's man-machine found a less fitting home in the leafy grounds of Eastwood Hall in Nottingham. Since 1998, the sculpture has pride of place in the centre of a roundabout on the busy St Helens Linkway, close to the site where the monster machine was birthed. Today, circled by cars destined for the adjacent Ravenhead Retail Park, the *Anderton*

The Miner (Anderton Mining Monument) by Arthur Fleischmann, unveiled in 1964. Photographed in its present location on the St Helens Linkway, where it has been since 1998.

Mining Monument is somewhat lost in his surroundings, yet another victim of progress.

By the time Stewart joined Bold Colliery in 1974, brute strength had long been outmatched by the power of ever more advanced machines underground. However, it seemed that the new generation of miners entering the industry felt less threatened by technology than their precursors. They were, after all, men of the first digital era, coming to maturity in the age of microwave ovens, Pong, the Apple computer, the Sony Walkman and *Star Wars*. Like Stewart, whose adrenaline used to pump whenever the mighty coal cutter roared past him, these young men relished working with 'big boys' toys' that would run like animals and proving they were strong enough to tame them. In this way at least, it seemed that machines had found their place in the masculine mythos of the underground.

Stewart started off as a haulage hand, at the bottom of the pit's hierarchy; but over time, he steadily climbed upwards until he was a coalface worker and one of the pit's 'big hitters'. Each pit had its own group of heavies, men who could be relied on to get the job done. As Ted had explained, in Durham, they were simply known as 'The Men', whilst over in worldly West Yorkshire, they were known as the 'yellow jersey guys', after the leaders of the Tour de France. As one former colliery manager explained to me, members of this group knew they were the kingpins and had no hesitation in letting you know, going around 'like the cock of the walk'. This bravado was not always confined to the pit and often extended into the club after work.

Eventually, like other big hitters, Stewart found himself on *big* money. At times, sustaining a lead position in the wages table led men to take risks, which could have fatal consequences, but as Stewart assured me, 'If you didn't cut corners underground, you wouldn't get a nugget of coal, simple as that.' On one occasion, Stewart's gang had been cutting corners whilst working in a tunnel and two of his mates had been killed outright. For a long time, Stewart had blamed himself for the incident as he was the gaffer, but 'we knew what we were doing, we knew we were doing wrong, but we was there for one thing, we was there to make money'. For months afterwards, jokes were made at his expense and people were warned not to work with him as 'he'll end up killing you, that one'.

When the strike came in 1984, Stewart's tolerance for risk grew unabated. Bold's striking miners managed to secure a decommissioned police bus to transport flying pickets around the coalfields. As Stewart explained, they came up with an ingenious plan to give the local Darby and Joan club the means to buy the bus on their behalf, with the agreement that after the strike it could be used to run old-age pensioners about.[30] He was particularly proud of the fact the constabulary was kind enough to sell the bus taxed and with a full tank of diesel, blissfully unaware of the vehicle's destination. Stewart subsequently drove the so-called battle bus across the warring coalfields, each time relishing the fact it would be erroneously waved through the police blockades.

The battle bus got Stewart into a lot of trouble over that year, but I had little doubt he took grim satisfaction in that fact, both at the time and in the retelling. On one occasion, they had picked up two strike-breakers who had wrongly assumed it was their police escort to nearby Parkside Colliery in Newton-le-Willows. Stewart conceded that the men must have been scared witless when they realised their mistake. They were subjected to a strip-search, in which the men's locker keys were the smoking gun that proved their identities as working miners.

Following the episode, Stewart and a colleague were arrested and charged with kidnap and assault. Later, the *Echo* told the story of the working miners' 'ride of terror', as it had been recounted before Liverpool Crown Court.[31]

Altogether, Stewart was banged up on five occasions for 'so-called picket line violence'. He argued that this was due to his larger-than-life presence on the picket lines. Of course, it could also have had something to do with the Molotov cocktails they concocted to set fire to police coaches. Or perhaps it was after he arranged for the local undertaker to send funeral wreaths to the homes of two 'scabs'. Regardless, by the end of the strike, even the usher of the court knew him as Bluto, a fact he took pride in.

When the time came to return to work in March 1985, Stewart made a point of ensuring he was one of the *last two* to march back in. However, their remaining time at Bold Colliery was to be short-lived. By October, the Coal Board had announced its intention to close the pit within six months. According to an official spokesman, the decision was one of financial pragmatism: during the strike, two coalfaces and over £2 million worth of equipment had been lost, and almost 200 of the 1,000-man workforce had already transferred to Parkside Colliery.[32] However, since then, production at Bold had been steadily increasing and many felt the looming closure owed more to the militancy of its workforce. The union's branch treasurer, Colin Lenton, summed up the views held by many Bold men, including Stewart, when he argued that shutting the pit was 'a punishment for the stand we took during the strike'.[33]

Despite the miners' opposition, the Coal Board got its way and on 26 March 1987, thanks to the efforts of explosives expert Derek 'Blaster' Bates, Bold Colliery's 150-foot-high pit headgear came crashing down to earth.[34] Mirroring the

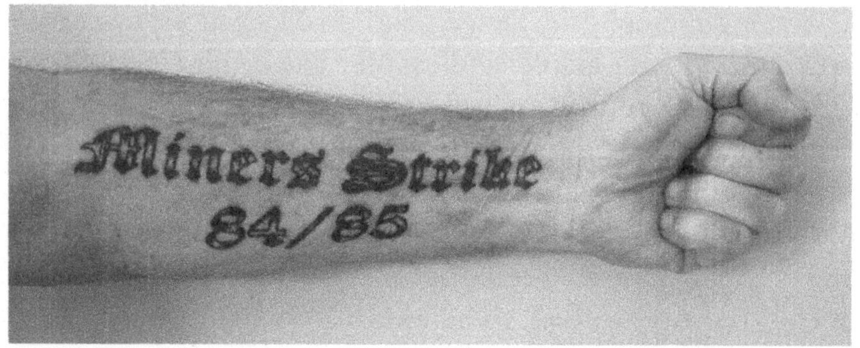

Photograph of Stewart's tattoo commemorating the 1984–85 miners' strike.

resistance of its former workers, the thick pillars of reinforced concrete above the no. 1 shaft defied extinction to the end, as Bates described how 'it was so strongly built it was almost impossible to get a drill into it'.[35] In a story that appeared under the exciting headline 'Whoomph!', the *Echo* recorded the more sobering fact that the demolition marked the end of 110 years of coal mining at Bold, and the loss of 2,000 jobs that the pit had provided at its peak.[36]

After being abandoned as an industrial wasteland, over the last decade the former Bold tip site in Parr has been transformed into Colliers Moss Common, an expansive green space, popular amongst dog walkers and horse riders. It seems appropriate that nature has reclaimed this site. Long before the Coal Board began using it as a dumping ground for spoil and waste from the colliery and power station, Bold Moss, as it was formerly known, was one of the last raised bog habitats in all of Lancashire. Older residents could remember running through this local wilderness as children, when it was still covered by verdant green sphagnum moss, purple sprays of heather, poor man's orchids and fluffy white cotton grass.[37] Once home to wagtails, blue finches, yellowhammers and scurrying rabbits, the Moss was slowly smothered beneath 9 million tons of spoil, ash and dark industrial sludge.

Today, like Lazarus, the Moss has risen from the dead. Life has returned in the form of birds, water voles, common lizards and no less than sixteen species of dragonfly. Walking around this revived habitat, the legend of the griffin and Robert the Bold seems far closer now than thirty years ago when it was an industrial refuse site. However, in recent years, the Moss has found itself engaged in a new battle against waste of the post-industrial age. The picturesque 'blue lagoon' at its centre, a renowned beauty spot, has become a congregation site for local teenagers whose leftovers include discarded drug baggies, used condoms and empty vodka bottles.[38]

The closure of Bold Colliery was only to be a small fault in the rich seam of Stewart's mining career. Despite the presence of several alternative pits in the local area, he was cautious about his next move owing to his reputation locally, particularly after the strike. He spent some time at Golborne Colliery near Wigan, 'a scab pit', but later transferred to Bickershaw Colliery in Leigh. In the 1970s, a £3 million development scheme saw Bickershaw become the focus of a new 'super pit' complex, the first in the North West, linking it with nearby Parsonage and Golborne Collieries, a move that was intended to give it 'a big future'.[39]

On arrival at yet another new pit, Stewart's friend shared his fears that the pair would once again find themselves at the bottom of the ladder. To address this, Stewart devised a way to solidify his status once and for all. On his first day at Bickershaw, Stewart kicked in the doors of the busy canteen and in front of the perplexed breakfast audience he stridently declared himself the Daddy of the pit, the nickname by which he was known thereafter.

Bickershaw was one of the deepest pits in Europe, a fact which, according to Stewart, had been recognised in the *Guinness Book of Records*. However, the reality was far less glamorous than the accolade. Toiling deep underground, tasked with digging a new tunnel, Stewart felt it was the nearest thing to working in hell, with temperatures easily reaching 45 degrees Celsius. Men would take 3-gallon bottles of frozen water underground, which would turn to slush half an hour into their shift.[40] The team often worked without clothes, which, as Stewart reminded me, was not a problem because he was working *with men*. Despite such testing conditions, he worked every day available and commanded upwards of £1,000 a week for his labours.

Much as money was a strong motivator for many big hitters, I got the sense that it was about far more than that for Stewart. Though men could be inclined to hyperbole in their nostalgia for an industry now long gone, it appeared that Stewart's affection for the pit was something he could neither rationalise nor control. As he explained, 'I was married to t' pit, and you must have talked to other men like me, and you look at pictures of men working underground, *what on earth* is the love affair with working underground, 'cause I don't know.' At one time, Stewart gave instructions to his wife that if he were to be killed in the pit, she should leave him down there, like Big Bad John, as he was happy there. I was struck by the sense that just like Ahab in his ill-fated quest for the white whale Moby Dick, had the worst happened, Stewart would have happily gone down with the pit, as if their fates were somehow inextricably intertwined.

As it transpired, fate had a different path in mind for Stewart. By the end of March 1992, Bickershaw, the oldest pit in Lancashire, had ceased production, at a cost of 620 jobs.[41] Gordon

Brown, then Labour's trade and industry spokesman, described the day when the announcement was made as 'another Black Friday' for Britain, with the dole queues growing ever longer.[42] As if circling the industrial drain, miners were shunted from pit to pit across the North West coalfield, each time with renewed hopes of long-term employment, each time having these hopes dashed. Time and again it was the *same shit, different pit.* Men like fifty-two-year-old George Foster, who transferred from Bold to Sutton Manor Colliery only to see it close just six years later, with no jobs left for blokes like him.[43] Redundant miners could do nothing but watch as thousands of tons of cheap foreign coal imports kept landing at Liverpool's docks, destined for British power stations.

Unlike many other men, Stewart's affinity with the pit outlived the death throes of the once-mighty British mining industry. Later, he joined a friend who was working in diamond and gold mining in South Africa. He retired at the age of fifty-seven, but even today, over a decade on, he is still called upon to oversee plans and give advice on how to bolt a roof, which helps keep the wolves from his door and his heart underground. He is also still a 'professional picketer', fighting alongside workers from Cammell Laird, Silentnight, the NHS, and Arriva. However, just like his own father, '*no way* would I ever let my lad go in a coal mine, *never*'. Yet, Stewart observed how his son is a master scuba diver, as just like him, 'it's in his blood, he has to go down'.

As headgear after headgear came tumbling down, like fallen castles on Britain's industrial chessboard, mining communities were left with a social vacuum. Communities like Concourse Way in Parr, St Helens – known locally as 'Cement City' for its pebble-dashed concrete houses – which was developed by the Coal Board when the industry was still growing in the 1950s. At first, the prevalent issues were unemployment and poverty, owing to the unparalleled loss of jobs, and an ageing population. However, over time, the character of problems experienced by the community shifted. Today, stories abound of residents being plagued by antisocial behaviour and disorder, often fuelled by drugs and alcohol and being committed by those as young as twelve. This situation was replicated in other former coalfields, as if the hopes, dreams and futures of whole communities had tumbled into the void left by the pit.

A hundred miles away, in the town of Cotgrave, I had met miners Andrew and Mick, who explained how their area had faced similar struggles in the aftermath of pit closures. Once a picturesque village in the Nottinghamshire green belt with a population of just 600, by the 1970s the village of Cotgrave had burgeoned tenfold, with around 2,000 men employed at its new colliery, including the Goliath Peter Gee.[44] Such developments were not welcomed by locals, who, according to the clerk of Cotgrave Parish Council, wanted to be 'left in [their] undisturbed peace', and were not keen to integrate with the legions of miners arriving from the far-flung North East of England and Scotland.[45]

When it came into production in the early 1960s, Cotgrave's distinctive Koepe towers were a beacon to the new age of mining and local prosperity. Even the 1984–85 strike failed to interrupt progress at Cotgrave, which like the majority of pits in Nottinghamshire, had continued working throughout. Despite its loyalty to the government, Cotgrave did not escape pit closures. By the early 1990s, this once most modern of collieries had closed, with access to its millions of tons of untouched coal reserves filled in with 6,000 cubic metres of concrete.

Sat in the optimistically named Cotgrave Futures community centre, of which both Andrew and Mick were trustees, surrounded by the cheerful hubbub emanating from the nursery next door, the two men dryly recounted the small town's extensive rap sheet. They told me how they had the first deployment of plastic bullets on British mainland, how the community centre, doctor's surgery, and the twelfth-century All Saints Church had all been burnt down, and people had grown frightened to leave their houses after dark. The colliery's twin towers were now immortalised on the stained-glass window of the church, installed after the arson attack of 1996, a reminder of what had been lost both when the pit closed and since.

Despite local opinion, it was not outsiders but young men born and bred in Nottinghamshire who had been terrorising their own community. Yet, Andrew had reserved the real punchline for the end: his discovery that the culprits were all from mining families, the sons and grandsons of big hitters. Their forefathers had the job, the status, the adrenaline rush of taking risks underground, the bloodied triumph of winning in a battle against nature and all the financial trappings that went along with it. However, after Cotgrave Colliery closed its doors, their sons could never experience this. As Andrew explained, 'It must be galling to hear 'em talk about, or hear us talk about the pit, and what we earned and all the rest of it, and they haven't got it.' Growing up listening to stories of their forefathers' past glory, these young men were like coiled springs with no means to prove themselves worthy of their family history.

Over the border in Derbyshire, a similar pattern had emerged in the town of Shirebrook, once home to a thriving colliery that dominated local life but that had finished production in

1993. Today, the sprawling headquarters of Sports Direct occupy the space where Shirebrook Colliery once stood. In 2016, the company's working practices were compared to those of a Victorian workhouse, with allegations that workers were not treated with dignity or fairness, and were subjected to unsafe and demeaning conditions.[46] The wider community continues to wrestle with anti-social behaviour, with stories of drug gangs and street drinking a regular feature of local news. Not long ago, the local secondary school had created a targeted scheme to address the 'persistent underperformance' of male pupils, as according to the Vice Principal, 'There are a lot of boys in our community who miss that male role model.'[47] I tried to imagine how life might have been different for some of the mountainous men I had spoken to, men like Stewart, had their energies not been channelled into anything positive, and had they not been tempered by the bigger, stronger men they worked alongside underground.

Back in St Helens, walking through the town centre, I came across The Landings roundabout and the monument that stands in its centre. Made of cast iron and ravenhead stone by local sculptor Thompson Dagnall, it depicts a mining family: a crouched collier swinging his pick, a pit brow lass stooping to sort the coal and a young boy seated, breaking up the coal. It had been unveiled in 1996 to commemorate 450 years of mining in the town.[48] The figures were still being carved as the last pit closed in Lancashire, just as so many young men, who like Stewart were 'built' to be coal miners, found they had grown into figures of the past.

As I circled the sculpture, I watched two young men exchanging a foil-wrapped parcel in the shadow of the town's grand YMCA building, that had been opened in 1903 by the

Earl of Aberdeen. Further down the road, a group of sweaty lads spilled out of a mixed martial arts club, whose logo was of one muscle-bound man holding another in a headlock. The club was recently awarded funding to deliver classes to help reduce anti-social behaviour amongst teenagers. I wondered what relevance, if any, this sculpture, dedicated to an industry that was once a lifeline for the town, had to its young people today. Were these iron figures just another reminder of a future they could never have?

Before leaving St Helens, I climbed the summit of the former Sutton Manor Colliery site to see *Dream*, a 20-metre-high sculpture overlooking the roaring M62 motorway. Standing as tall as the Angel of the North, the sculpture was unveiled in 2009 by Spanish artist Jaume Plensa, after the location was nominated by former miners in a Channel 4 initiative to create new public art. The miners rejected Plensa's first design, which would have taken the form of a miner's lamp, as it was felt to be too closely connected to the past.[49] Instead, *Dream* is an out-of-perspective sculpture of a young girl's head, in gleaming white Spanish dolomite, on a plinth designed to resemble a miner's tally.

According to Plensa, the *Dream* concept was inspired by the idea that 'in our dreams anything is possible', as well as the miners' dreams of light whilst toiling in the darkness underground.[50] However, though the statue heralds the future and dreams yet to be realised, the words on the many flame-shaped markers that rise up from the site, created by Bernadette and Collette Hughes in partnership with the children of Sutton Manor Primary School, speak of wisdom in 'the bones', past dreams and 'scattered memories'. In 2013, the town's motto, *ex terra lucem,* light from the ground, was

Dream by Jaume Plensa, unveiled in 2009 on the former site of Sutton Manor Colliery in St Helens.

restored following a public consultation, in which respondents described the motto as their 'birthright', their 'heritage' and their 'identity'.[51] Miners, like Stewart's father many decades earlier, may have dreamt of a better future for their children, in the sunlight and away from the dust. Yet, in a world where pride was increasingly being eroded from work, at a time of zero-hour contracts, when the cost of living was spiralling but pay was low, where it seemed the only thing to fight for were gangs and passions were numbed by drugs and alcohol, what would the young men of St Helens dream of today?

One of six markers that form a trail around the former site of Sutton Manor Colliery, designed by artist Bernadette Hughes with poetry by Collette Hughes, in partnership with Sutton Manor Primary School and the wider community.

5. You've Just Got to Laugh

They'd wait until you were doing summat and they'd shove their fingers up your nose, right, after they'd been round their bum, and they'd say things like 'er have you met me wife?' . . . But that's how it was, you know.

Unlike some men, who shied away from divulging the lewder aspects of life underground, Stoke-born John was happy to tell it how it was, fingers up the nose and all. Perhaps his directness owed something to the unique context in which we unexpectedly found ourselves speaking – instead of meeting in person, as planned, we conversed over laptop screens, 200 miles apart. Somehow, despite the government-enforced distance between us and my (much-criticised) non-alcoholic lager, as the interview progressed it felt more like we were sat across the table at the pub, as we raised a glass to good company in strange circumstances. John's Potteries accent and infectious humour filled my kitchen and the darkness of the pandemic faded into the background, while we spoke late into the evening about his memories – good, bad and unpleasant – of his former life underground.

John was born in Boothen in the heart of Stoke-on-Trent in 1957. At the age of four he and his family had left the city, relocating 7 miles north to the small village of Newchapel. The community there owed its mining pedigree to the Birchenwood Colliery Company, which had opened a colliery nearby at the end of the nineteenth century.[1] The pit had long gone by the time John and his family set down new roots in Newchapel, though as a child he enjoyed playing in the old mine workings and coke ovens.

John had little to do with his biological father growing up, and was raised by his mother and stepfather as the middle child of three, with two sisters. It was John's mother, Elsie, who provided the family's role model and was responsible for instilling values in her brood, morals that John hoped he had retained to this day. Hailing from a family of fourteen, Elsie had a massive heart and was firm but fair, and 'very streetwise'. She was a small woman, 'in fact she was tiny', an observation which made John chuckle, as both he and his sisters dwarfed her, something he attributed to his mother's abilities as a cook. Elsie had always been a hard worker outside of the house too. During the Second World War, she had helped make aircraft tyres for the Michelin rubber company in Stoke. When the work dried up in peacetime, Elsie found a job in the pottery industry, which had long been one of the county's biggest employers.

Frank, John's stepfather, was the head wine waiter at the prestigious British Pottery Manufacturers' Federation Club, located in an imposing art deco building opposite Stoke-on-Trent railway station. The Potters' Club, as it is still known today, was established in 1951 as a place for local industry leaders to entertain their esteemed guests.[2] As John recalled, back then it was all 'proper dickie bows, white ties, and penguin suits'. During his time there, Frank had served Queen Elizabeth as well as Princess Margaret, on several occasions, after the latter was appointed the first Chancellor of nearby Keele University in 1962.

John's only family connection to mining came via his

paternal grandfather, who hailed from the village of Monk Bretton in Barnsley, which, as John reverently observed, made him a 'grandson of Yorkshire'. John knew of several relatives who had worked in the pits around Monk Bretton, including at the Oaks Colliery, which, as he reminded me, 'was the one where they had the disaster'. I had read of the terrible events that had occurred at the Oaks in December 1866, with two explosions resulting in 361 deaths, the worst mining disaster under English soil. I thought of the harrowing stories told in Stephen Linstead's film *Black Snow* and Graham Ibbeson's recent memorial in the centre of Barnsley, of a woman stoically carrying her child forward into an uncertain future, above her husband entombed in the pit below, a dark stream of coal cascading down her back.[3]

John's grandfather, Arthur, was not a miner but a foundryman, who had been talent-spotted whilst playing football for Frickley Colliery. Looking through old newspaper clippings, I learned that several league clubs had made overtures for this strapping South Yorkshireman's services as a full-back until his celebrated signing to Stoke City – known as 'the Potters' – in September 1926, at the age of twenty-one.[4] As it happened, Arthur's fate was decided by the stoppages in the coal industry that year, which meant the weekly levy paid by miners in support of the team – the club's primary source of income – had dried up. At the same time, local fans had no money in their pockets to pay for match admission, which had meant Frickley Colliery had no choice but to part with their star player.[5]

Six years after his transfer, Arthur was still with the Potters and named as the 'man of the moment', and one of the finest left-backs in the Second Division.[6] In October 1929, his photograph appeared in the local paper, clutching his fedora as he stood proudly alongside his new wife, another Elsie, following their marriage in Trent Vale.[7] Less than five years later, in February 1934, a smaller notice was printed in the same paper, announcing that Arthur's beloved wife had passed away at the age of just twenty-six, after a long illness.[8] The following week, beneath a story publicising the mechanisation of North Staffordshire's mines, there was an account of the funeral, in which four Stoke City players had acted as pallbearers.[9]

Notwithstanding his intertwined connections to the coalfields of Yorkshire and Staffordshire, John had no real knowledge of mining until he was a teenager, and even then he took little interest. Rather, his own entrance into the industry was, in his own words, the result of 'a balls up'. In 1972, at the age of fifteen, John had travelled under his own steam to Birmingham, to undertake the medical examination required to join Her Majesty's Naval Service. All in order, a fortnight later, a large brown envelope dropped through the family's front door, confirming John's place at sea. As he recalled, much to his misfortune, the envelope had RN stamped on the front, in great big blue letters, and his mother 'knew what it was and she *hit the roof*, honest'.

John fervently wanted to join the Navy, which in the 1970s offered fledgling seamen a life 'like nothing on earth'.[10] His stepfather thought it was a brilliant opportunity, having served twelve years himself. However, as John was under sixteen, he needed to have written permission from his guardian, and his mother refused to sign. John remembered the heated discussions at home clearly: 'Dad was going nuts, she was going nuts'; 'She says, "If you want to go in the Navy, go in the Merchant Navy", "He's not going in the Merchant Navy, it's full of poofs!", and all this, you know.' To restore the peace, it was agreed that when John turned eighteen, he could please himself, but until then he was to remain on dry land.

While John felt 'really really sneeped' that, unlike him, his two best friends were given the consent required to set sail with the Navy, he carried on at school until he was sixteen, leaving with a couple of O-levels under his belt. Not long after, the family's next-door neighbour, who was a draughtsman for the National Coal Board, told John he had found him a role there. However, as events transpired, they did not have an opening until the following Christmas, in eighteen months' time. John needed a job and instead the Coal Board offered him an apprenticeship in mining engineering 'there and then', which he readily accepted. John was asked which colliery he wanted to join and he is still bemused as to why he had said Wolstanton, ''cause I didn't even know where it was'.

Following a brief interview at nine o'clock on the Monday morning, John was 'signed on' at Wolstanton by that afternoon. When he returned home that evening, his Mum went 'ballistic, *absolutely mental*', voicing the standard refrain: 'No son of mine's going down the pit!' Though John's stepfather was 'sort of proud of it really', his sisters were worried and so was his Nan, because she could still remember the old disasters. Undeterred, John began his apprenticeship, safe in the knowledge that when he was eighteen, he could please himself and join the Navy.

I had heard many positive things said about the National Coal Board's apprenticeship scheme. Ron, another former Wolstanton miner I spoke to, had been selected to take part in a 'British Apprentices to Europe' study tour, where he had visited the Ruhr coalfield in West Germany.[11] As John confirmed, the opportunities on offer to new recruits were '*unbelievable*', and they could even take day release to attend college and 'get paid for it'. With a glint of humour in his eye, John confessed that he remained 'absolutely *convinced* to this *day*' that if he had asked to be trained as a gynaecologist, in case one of the canteen girls got pregnant, the Coal Board would have agreed.

In the first stages of the apprenticeship, there was no distinction made between those marked out to be skilled craftsmen, with all the new recruits to the industry undergoing basic underground training together. It soon became apparent that some of the trainees John found himself amongst had not benefitted much from their education to date and were, as he recalled, 'really thick as bricks'. Several lads had endured difficult upbringings, '"Dad was a drunk" and you know, wasn't very nice', and as a result they also lacked basic life skills, like how to have a proper wash. Accordingly, at the training centre, they were shown not only how to mine but how to get themselves clean. Years later, some of these same lads had ended up as senior managers. As John observed, this was down to their own hard work, and the fact someone further up the tree had given them a chance: 'At first he'd be, "Well I can't read or write", "Well that don't matter 'cause we'll teach you", and that's what they did, it was *amazing*, you know.'

No matter what else was said about the Coal Board, especially in later decades when promises of a job for life were proven hollow, John would always credit it with giving him and many other young men skills for the future. Of course, the mining industry was not alone in providing such opportunities. Following the Industrial Training Act of 1964, which established Training Boards in no less than twenty-six different industries, the number of apprenticeships in Britain

National Coal Board recruitment advert from the 1970s.

burgeoned with almost a third of boys taking up a place in 1969 (though fewer than one in ten girls, who were mainly trainee hairdressers).[12] Such opportunities declined radically from the late 1970s, in the face of deindustrialisation, rising unemployment and a lack of government support, as John bemoaned, 'Obviously all that's gone now, ain't it.'[13]

Having ventured down the shaft of nearby Chatterley Whitfield Colliery as a schoolboy, John thought he had a good idea of what to expect underground, but this was swiftly proven 'wrong, totally wrong'. Wolstanton had some of the deepest mineshafts in Europe, and as John explained, the speed of descent 'was just bloody incredible' but seemed to last forever. The pit bottom was 'massive, absolutely *massive*', and well-lit but torturously hot. The airspeed from the giant fans, installed to suck the foul air out of the pit, was so forceful that you had to lean into it, making walking through the roadways even more challenging. The apprentices' first job was to salvage equipment, including electric cables, rail tracks and conveyor belts, from a decommissioned coalface. As John recalled, in some places, the roof was so low that they had to dig their way out to get the salvaged materials through.

Looking back, John described how he '*never ever* expected it being like that, you think, God I'm only sixteen, just out of school, I come from a small village, and then to be suddenly thrown into the bloody fires of hell, and it was, it was hell'. Quite a few of the boys never returned after these first forays underground, 'That was it, they went up the pit, they had a bath, and I never saw them again.' I asked John what had made him stay, particularly when others had left and when, unlike many, he had no family reputation to uphold in the pit. He replied that it was 'stubbornness more than anything', accompanied by the fact that he would not dare to return home and say that he had given up, ''cause that's the way we were brought up, we were brought up to not fail, we were brought up to, you know, never give in'. I imagine John owed such grit to his mother as well as the fact he, like many of his peers, was raised on a full-blooded diet of Kirk Douglas, Robert Mitchum and John Wayne films.

John's first experience of the pithead baths was another memorable moment, as he explained: 'That's an eye-opener, for a young boy, 2,500 naked men, all messing about, it's enough to make a young lad run home.' One thing he learned early on was *never* to close both eyes, 'even when you were washing your face, you kept one eye open, you only had to close your eye for one millisecond, and you had the *lot*'. Through the steam, John had been approached by a large black man, Harry,* the 'biggest, *massive* lad, good-looking

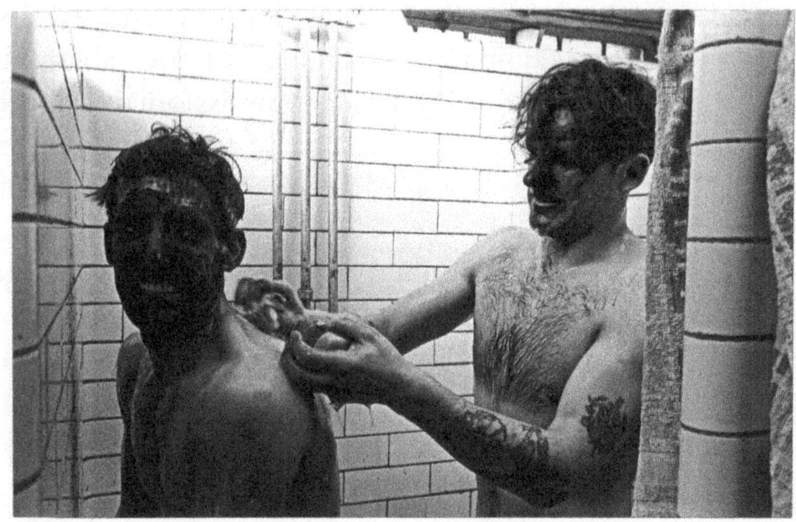

Miners showering in the pithead baths after finishing their shift underground at Horden Colliery, County Durham, in 1966. Photographed by Patrick Ward as part of an assignment for *The Sunday Times Magazine*.

lad', who had come to Wolstanton from Jamaica, via Liverpool.[14] John recalled their interaction: '"Wash me back white boy", and I looked at him, I were just cowering in the corner, and I'm washing his back, you've got to say something, and I said to him, "Harry, how do I know when you're clean?", and he turned around, and he said "I shine brother, I shine."' From that moment on the two men were friends and remained so right up to Harry's death decades later.

John recognised himself as part of a 'new breed' of men who were entering Britain's pits in the 1970s, 'We all didn't live in terraced houses, you know, we all didn't go to the working men's club, or the miners' welfare', and most of them had cars. However, though the 'grandad mentality' – as John termed it – may have been fading out, older, more experienced miners 'were still the same as their dads were', and as a result incomers did not get an easy ride underground. Alongside invitations to 'wave goodbye to the sun, just in case you don't see it again', naïve recruits would be sent on impossible quests to fetch 'a bottle of elbow grease', 'a bucket of steam', or 'skyhooks'. I was also told about a time some older miners brought seaweed into a pit that extended under the North Sea, to convince their guileless colleagues that water had broken in.

John explained how he and the other 'kiddies' faced '*constant* questions' from the established miners underground. A favourite topic was their mothers: 'How's your mother?', 'I think I've met your mother', 'Bill, he looks a bit like you, have you been with his mother?', 'Have you ever seen your mother naked . . . do you want to buy some pictures?', 'Have you got any sisters?', 'Do they put it out a bit?' If you chose to ignore the inquisition, 'they would be onto you *constantly*', whereas if you gave them 'a daft answer', and showed that it did not bother you, 'then you fitted in'. As John explained, it was their way of rooting people out.

I heard many different accounts of such pit 'hazing' or 'pillocking' that had been endured by men of different generations throughout the British coalfields.[15] Such initiations forced new recruits to submit to the hierarchy underground and, as former miner and historian Keith Gildart observed, at times they could be 'tantamount to physical and sexual violence'.[16] One man I heard from, who undertook his apprenticeship at Chislet Colliery in Kent, recounted how as part of his initiation he had been spread-eagled over a large motor, with Castrol grease 'ceremoniously applied' to his gonads and 'thoroughly rubbed in'.[17] Although at the time he was powerless to resist the assault, he later saw the experience as 'a badge of honour' that signified his membership of the group. As one Yorkshire miner confided, there would be a claim made every day now for harassment, '*But*, we sort of looked after us own.' The flip side of such initiations was that once you were accepted, your colleagues would do anything for you, and, as John explained, if you ever got hurt, 'They'd shift heaven and hell for you.'

Of course, there were people who did not fit in or could not tolerate the culture underground, where nothing was sacrosanct. In the pit there was no room for political correctness, nor any 'mamsy-pamsy attitudes', as John termed them. Likewise, there was no point in reporting issues to management because the men would 'stick together like glue' and make your life even worse. It was still a hypermasculine world, albeit one that from the 1970s was more concerned with cars, tattoos, bodybuilding and playing squash than performing feats of strength underground, as in generations before. Bigheads, brown-nosers and liars were not tolerated, and neither was homosexuality – at least as far as anyone was aware – though other men I spoke to knew colleagues who had emerged from the closet after leaving the pit. Simultaneously, as John recalled, men would play at the boundaries of acceptable heterosexual behaviour: 'One of 'em would put their arm around you and kiss you, and then when they'd done it, they'd spit tobacco in your ear or summat like that.'

After completing the first two years of his apprenticeship, John could finally fulfill his long-held ambition to join the Navy. However, instead he decided to stay on and complete the next two years of study. His decision was unquestionably bolstered by the generous pay on offer, which even then, for a young lad, was 'really good'. Under the tutelage of older, experienced miners, he worked on the winding engines, the compressors, the methane plant, the coal preparation plant, the surface locomotives and the fitting shops, 'all of it'. Completing his apprenticeship after four years was a proud moment, which gave John a sense of achievement. Now aged twenty, he could still have gone to sea, but by then he was doing a bit of courting and the prospect of being confined to a ship full of men was losing its appeal.

Though the work was hard and the conditions could be brutal, daily life underground was rarely dull and often felt like an extension of being at school, though it was older men who were typically the instigators of mayhem. Sometimes it would take over an hour to have a shower, because the men were in the mood to make mischief, and 'if you didn't take part, you didn't fit in'. As John recalled, at Wolstanton, no matter what you were doing, if somebody shouted 'happy half-hour', the men would 'just go nuts', and their superiors would sit there and let them get on with it: 'There'd be buckets of water chucked all over the place, everything, it was just mental, yeah mental.'

One of the first coalfaces John worked on held lying competitions whenever it was snap time.[18] The men split themselves up into two teams, with each scoring points for telling the biggest lie. John gave me an example of how one competition had unfolded: 'One started off, he says, "Me and my Mrs", well that was a lie, 'cause he wasn't married, "flew over to Canada at the weekend", well that was a lie, 'cause he was working, he says, "and we went to Niagara Falls", so that's another lie, and "we were on the Maid of the Mist, and I look at the Falls and I think to meself, that's easy-peasy, that is", he says, "so I threw me shirt off, dived in, and I swam and I went straight up the Falls, and I got to the top and I'm shouting to my lady, 'aye up Duck, I'm up here!'"' Everybody was in stitches by this point, and the team was justly awarded twenty points. Then the opposing team began: 'He says, "You know when you went to Canada this weekend", he said, "Yeah", "Well I went", that was a lie, he said, "I went to Niagara Falls and all this business", he says, "Do you know when you jumped in the water and swam up the Falls", he says, "Yeah", he says "I bloody saw you do it!"'

Practical jokes were also a regular occurrence, particularly when men saw the chance to prey on a colleague's vulnerability. John had been a victim of such a prank when he was working on a broken-down machine on the coalface. He unscrewed the bolts that were holding it together, took off the lid, which was 'big as a table' and realised that the issue lay with the internal pump. John bent over the machine, reached his hands into the oil, felt around for the pump, then carefully turned the bolt on its side, releasing the spring and ball bearing within, so he could give it all a good clean. Laughing, he explained how, thanks to his workmates, events did not unfold as planned: 'So I got hold of it, and they said, "Have you got it?", I says, "Yeah", "You're not going to let go, are you?", I said, "No", and then next thing, they started lowering the roof supports down on me, and the oil was filling me mouth, and "You're not going to let go are you?", and I said, "No", next thing, shorts down, and they're doing all sorts to you aren't they, and you've just got to laugh haven't you? 'Cause if you didn't laugh, they'd make your life hell.'

Though Wolstanton's miners were awarded a plaque for safety in 1979, after cutting down their accident rate by two thirds, deaths and serious accidents still punctuated life underground.[19] Recalling such occasions, John explained how they were made more surreal by lamplight, but even then, humour was never far away. John shared the story of two mining brothers he had worked with, and how one of them suffered an accident in which his leg was cut off. When the other brother discovered what had happened to his sibling, the humour came instantly, as John recalled how he had sanguinely observed: 'Well, he was never any good at dancing.' As John explained, that's how they dealt with it.

Another time, John and a colleague had gone to help a man they heard shouting for assistance and discovered him sitting there with a bandage wrapped around his index finger. John recounted their interaction: 'He said "I've cut the end of me finger off"; when asked how he did it, he replied "I stuck it in the end of this electric motor", and the other man says, "*How on earth* have you done that?", and he picked his left hand up and shoved it in, and he said, "Like that", cut both fingers off.' At the time, John 'couldn't do anything for laughing, honestly I was laughing that much, that was it'.

At the weekends, John would help with shaft maintenance. This was considered one of the most dangerous jobs in the pit, but he saw the positives: 'twelve-hour shifts, money, loads of money, it was great.' There was no denying that the conditions could be challenging, like when he had to work in the downcast shaft during the winter months and it was '*absolutely freezing*'. The plight of Wolstanton's miners had appeared in the local newspaper in 1983, after they appealed for thermal underwear for use at the pit bottom but had received a typically 'icy reception' from the Coal Board.[20] Nevertheless, after a few years, John had joined the shaft maintenance team on a permanent basis, and as he told me, at that time, he was the youngest shaftsman ever to be employed by the Coal Board.

When the strike was called in 1984, John came out, 'to stop the pit closures, and the loss of mining jobs'. At first, the picket lines at Wolstanton were reasonably quiet, while the local bobbies were the ones policing them, but later the Metropolitan Police were brought in, and, in John's words, 'that was when it really kicked off'. After that, he and his fellow strikers would turn up for picket duty to be met by 'a thousand coppers on horses'. John observed how 'they beat the shit out of us to be honest with you'. Fortunately, as they were still young men, 'full of muscle' with 'plenty of grunt' in them, they could give as good as they got. Wolstanton was Staffordshire's last pit at a standstill until October 1984, when over 300 men, around half of the workforce, had returned and production resumed.[21]

As John told me, during the strike, there had been a big problem with movement in the main coal drawing shaft at Wolstanton: a large section of concrete, which 'must have been the size of two double-decker buses', had pushed into the shaft, preventing the cages getting through. The damage was so significant that the Coal Board could easily have condemned the whole pit, but they chose not to. Instead, the management came down onto the picket lines, spoke to the unions, and asked if the shaftsmen could return to work to rectify the problem. John and his colleagues did not agree at first, but the unions did, and asked them to go back in and sort it, as otherwise the pit would shut for good, 'It's as simple as that.'

As John and his colleagues followed the union's instructions, leaving their mates on the picket lines and reluctantly walking into work, somebody shouted scab, and for John, 'That was it, I'll never ever, ever, ever put myself in a position like that again, and I'll *never ever* work to save somebody else's job, 'cause I thought you ungrateful bastard.' Other men, who broke the strike under their own volition, undoubtedly fared worse. In July 1984, the *Daily Mirror* reported how one thirty-three-year-old Wolstanton miner, who had returned to work after fourteen weeks on strike due to money worries, was discovered dead in his garage, with his car engine running, after being spat at by his colleagues on the picket line and receiving threats against his twelve-year-old daughter.[22]

Notwithstanding such desperate stories, according to John, the atmosphere at Wolstanton was not too bad in the strike's aftermath, as management kept strikers away from 'them that had scabbed'. However, the pit itself was a shadow of its former self, and by 1986 it had closed due to escalating financial losses.[23] The closure was waved through by the 650-strong workforce, who were offered a choice of transfer or redundancy, with some of the colliery's more senior men set to receive a reported £70,000 in redundancy payments.[24]

I had seen a black and white photograph of Wolstanton's demolition two years later, its rigid concrete Koepe winding towers, like a child's Lego creation, cast asunder. It reminded me of times when my father and I would watch repeats of the inimitable Fred Dibnah felling factory chimneys on the BBC. Back then, my childish gaze was drawn to the clouds of dust on the television, and I failed to notice the steeplejack's sadness that these totems of Lancashire's textile industry were almost all gone. At Wolstanton, the detonation button was pushed by two 'excited' local schoolboys, whose mother had been knocked down and killed by a drunk driver twelve months earlier.[25] The following year, the brothers returned to unveil a plaque at the new Asda superstore, part of the multi-million pound retail park built on the colliery site.[26]

Like many of Wolstanton's younger workers, John was found a new position in the industry, in his case at nearby

The demolition of Wolstanton Colliery, January 1988.

Hem Heath Colliery.[27] For the first twelve months, he did not really like Hem Heath – it was a similar size and design to Wolstanton, but he found his new colleagues peculiar: 'They didn't trust anybody, you know, didn't like strangers and it did take a long time for me to settle in.' Nevertheless, John persisted, and after a year, he was sent back to college, where he completed a degree in mechanical engineering. When he returned to the pit full-time, he was asked to shadow the shaft engineer for three months, until his retirement, and then John took over his job, with an extra promotion to the position of assistant engineer.

As the new assistant engineer, John managed his team of twelve according to his tried and tested formula of 'don't tell them to do something, ask them to do something'. If he encountered a particularly 'gobby bugger', his unconventional solution was to put them in charge, as he explained: '"I'm not doing this at weekend, I'm not doing that at weekend", "Well, you've got two choices, you either do it, or you stop at home, if you want to stop at home that's fine with me mate, but if you want to come working weekends, you're in charge", "I'll do it!"'

At first, John's own experiences of senior management at the pit had been positive, when such roles were filled by men who had worked their way up the ranks and knew every aspect of the job. He remembered a lot of good-hearted banter between such managers and the men. Sadly, over time, this had changed as the Coal Board brought in new officials who were straight out of university. As John pointed out, there was a *massive* difference between the theory of mining and actually mining, and as a result these managers would clash with the men, 'who'd had *years and years and years* of experience'. As the Coal Board evolved into the British Coal Corporation in 1987, managers appeared to be on a mission to 'psychologically degrade' the men, and when redundancy packages were offered, they jumped at the chance to leave.

John left the industry in 1993, just shy of completing twenty years underground. He felt senior management had 'planted that much hate' that continuing was no longer an option. Hem Heath closed the same year but reopened under new ownership in 1994, with over 1,400 men from as far afield as Wigan, Bradford and Sheffield applying for jobs there, a ratio of 10 applications for each of the 130 jobs available.[28] Though former energy secretary David Hunt had promised it was 'the future for the coal industry in Britain', two years later, Hem Heath was given up as a 'lost cause' and closed for a second time, leaving its 200 workers without a job, many for the second time in as many years.[29]

Not tempted back into mining, John was self-employed for a while, selling safety equipment, but after finding that he was a 'shit' businessman, he went to work for Staffordshire County Council as a property surveyor. He was put in charge of 9,500 acres of land, and over 100 smallholdings, which he relished. Other men I spoke to had found it difficult to tone back their humour when they left the pit, struggling with colleagues who seemed to be quick to take offence or who did not understand how taking the piss was part of incorporating them into the team. John, on the other hand, seemed to adapt well to his new role and after initially being employed on a six-month contract, retired twenty years later.

After over two hours chatting, John observed that they would not put dogs underground now. Though '99.9 per cent' of his experiences had been positive, he had not walked away from the mining industry entirely unscathed: he suffered with vibration white finger, damage to both knees, arthritis in both hands and dust on his lungs, but, as he concluded, 'apart from that' he was 'alright really'.[30] Though he was not too proud to admit he would struggle to do the work now, John still missed the banter and comradeship he had found underground. Likewise, though he never made it into the Navy, in mining he had found an equivalent: 'It is serving your country, ain't it? You know, and we did keep the lights on, I don't care how anybody said, we did, you know, it was us that did it, and that's it, really.'

As John left our virtual meeting room, I closed my laptop and returned to the quiet darkness of my kitchen, the red digits of the oven clock warning me it was past ten o'clock. I thought over the many times I had been told that I would not understand the culture underground, as an outsider, as a woman, as a millennial, as someone who had never crawled through the dark bowels of the earth, day in day out, year after year. Pit humour could be hilarious, childish, disgusting and at its worst downright cruel, and I had little doubt that some men had emerged with different scars as a result. Yet, I *could* understand why miners behaved in this way, why given the mad conditions they endured underground, they needed to let off steam in a happy half-hour, why a laugh had to be found in even the bleakest circumstances and why new colleagues were tested in the extreme, because when all was said and done, it was these men that you relied on to watch your back, to put *everything* on the line and get you out.

A few days later, John emailed to say that he had told the boys our interview was so successful it was being turned into a full-length feature film, with Russell Crowe playing the lead role, 'you can just imagine the replies.' Yes, I could.

6. The Meaning of Camaraderie

Dad went to visit Frank and Frank said, 'I'm ever so sorry to hear about your John', and he says, 'What do you mean Frank?', he says, 'Well he's dead ain't he?', and he said, 'No Frank, you pushed . . .', 'pushed him, out of t' way', so erm . . . I'm here, because of Frank.

I never knew the worlds into which we would venture during an interview. Whether we would be laughing over pranks in the pithead baths, as in the last chapter; reluctantly shuffling into the cage for that first memorable descent; shouting from the picket lines as strike-breakers went into work or peering through the bus's mesh-covered windows at the angry crowds, filled with apprehension about the return and its repercussions. When I pulled up outside a neat 1970s semi on a pleasant road just outside of Dinnington in South Yorkshire, I had no knowledge of the accident its occupant had been involved in. Sitting in John's warm living room, the last of the March afternoon's sunshine streaming through the venetian blinds, he broke down in tears as he took me into the darkness and recounted the day his life had been saved.

Although I grew up less than 15 miles away, I knew little about the community of Dinnington, aside from the fact my parents had once considered moving there. It began as a small farming settlement, with two churches, a public house and a school, the main focal points of local life.[1] Since the mid-eighteenth century, the grand Dinnington Hall, set in its own parkland, was home to the Athorpes, the Squires of Dinnington, whose family crypt was in nearby St Leonard's Church.[2] Before 1902, most locals worked the land or were in the employment of the Hall, with a few men employed at local quarries or making a 6-mile round trip, six days a week, to Kiveton Park Colliery, sunk in 1866–67.[3]

Just like many other rural communities in South Yorkshire, in the early twentieth century Dinnington found itself caught up in what one newspaper described as an irresistible 'tidal wave of industrialisation'.[4] After black gold was struck via the Barnsley seam in 1904, at a depth of some 668 yards, Dinnington was transformed into a bustling mining community.[5] The census charted the town's rapid expansion, with just 250 residents recorded in 1901, which had ballooned to 5,000 a decade later.[6] The first mining settlement, known as 'Tin Town', was made up of squat two-roomed huts, with corrugated iron coverings, erected quickly and cheaply and overlooked by the pit tip.[7] In time, these were replaced with more aesthetically pleasing brick terraces, built by the Dinnington Main Colliery Company. Though some locals decried the area's evolution, alongside new houses, the industry also brought the railway, a new school, allotments, a miners' institute and sporting facilities including a football ground, cricket field, running track, bowling greens and tennis court.[8]

Arriving in Dinnington at the turn of the new century, entrepreneur James England became a keen supporter of the town's blossoming sports and societies, and was instrumental in building local infrastructure like the post office, the bank, The Lyric Theatre and Palace Cinema.[9] The cultural life of the changing town was connected to the colliery. The Dinnington Choral Society was founded in 1922, with rehearsals held in the Colliery Institute.[10] Later, in 1938, Francis Davies, the manager of Dinnington Main Colliery, took it upon himself to relaunch the group – now known as the Dinnington and District Amateur Operatic Society – with packed audiences enjoying their production of Gilbert and Sullivan's comic opera *The Gondoliers* at the Lyric that October.[11] There was also a colliery band, formed in 1904 by miners who had relocated to Dinnington from Durham, which consistently placed well in local and national competitions.[12]

The history of the pit itself, which lay at the edge of the South Yorkshire coalfield, was, happily, largely uneventful. In 1913, representatives of the Admiralty, War Office and the General Post Office paid Dinnington Main a visit as it was the first coal mine in Britain to have 'wireless telephony' installed.[13] The system, invented by one J. H. Reinecke of Bochum, Westphalia, had already been successfully adopted in Germany.[14] By virtue of these revolutionary portable instruments, weighing around 20lb each, in the event of an accident, entombed miners would have the means to seek help. Thankfully, Dinnington never faced a large-scale accident that would have necessitated their use.

In 1928, the Chelmsford Mining and Technical Institute was opened in Dinnington by the Viscount of Chelmsford, Chairman of the Miners' Welfare Committee, after whom it took its rather confusing title.[15] Hailed as a 'landmark' in the history of technical education in mining areas and supported by a grant of £17,500 from the Welfare Committee, the institute offered complete training in mining, mechanical and electrical engineering, as well as 'domestic subjects' like tailoring and dressmaking.[16] As the Viscount observed when opening a similar institute in Wakefield the following year, what the industry hoped to achieve from such colleges were not 'better miners', but 'better citizens and better men'.[17]

John had lived near Dinnington all his life. He was lucky, being born five years after the end of the Second World War and having enjoyed a 'fantastic childhood' with his brother and sister. John's parents had both been 'grafters'. His mother was a 'jack of all trades', and his father was a miner, who finished up as colliery overman. Growing up in that part of South Yorkshire, John felt he only had three choices in life: 'You either went to the steelworks, you went to pits, or you went in forces.'

As a youngster, John was always *adamant* he would be a naval man, but ultimately, he had 'bottled out'. This, he explained, was because he had always been on his mother's apron strings. In the end, he took the shorter path to the pit, reasoning that he could start on Monday and if he did not like it, he could always pack it in and go to the steelworks. As he observed, kids in Dinnington today did not have the same choice. John's father welcomed him having a try but warned him, 'Don't think you're going to be a collier', 'you're not even going to be a fitter, go and be an electrician'. Reflecting on this advice, John explained how nobody would want you to be a fitter because it was not the safest job in the world and required 'a bit of nouse'.

John's father had never really spoken about his work whilst at home. The only insight his son had gained was from his father's repeated requests for him to turn the wireless off, as he had to listen to machines running all day and could not stand such 'bloody jungle music' at home. One time John had refused his father's appeals to turn his mother's portable radio off, and in response his father had hurled it down the garden. Laughing, John remembered how 'it must have bounced forty times, and when it stopped it was still playing'. I could not imagine a portable speaker faring so well today.

John never made great progress academically but he did manage to get a place on the Coal Board's apprenticeship scheme, which he started in 1965. In time he was followed by his younger brother, who had also gained a place as an apprentice electrician. By the 1970s, Dinnington Main Colliery had a workforce of around 1,000 men, responsible for an annual output of over 308,000 tons of coal.[18] Although John was ultimately responsible to his father, as the overman, underground their two worlds rarely collided: 'Me Dad got on with his job, and I got on with mine.' Nonetheless, given his father was in a position of authority, some of the other lads used to tease John, and he could remember their taunts: 'Have you got your white pumps on? Your Dad is shouting for you, put your pumps on and go to your Dad.' Despite this, after going down the pit at the age of sixteen, John never really wanted to do anything else.

Above ground, John's passion as a young man was athletics. He was a member of the Rotherham Harriers, a local running club founded back in 1887 'with the object of affording a means of health-giving recreation which otherwise could not be obtained, viz., frequent trips into the country'.[19] John trained six or seven days a week, and had competed in many events, to a good standard. He won his first county title at Clairville in Middlesbrough in 1970, a much-loved stadium which was demolished in 2015 to make way for housing. Back then, there were no cash prizes, so men competed for cigarette lighters, ashtrays, clocks and candlesticks, and the simple love of running.

One weekend, John won the 2-mile race during half-time at Bramall Lane, home of Sheffield United Football Club.

When he came up from his shift in the pit the following week, he had a message on his tally asking him to go and see the engineer, 'I thought, oh God, what have I done wrong now.' He knocked on the door and hesitantly went in, expecting the worst. To his surprise, John's boss, who was a United fan, congratulated him on the race. All seeming amicable, John took the opportunity to ask him if he could work the day shift regularly because his new coach wanted him to train twice a day, 'and if you're working three shifts your body clock never works'. John could still remember the other man's deep intake of breath and uncompromising response: 'You work for the Coal Board; the Coal Board doesn't work for you. So, carry on, on three shifts.' John kept running but over time he lost his mojo. Even now he looks back and wonders what he could have done, given the right opportunity.

The more miners I spoke to, the more I became familiar with the stereotypes associated with different groups of workers underground. Unfortunately, electricians had the rather unenviable reputation of always being asleep on the clock. They were the butt of a joke made at the recent unveiling of a new memorial and, even in 2023, the audience all seemed to be in the know, such was the response it elicited. This reputation appeared to be largely without foundation, although as a young man, John had been known to come home from a nightclub, collect his snap and go back out to work in a less than fit state, spending much of his shift dozing in his 'perch' and trying to avoid being discovered by his father on his rounds.

Due to the heat underground, John often found himself fixing motors that ended up full of his own sweat. However, though he conceded that the conditions were 'terrible', for

John, 'it were the people you worked with that made mining what it was. It was brilliant'. Sure, they would take the mickey, and if they found out anything embarrassing about you, it would not be long before it was broadcast over the pit's tannoy system for all to hear. Yet, at Dinnington, they were 'brothers in arms', who would never see you struggle or let you down, and in John's words, 'If you hurt yourself, or anything like that, they were there.'

Though there had been no major disasters in Dinnington's history, I had found two stories whose similarity made them stand out. In 1956, Robert France Miggels, a thirty-year-old Polish miner, who was married with two children, had been awarded £13,800 in damages against the Coal Board after he suffered a fractured spine in a road fall at Dinnington.[20] Sadly, this accident on its own was not remarkable: I knew several men whose friends had sustained such lifelong injuries underground. However, a mere four years later, another incident at Dinnington had made national headlines, when forty-two-year-old Christopher John Brace was awarded £17,666, after his back was broken when overhanging coal fell on him at the coalface.[21] Just like Miggels, after the accident Brace was resigned to spending his life in a wheelchair, as 'an object of considerable pity'.[22] The circumstances surrounding the accident caused the presiding judge particular concern, as he was reported as having 'a very uncomfortable feeling indeed that the colliery deputy has been trying to cover up his own shortcomings'.[23]

I asked John whether he had ever witnessed any accidents underground, and he quietly conceded that he had. In the early 1970s a group of them had been undertaking a job in the Swallow Wood seam, located around 80 yards below the Barnsley seam, which drifted down from the summit at a gradient of around 1:20.[24] It was quite steep and there was no paddy train, and John remembered the difficulties they encountered transporting the heavy ten by ten girders down the slope. John and his mate had been tasked with carrying a particularly cumbersome control unit. His friend decided to come down with it on his own, and instructed John to go down ahead of him.

At the bottom of the drift, John had met four or five colleagues, and they all sat together chatting, blissfully unaware of what was about to take place. As John recalled, 'I don't know, I don't know what, what happened . . . but we could hear a rumbling and all I felt was somebody push me in the middle of t' back, and I'm bawling, and I'm shouting and swearing at him, and next minute when I look up there were *clouds* of dust and there was sparks, 'cause all t' light fittings had been hit, and they were short-circuiting.'

As the dust settled, John shook himself and surveyed the aftermath. He realised he was the only one of the group still conscious: 'I, I panicked. I didn't . . . one guy, it had chopped his leg off and erm, and I've, I've never seen anything like it . . . there were blood.' Frank, the man who had pushed him from danger, had been seriously hurt, with a bad gash to his head. In shock and without the confidence of first-aid training, John had no idea what he was doing. 'One guy, I thought he were, he were moaning, and I went across to him, and it's the, it's the funniest sensation I've ever had in my life, I put my hand to his chest and there were no chest, you know what I mean, *horrible* . . .'

Dinnington was blessed with some really good first-aid men and, despite only being 'a couple of minutes on t' job', one appeared, and sent John out of the pit. One of his colleagues died instantly, and another succumbed to his injuries on the way to the hospital. Fortunately, Frank survived his head wound and John's father had gone to visit him while he was recovering. As in the lines opening this chapter, hearing no different, Frank had assumed that John had been killed. It was only later that John's father told him how his actions had saved his son's life. John broke down recalling this conversation, as he was reminded that the rich kaleidoscope of life he had lived since that day was the result of a decision made in a split second and the selfless actions of one man, who instead of saving himself, had chosen to push his colleague out of harm's way.

I asked John if the accident had ever made him reconsider returning underground, a question he remembered his father asking him at the time. As it transpired, John had time to think – the accident happened on a Friday and the pit was on strike the following Monday. Two weeks later, he had decided to return along with everyone else. Arnie, his assistant engineer, a man he had worked with for years, sent him back to finish the job he was supposed to do that fateful day. 'He said to me, "I want you to go back to that job, John", and I said, "I don't think I can, Arnie", he says, "It won't happen again."'

It was a risky move, instructing someone to return to the place where he had seen two colleagues mortally wounded, and I doubt it would ever be allowed today. However, this action was far more than a simple admonition to 'get back on the horse'. Visibly emotional, John recalled how unbeknownst to him, Arnie had 'put people in place all the way to the job, so that I would go'. Revisiting the scene of the accident to complete the job he was 'supposed to do', bolstered by the silent support of colleagues posted along the route, seemed to have provided John with a sense of catharsis; though bruised, the pit had not broken him.

Everyone at Dinnington was a member of the NUM, and John had been involved in all the previous strikes called by the union. As a result, when the strike began in March 1984, he and his wife Anne assumed for a while it would be alright, 'like a month on holiday'. In those novel early weeks, they had little notion of how the strike would come to stretch all their resources, both financial and emotional, to the limit.

As Anne told me, at the time their daughter was two and their son was just six months old, and she was not working. She had no maternity leave, so as the weeks on strike turned into months, the couple 'spent everything' they had. They 'didn't get nowt from nowhere' other than their two bags of coal a fortnight, the occasional food parcel and donations from a friend, who would give them a bag of basics – flour, sugar and teabags – when she visited. Though John admitted his previous tendency to spend money 'like a man with no arms', Anne had always been a saver, but by the end, despite her best efforts, they 'were skint'.

On 12 November 1984, the South Yorkshire coalfield was the site of a 'night of fire and fury', when the police station in Dinnington was besieged and shop windows were smashed as more men began to trickle back into work, lured by the promise of Christmas cash.[25] Nonetheless, before Christmas, the strike effort in Yorkshire remained solid, with only around 5 per cent of the county's miners returning to work.[26] Whilst the majority of men at other South Yorkshire pits like Maltby, Silverwood and Kilnhurst remained out, Dinnington, like its neighbours Kiveton Park, Shireoaks and Manton, had over 50 per cent of its workforce back at work by the beginning of March 1985.[27]

Ten days before the strike officially ended, John had gone

to visit his father. He told the older man how his family had nothing left, and his father advised him 'tha's got to do what's right for thee own family'. So, with no end in sight and his family on the verge of losing everything, John decided to return. Very early in the morning, he got onto a bus that had been blacked out and meshed up, to make the tortuous journey across the picket lines. For months newspapers had carried stories of what was happening to those who had returned to work: their houses daubed in paint, windows smashed, their families surrounded. As Anne recalled, 'It was frightening, it really was frightening, it was horrible.'

Some strikers could never forgive 'scabs', regardless of the situation they had found themselves in. For others, the measure of a man's worth was weighed by how long he had endured the strike and how much he had sacrificed along the way.[28] Just as in the pit, men who did not have the strength or stamina required for the job could be forgiven if they gave it a 'go'. I remembered how Paul, the first miner I interviewed, who remained solid throughout the strike, told me of the pathos of one man who decided to return to work after Christmas, after losing his wife, his kids, his house and his car, after giving 'everything' he had. As Paul sagely reflected, 'So he went back to work, so he's a scab. Now how can you call him a scab? What did I lose? I couldn't call him a scab.'

Following his return, John and his brother, a 'union man' without a young family, did not speak for a year afterwards. Anne reflected how some friends had responded in a similar fashion, forgetting that their wives were working, bringing home some money each week. Although he told me he was not 'bothered', it was clear John still dwelt on his decision to return, 'I suppose had I known that, that there were, you know, ten days before it ended, if I'd have known that I'd only got to manage ten days.' But back then, how much faith could be placed in the promise of ten days after a month had already turned into a year, when debts were mounting, children were growing, cupboards were emptying and there 'didn't seem to be any end'? As John conceded, maybe in a parallel universe they would have won, but 'everybody's pain levels are different' and at times, hindsight was a cruel thing.

While her husband had a police escort into work, Anne had no one to shield her from the court of public opinion. As she walked into town with their two young children, she greeted everyone she passed with the same good morning, as she had always done, but people no longer responded. As Anne admitted, this was better than the alternative, as 'at least they didn't say anything to me, in a, you know, a horrible way.' Having young children of my own, I remembered how vulnerable I felt during these first forays into society with a toddler and a baby, and how just one interaction outside the house, a passing hello or brief good morning, might be the only adult conversation all day. I could not imagine the grit it took to venture out knowing you would be met with hostility.

Though Anne's mother had encouraged her to follow her example of staying at home to look after the children, having witnessed everything the couple was going through, she changed her mind. With grandparents agreeing to share the childcare, Anne managed to find a job for two days a week and gradually the young family was able to break free from the shackles of debt. At the time, Anne had 'lost an awful lot of weight'. However, she could still recognise what the experience had given them: 'It makes you realise how you can manage with very little, you know, if you have to.'

John's father retired through ill health in 1986. Six years

later, the pit he championed was also shut down: the last shift finished on 27 September 1991, and the mine was abandoned the following spring. Over its ninety-year history, the men of Dinnington Main Colliery had brought some 48 million tons of coal from the darkness into the light.[29] Ged Wilbourne, NUM branch secretary, observed that the pit would 'bow out' in profit, with a wonderful reputation for safety and one of the best industrial relations records in British Coal.[30] Notwithstanding these noble achievements, after the pit closed the town was left with a gaping hole in its local economy. In the House of Commons in October 1992, Kevin Barron, a former miner and Member of Parliament for the Rother Valley, noted that just sixty-eight vacancies had been advertised in the job centres of Maltby and Dinnington the preceding month, a pitiful ratio of one vacancy for every sixty-six people registered as unemployed in the local area.[31]

Two years after the pit closed, a new memorial to the miners of Dinnington was unveiled in the town's St Leonard's Church. Made from wood and panels of etched glass, a sort of modern-day rood screen, it features a tree of life sprouting up from the pit below. Running through the middle are mosaic panels created by local people. It lists the names of the seventy-four miners who lost their lives at the colliery across its history.

The memorial was the passion project of Dinnington's rector, the Reverend Simon Bailey, for whom it would be a lasting testament not only to the community that had welcomed him, but his own legacy in the town. Bailey had arrived in Dinnington the year the miners' strike reached its sad conclusion. It was a difficult time both for the community and their new rector, who had learned he was HIV-positive shortly before his appointment. As his health worsened and he developed AIDS, Bailey bravely decided to share his burdens with his flock, believing it was something both society and the church needed to 'face up to'.[32] His story was so compelling the BBC chose to make a documentary about it, first broadcast in January 1995.[33]

There were obvious anxieties concerning how the parishioners of this 'tough' mining community would react to not only having a homosexual rector but one with AIDS, a disease which brought to mind the gigantic tombstones of the recent television campaign.[34] However, in the end, it was an unlikely union for a community and a priest both facing an uncertain future. Out of a congregation of eighty, only four of the flock were lost.[35] Though some were still conflicted about Simon's sexuality, having grown to know the man behind the label, when he needed their support the parishioners gave it freely, creating a rota to provide care. Until Simon's death in 1995, at the age of just forty, his parish lived up to their motto, 'Unlimited, unconditional, unquestioning love, freely given with no expectation of return, with comradeship and equality for all.'[36] It was, in its own way, an extension of the protective camaraderie underground: where miners would watch each other's backs, regardless of personal differences.

After Dinnington Colliery closed, John, like many others, had transferred to nearby Rossington Main Colliery, where he was able to work regular day shifts. However, he found the culture there was totally different: men seemed to want a bonus for 'doing *nothing*', and they did not have the same cooperative spirit that John had grown accustomed to at Dinnington. He told me how Rossington became known as a 'sleeping giant', as it could have been a fantastic pit, but 'the people were wrong'. Eventually, John decided to follow a friend to Silverwood Colliery, located near the village of Thrybergh in Rotherham, which, though still not quite the same as Dinnington, suited him better. Silverwood closed on 23 December 1994, despite the fact there were, according to the NUM, 'a good fifteen years' life left underground'.[37]

Not long afterwards, John was invited to return to Rossington, which at that point was being managed by Richard Budge, owner of the Doncaster-based RJB Mining company.[38] He spent the next few years as an electrical project engineer, along with men selected from other ailing pits: 'It were really hand-picked, and it, oh it *sailed*, I think we made 90 million quid profit first year'. For John, it was a 'brilliant job', which he loved, particularly as there was a great atmosphere, working with lads who '*wanted* to make it happen, they *made* it happen', 'the *morale,* it were lovely, it were a pleasure to go to work'.

Over time, a new manager had been brought in, 'aptly nicknamed the treader, 'cause that's all he did, he trod on everybody'. Those who refused to submit would be summoned outside the pit gates after work. According to John, it appeared this manager's remit 'was to kill the spirit of the pit' and, as a result, 'gradually Rossington sort of *imploded*, the morale at t' pit died'. Rossington closed for the final time in 2007. One of the things both John and Anne found most objectionable was the waste of resources, which Anne described as 'unbelievable'. Alongside the coal that was ready and waiting to be cut, men were also told to leave all the machines underground, despite the fact they were worth £150,000 a piece.

Moving again, John was placed in charge of the machinery at the Selby coalfield after its closure in 2004, making sure the pumps were working so water from the mines did not contaminate the local water table. By the time he was made redundant from this role, John had totted up forty-one years in mining. He later worked for Baldwin & Francis, a Sheffield-based company, dating back to 1919, that produced electrical equipment for mines. John helped to plan new pits in India, China and Poland, 'everywhere were opening pits, and we're shutting them'.

Now John and Anne are retired and mortgage-free, with a car each. Anne conceded the latter circumstance may be a bit extravagant, but she was allowing herself to enjoy what they had, because 'we've earned it, it's ours, you know, and we don't owe anybody any money, and we can do it'. Nevertheless, she had maintained her survival instinct from almost forty years earlier as 'if anything happened, we'd sell the car, that's fine, I can catch a bus, it's no problem, but it does make you stronger, really, yeah it does'.

Thirty years later, John still suffered for doing what he felt was right for his family back in 1985. Earlier that day, the couple had been out having a coffee and reminiscing with old colleagues. When John stepped away from the table and out of earshot, his friend had asked if he had been a scab. Anne could understand people's frustration, the incident another reminder that 'in those people it's still there, you know what I mean, although people don't generally talk about it, it's still something that is . . .'.

Dinnington's mining heritage is still alive. In 2010, with the help of a BBC documentary presented by Sue Perkins, the colliery band had been brought back from the brink of extinction, and nine years later, with the support of the National Lottery Heritage Fund, a new mining memorial was unveiled in the town's Coronation Park.[39] As John told me, it was for all the people who had worked at Dinnington

Main, not only the ones who had died underground. John had sponsored a brick for himself, his father, and his brother: 'So the monument's there for when we've gone, and my grand-kids can go and have a look and say, "Look there's grandad's name there."' Notwithstanding his own trials, for John, the most important aspect of the mining industry was still the camaraderie: it was that which had bound the village together, and given it its heart, and that is what they had lost, 'Did you drive through Dinnington? It's like going through Beirut.'

Parts of Dinnington recently appeared within the most deprived 10 per cent of England, and in 2019, the town's dance school and florist were gutted in an arson attack.[40] When I visited, the charred remains were yet to be cleared. In the Neighbourhood Plan, 'From Tin Town to Great Town', David Smith, a former miner and now a member of Dinnington St John's Town Council, described fears that future generations would inherit a community with less 'heart' and fewer opportunities, green spaces and facilities.[41] Though the town had missed out on cash from the levelling-up fund, in March 2023, the government promised £12 million to regenerate Dinnington's high street.[42] Yet, as one local reporter opined, the money was 'a token pot of cash', which was perhaps 'too little too late'.[43]

I drove back through Dinnington in the darkness. Despite John's warning, the streets were quiet. Parking up, I walked across the damp grass towards the new memorial: it was beautiful, all lit up, just as Anne had said it would be. Neat black plaques lined the red brick wall, remembering local colleagues who had once laboured together underground. On a low plinth in front was a solitary miner, a white apparition, helmet on and pick in hand, walking steadily into the night.

Memorial designed by the Dinnington Old Boys Committee, unveiled in Dinnington, South Yorkshire, in 2019.

I wondered what would be next for Dinnington, this once rural community that had evolved as the pit brought not only industry but culture, sport, education, friendships and families. Only time will tell if an injection of cash will be enough to keep the town's spirit alive. For now, at least, it feels like a community that is still in the dark as to what its future may hold. As I thought back to the names on the memorial wall, the colliery band and the congregation of St Leonard's, the speech made by Pete Postlethwaite's character in *Brassed Off* felt particularly apt in this 'forgotten' part of South Yorkshire: 'If this lot were seals or whales, you'd all be up in bloody arms. But they're not, are they, no, no they're not. They're just ordinary common-or-garden honest, decent human beings.'[44]

7. The Enemy Within

I remember an old Geordie guy, Tommy, as nice a guy as you'd ever wish to meet; he went to Orgreave one day, and this copper chased him into this derelict building that were on Orgreave old side . . . He says, 'He came at me, and I knelt down like that [covers his head] and he went as far as there', and got near to hit him with truncheon and he didn't hit him. He had a nervous breakdown over that, that guy. Never same guy again, like that for the rest of his life, Tommy, and a great bloke, and a great worker and all . . . great, you know, hard grafter, and he never got over that, Tommy . . . it was a war, it was without any doubt a war.

There is no memorial to the Battle of Orgreave. Unlike the multitude of markers commemorating other battles fought on British soil and blood spilt on foreign fields, there is nothing to remember what happened at Orgreave. The absence speaks volumes, just like the way the name of this small Yorkshire village has become a byword for injustice – like Hillsborough – a powerful, loaded word to be spoken solemnly, forcefully. It is a word that has been emblazoned across many memories and lifetimes, so it cannot be forgotten no matter how hard some might try. The events that took place at Orgreave on 18 June 1984, when over 5,000 police officers clashed with an estimated 8,000 striking miners outside a coking plant, remain an aching wound in working-class history.[1] At the time, Tony Clement, the Assistant Chief Constable of South Yorkshire and the man in charge of proceedings, said it was a 'miracle' no one had been killed.[2] It is true, no one died that day, but many were injured, some badly. Others, like Tommy, who were not beaten, were forever bruised and broken by what happened.

When I first started speaking to men about their career in mining, I never began with the 1984–85 strike. Some men's time in the industry had ended long before Thatcher came to power, whilst for others the strike was just a brief hiatus in a much longer journey underground. I did not want to disrespect an industry and a career that should be defined by so much more by focusing on the most sensational aspects and aggravating old scars. Yet, during some interviews, it seemed as if we were being propelled towards disaster, like passers-by slowing to rubberneck over an accident from which it was impossible for either of us to turn away. A handful of men acknowledged the elephant in the corner, stopping me to ask: 'Are we going to talk about the strike?' Whilst others shifted in their seats and danced around the topic, only later revealing why.

I heard many stories of pickets and police, of cat and mouse games and tit for tat. Often these were told in a jocular style, one that both expected and embraced the push and the shove of the picket lines. Rarely did men shy away from recounting the damage they inflicted on police officers on these occasions, as one Yorkshire miner confessed 'some of them got hammered'. Another, a Kent miner, took grim satisfaction in explaining how he had thrown ball bearings instead of bricks as the police horses didn't like them.

Watching warring police and pickets from old news footage, it seems more like drama than reality. Hearing men recount what happened to them and their friends, events seemed at once immediate and real, but so shocking as to be almost implausible. However, the emotion in the narrators' voices, the pregnant pauses and hesitations, their hand-wringing and downcast eyes confirmed the truth.

Evoking the scenes on the picket lines of 1984, many men drew parallels with the 1964 film *Zulu*, which told the story of the Defence of Rorke's Drift in 1879, when a garrison of some 150 British and colonial men defended against an attack from around 4,000 Zulu warriors.[3] Pickets recalled how police officers would rattle and bang their riot shields 'as though they thought they were Zulu warriors'. It was interesting how such surreal experiences were given coherence through the cultural repertoire available at the time. I could imagine how striking miners would have been drawn to this film, which, as the trailer proclaimed, showed men 'fighting for their lives' in times 'of fury and honour, of courage and cowardice'.[4] Of course, in their narratives, the miners put themselves in the place of the beleaguered battalion, whilst at the time, the state and mainstream media were more inclined to frame the strikers as the 'savages' of the piece.[5]

Other accounts I heard from men who had been part of the especially violent clashes that occurred at Orgreave, Gascoigne Wood and Maltby were told almost surreptitiously, unexpectedly. They were not asked for but came out, like a quiet and painful catharsis. There were few comparisons made to grand cinematic moments, and there was little sense of heroism. I was not the first person to be told these stories, but I grew to understand how such self-revelation was simultaneously healing and damaging. As if each time the narrative was played out, blow by blow, its potency might be both enlivened and eroded, like a match reignited and burnt down.

For many miners and their supporters, Orgreave was the altar upon which trust was burned to ash. Young men, who had come out on strike alongside their mates, keen to be part of the action and perhaps make their forefathers proud, had the scales fall from their eyes. Older men, who had already gained their battle honours in 1972 and 1974, found their expectations of how events would unfold entirely wrong. As I was constantly reminded, there were *always* rules in a strike, and picket lines were expected to follow the 'old school rules of engagement', where the balance of power was determined by the push. Orgreave saw the end of all rules, and all that remained was blood, sweat and fear.

Even now, four decades on, men were still trying to piece together exactly what happened that June day. How they, who had arrived wearing trainers, T-shirts, and stonewashed denim, ended up chased by cavalry and bloodied by police batons and steel-toed boots. At the time, the artist Barrie Ormsby had tried to capture the visual incongruity of the two opposing forces in his painting *Miners' Strike* (1984).[6] In it, the sea of miners – who like Seurat's bathers are seated, many of them topless – is contrasted against the black mass of police opposite, the sun bouncing off their riot shields, which segregate the miners from the community seen behind. Where was the 'in between', the moment when it all changed, the invisible line that turned from blue to red?

It was a sunny Monday on the 18th of June 1984, the ninety-ninth day of the strike.[7] The miners had been rallied to attend a mass picket at the site of the British Steel-owned coking works in Orgreave, just outside of Sheffield. Pickets had arrived from all over – North Wales, South Wales, Scotland, Durham, Nottinghamshire, as well as from across

Barrie Ormsby, *Miners' Strike*, 1984.

Yorkshire – to show their support. It was just a few months into the strike, morale was still high, and who would have turned down an excursion on such a lovely day?

I could imagine the atmosphere on the coaches, friends joking, laughing, singing and looking forward to standing together for a healthy dose of push and shove. As the miners pulled in, they were surprised to be greeted by an affable reception, with police directing them as to where to park, as though they were coming for a music festival or a football match. One miner told me how 'they'd have parked your car up for you if you'd have asked them'. Later, several men observed that this was the point they should have known things were not all they seemed.

Huw, a twenty-four-year-old picket, had travelled over 200 miles from a mining community in South Wales to be in Orgreave that morning. By this point he, like many others, was already a seasoned striker, having picketed the Essex ports of Wivenhoe and Colchester a month earlier and already experienced the iron fist of the police.[8] On the long drive to South Yorkshire, Huw and his fellow passengers were surprised not to be stopped, as in the past they had inevitably been pulled over when police recognised the car was registered in South Wales. Yet, on the 18th of June they didn't have *any* problems getting to Orgreave, 'none whatsoever'. It was only later that Huw concluded this was because the powers that be had wanted them there, 'to give us a kicking, to teach us a lesson'.

Twenty-year-old Paul, who was on strike from Dodworth, near Barnsley, had a much shorter journey to Orgreave that morning. Despite his relative youth, Paul had a family history steeped in mining, with uncles, brothers and cousins all working underground, most at the same pit. As he told me with pride, his great uncle was Jack Woffenden, the former President of the Dodworth branch of the NUM, whose bespectacled face still looked down earnestly from the branch banner, promising members of a past generation a shorter day, better conditions and a longer life. Though Paul's father and older brother were both 'rock solid' during the strike, neither of them had ventured onto the picket lines. Paul, on the other hand, had 'single lad syndrome' and no qualms about getting 'stuck in'.

Like Huw, Paul had already had a brush with the long arm of the law. During the first fortnight of the strike, the union had been hiring coaches to send flying pickets from Yorkshire into Nottinghamshire and Derbyshire, which was seeing some success as 'when faced with an actual picket line, a lot of people would not cross'. However, within a few weeks, these same coaches were being sent back as, in Paul's words, 'it had been turned into a police state'. A short time later, the car he was travelling in, along with three other pickets, was pulled over by police on the A1 near Blyth.

It was suggested by the officers that if the car were to reach its intended destination there would likely be a 'breach of the peace'. When the driver refused to turn around, the police arrested all four passengers, and Paul, the youngest member of the party, subsequently found himself in police cells at Mansfield. It was five o'clock in the morning when he was arrested, and it was not until five o'clock that evening when they were brought before a 'kangaroo court'. To avoid facing more serious charges, Paul was advised by the NUM's solicitor to plead guilty to obstruction. Doing as he was told, he was issued a fine of £75 and sent on his way.

At the time, the experience had not been a frightening one, because Paul was running on adrenaline. More feared was the sobering prospect of having to reveal to his parents that he had been sat in police cells all day. There was still a stigma attached to being arrested, even though by the end of the strike over 10,000 miners would find themselves in the 'same pickle'. Still, Paul remained undeterred: having left police custody on Thursday, by Monday he was joining the assembly at Orgreave.

Unlike many others, who found themselves arriving in Orgreave for the first time on the 18th of June, Kevin, a thirty-five-year-old miner on strike from nearby Barnburgh Main Colliery, had already notched up considerable time picketing there. Curtailed from leaving the county by police roadblocks, he and what started off as just a handful of other strikers had decided to picket closer to home. When Kevin first arrived at the coking plant in Orgreave, there were just six pickets and four police officers and it was still possible for miners to stop the coal lorries and put their case forward. To address this, non-union drivers were increasingly employed on the route. As the days went on, more pickets arrived, unable to get to other parts of the country, and more police came in response. By late May and early June, there were mass pickets regularly assembling outside the coking plant.

As one *Socialist Worker* placard proclaimed at the time, there were ambitions to 'Turn Orgreave into Saltley' and recreate the symbolic victory of 1972, when massed pickets had closed the gates of a coke depot in Birmingham. Yet, despite the number of pickets at Saltley and the heroic mythology surrounding it, the picket line confrontations with police that day had been comparatively restrained.[9]

Over a decade later, the miners found themselves ushered onto a very different playing field. In the words of Kim Howells, who was responsible for directing the Welsh pickets at Orgreave but is perhaps better known for his later career as a Labour MP, '1972 and Saltley was an age away. It was a government of a simply different order from Heath.'[10] In 1977, Conservative backbencher Nicholas Ridley had already pre-empted another national strike in a 'vulnerable' industry like coal.[11] His so-called Ridley Report provided a blueprint of how to tackle the 'problem of violent picketing' by means of 'a large, mobile squad of police', who would be 'equipped and prepared to uphold the law against the likes of the Saltley Coke-works mob'.[12]

The police who arrived at Orgreave were a changed force compared to the one that had manned the picket lines twelve years earlier. In 1972, the National Reporting Centre had been founded by the Association of Chief Police Officers of England, Wales and Northern Ireland, to coordinate the response to nationwide disputes from New Scotland Yard.[13] So-called Police Support Units, or PSUs, were devised to amplify resources in a particular location, and following the urban uprisings of 1981, specialist 'riot squads' had been trained to effectively disperse crowds.[14] Like the sea change that took place in the opening months of the First World War, when men trained with the antiquated weapons of the last century were outmatched by new machine guns, mortars and grenades, the miners found themselves wanting, following the advent of new 'paramilitary policing'.[15]

As summer loomed, temperatures at Orgreave began to rise. Remarking on the violent clashes at the end of May, Thatcher commended the 'magnificent police force', who were acting 'bravely and impartially', and declared: 'The rule of law must prevail over the rule of the mob.'[16] During one ruckus on the picket lines at this time, Kevin had found himself crushed and lifted off his feet. When he came back down to earth, he tripped over something lying on the ground, it was a man, who was blue and bleeding from his ears and mouth. When Kevin eventually freed himself from the melee, he vowed he would never go back on the front line, but he was lying to himself. That was how, a couple of weeks later, he found himself returning to Orgreave once again, at six o'clock on the morning of the 18th of June.

Kevin's group parked in the village and, like Huw and Paul, walked to where the pickets were assembling. As they came over the old pit tip, the sight of the field below took their breath away: thousands of police, moving in lockstep, accompanied by dogs and horses. Another miner, also there that morning, told me how the view from the hill was like a scene from Mankiewicz's *Cleopatra*, where Roman centurions were marching in formation.[17] At that moment, Kevin knew they should have turned back, but even with the benefit of hindsight, he could not bring himself to do so, as he told me: 'We were there to do something, and we did it, we went.'

On his way down Kevin became separated from his friends and was stopped by a policeman who asked if he would help him shift the remains of a stone wall that had been knocked down earlier in the morning. 'There's ambulances waiting to come, with injured pickets.' Kevin agreed to help, and he and some other lads set to work clearing the road. However, when they had finished, it was not ambulances that came rushing through, but horses. As Kevin reflected, 'We'd sort of, you know, been a bit naïve again, hadn't we?'. I wanted to point out that accusations of naivety could only be justified with the benefit of hindsight. Despite everything going on around them, these men were still upholding the principles that had been instilled in them from their first days underground: to not walk by when they saw someone struggling, and above all, watch each other's backs, in this instance by ensuring medical aid reached those who needed it.

Several veterans of Orgreave have published diaries of the 18th of June, each chronicling their own perspective of how events suddenly escalated from the expected push and shove to scenes befitting a medieval battlefield.[18] By all accounts, the day had started peacefully enough – some pickets kicked a football about on the grass, while others milled about introducing themselves to miners from other areas and exchanging badges. Men unafraid to make a spectacle of themselves toyed with the police on the front line, others were photographed playing a game of pitch and toss against a background of riot shields.

As the lorries made their way into the plant one after another guarded by the impenetrable wall of police, the pickets became increasingly frustrated. A small minority of men threw stones over the police lines. After a 'ritual push' on the picket lines, a command was given: the glassy sea of riot shields parted, and cavalry flooded out into the crowds of miners.[19] Contrary to Tony Clement's later court testimony, the horses did not advance at a 'walk or a trot' but came galloping into the field, as was evident in later footage.[20] Short-shield snatch squads followed behind, grabbing any pickets who were not already desperately fleeing the scene.

Paul remembers the horses charging through and how as a result 'all hell let loose, it were complete Bedlam'. He found himself in a group that was being chased up the field, stuck between a rock and a hard place, with the choice of a wall on one side and woods on the other. Some men chose to run into the woods and Paul could hear their screams as the police set the Alsatians onto them. Fortunately for Paul, he determined to run up the field and down the steep railway banking, where the horses could not reach him. He traversed the railway line and climbed back up the other side, where another wave of horses was waiting to chase them through the village. Paul's comparative youth was to be his 'saving grace', as he could 'still run a bit'.

Other, older miners naturally fell behind, out of breath after desperately trying to keep pace with their younger comrades. In his diary entry from the encounter, Bruce Wilson, a striking miner from Silverwood Colliery in South Yorkshire, described coming to the aid of 'an elderly miner, on his knees [. . .] couldn't get his breath, the riot police were closing in'.[21] Younger miners, who had grown up admiring older men underground, witnessed their heroes being beaten and humiliated. Though Paul saw many people with cuts, bruises and bloodied heads, the singular memory that stayed with him, above all others, was not of any personal harm or violence he had witnessed. Rather, the very worst thing he had seen was a bloke in his fifties who had stood there with his hands on his head and who had wet himself, paralysed in terror, 'just stood stock still with fear'.

Kevin had run down onto the field just as the lorries arrived. There were 'spotters' in the crowd, and as he explained, 'I must have been pointed out, because as soon as the wagons came and I went to the front, I got a shove in the back and that were it, I'd gone.' I had heard stories from other men about the prison vans used at Orgreave and how some unfortunates found themselves contained within them for up to twelve hours, in temperatures of 'eighty-odd degrees Fahrenheit', with no access to food or water. Kevin was put on one such bus, 'roughed up a bit' and eventually taken to Sheffield. All day long, he and his cellmate could hear more people coming in, shouting, crying, screaming and 'all sorts', harrowing, disembodied sounds that echoed off the bare walls and terrified the captive audience inside.

Luckier men, who had managed to flee the field and reach the village, were offered refuge in local houses. One of these was another Paul, an eighteen-year-old Yorkshire miner, who police had chased into Catcliffe. They were closing in when he and a friend found themselves in a cul-de-sac, with no way through. Paul thought his luck had run out when an old woman emerged from her front door, beckoned 'in here love', and they dove into the house. Inside, as Paul recalled, 'there must have been 12,000 miners', including a guy hiding in the cupboard under the stairs, terrified that if the police were to catch him, they were going to 'lock him up and throw away the key'.

The unexpected house guests were all red-faced after running for their lives, many for the first time since leaving school. In the background, the television was playing scenes from another world over in Birmingham, where it was the fifth day of a fraught test match between England and the visiting West Indies cricket team. Paul found a place to perch, and the hostess offered him a cup of tea and a custard cream, which he eagerly accepted, such civilised proceedings a stark contrast to the mayhem outside. Soon enough the garden was full of police, like a dozen uniformed Mr McGregors hell-bent on finding rabbits. Fortunately, the man of the house soon let them know in no uncertain terms that it was *his bloody garden* and *his bloody house*, and they could *sling their bloody hooks*.

Black and white images of Orgreave, taken by a handful of intrepid photographers who negotiated the battlefield armed with nothing but cameras, are often reprinted on the anniversary of the strike. Police took a dim view of such independent observers, who, if seen, could have their cameras confiscated or even face arrest.[22] It is only thanks to their individual bravery and unwavering determination that we have photographic evidence of events that day. Martin Jenkinson, a former steelworker, captured the scenes of cavalry chasing bare-chested miners through the streets. Another of his images showed a mounted police officer with baton raised in readiness to descend upon a group of miners surrounding an ice-cream van, marked with the infamous Bobby Ball catchphrase 'Rock On Tommy'. Recently, a print of this image had been presented to one of the young miners photographed, as an ironic gift to mark his own retirement from the police force.

Martin Jenkinson, pickets and mounted police at Orgreave during the miners' strike, 18 June 1984.

Another photographer, Lesley Boulton, inadvertently found herself the focus of attention. Boulton had been picketing with Women Against Pit Closures since April, but this was her first visit to Orgreave, despite the fact it was only a 10p bus ride from her home in Sheffield. Later, she reflected on how, if she had had prior knowledge of the violence that would be enacted that day, she may well not have gone.[23] When Boulton first parked up in the Asda car-park in Orgreave, there were few portents of the events to come; rather, all she could see were pickets buying cokes and eating ice creams, 'really rather a carnival atmosphere at the time'.[24]

A few hours later, Boulton was captured in the now infamous photograph, taken by John Harris, of a mounted policeman swiping at her with a baton, as she stood at the sidelines, with one arm raised and her camera in the other hand. Later that week, the image was printed on the front page of *Labour Weekly*, above the line 'She was only trying to help . . .'.[25] Boulton had been calling for medical assistance for a wounded man, whom she had found lying in the street, suffering from what she believed to be broken ribs.[26] Fortunately, a picket behind her was able to pull her out of harm's way and the baton missed her 'by the skin of [her] teeth'.[27] The police would later claim the image had been doctored, and when Boulton took the matter further, she was told there was not enough evidence.[28]

In his 1989 book *Talking Blues*, Roger Graef interviewed a handful of officers who had been involved in policing the 1984–85 miners' strike.[29] There were local bobbies who deplored the behaviour of those who had been brought in to assist, particularly from London's Metropolitan Police.[30] Outsiders who would flash £10 notes to taunt 'proud men', who had been out of work for months, some who reported for duty drunk and others who had allegedly perpetrated much more salacious acts, ominously reminiscent of recent crimes committed by 'a few bad apples' in the force.[31] Graef also heard from officers who seemed to revel in the violence, finding it both exciting and intoxicating.[32] One thirty-four-year-old Police Constable from a 'northern force' applauded when the horses went into the crowds at Orgreave: 'It was great to see them smashing into all them bastards who'd been giving us grief all day.'[33]

Official images of the picket lines were often taken from the police side of the action, inevitably skewing the story to make the miners appear the aggressors.[34] One 1985 study suggested that at times the police may have 'stage-managed' incidents to gain the sympathy of the public, exaggerating injury to officers and horses alike.[35] Indeed, Malcolm Pithers, the correspondent for the *Guardian*, overheard a policeman at Orgreave yelling at press to 'take photographs of a hero', pointing to an injured police officer.[36] However, Pithers, unlike many other reporters, also acknowledged the losses on the other side and the 'sickening' sound of 'policemen clapping and cheering as a picket, bleeding heavily from a head wound, was helped into an ambulance'.[37]

Toeing the Conservative party line, much of the press had already turned their backs on the striking miners.[38] The most severe criticism came, perhaps inevitably, from the *Sun*. A month before the clash at Orgreave, it had attempted to compare the leader of the NUM to Adolf Hitler, with a front page showing Arthur Scargill raising his arm in a gesture akin to a Nazi salute, beneath the headline 'Mine Fuhrer'. Fortunately, due to opposition from union members at the printer's, who refused to handle the picture and print the headline, the edition 'reluctantly' went to press without either.[39] Just five years later, this same newspaper would make appalling and entirely erroneous claims about the victims of the Hillsborough disaster.[40]

On the 19th of June, two pages of the *Daily Mirror* were dedicated to the 'DEATH TRAP' at Orgreave, reporting how police horses faced a 'barrier of spears' and how officers were bombarded with stones, sticks and bottles.[41] Conversely, the *Daily Mail* focused its attention on Scargill's leadership, claiming that the 'real assault' was on democracy, with scant mention of the huge numbers of casualties.[42] Television representations followed a similar trajectory, with the BBC famously reversing the footage of the confrontation between the police and pickets at Orgreave, foregrounding the miners' violence, with a police cavalry charge shown to have been in response.[43]

It was the mining banners that were left to tell the real

story of what happened at Orgreave and on other picket lines during the strike, when the once-mighty miner, the hero of the working class, collided with the faceless arm of the state. If pictures could talk, these banners would howl. The bare-chested miner was no longer Herculean, as on earlier banners, but instead appeared as a martyr, beaten down, banged up. The Gascoigne Wood Branch banner carried a single, quiet voice of optimism: beneath scenes of miners charged by horses and carrying fallen comrades off the field, it solemnly vowed, 'Our Spirits Were Bruised . . . But Never Broken.'

When Paul finally made it home that evening, he sat down with his parents to watch the news and witnessed first-hand how the footage of Orgreave had been altered. It was a watershed moment as for the first time he saw how the media was capable of distorting events. Paul explained how he now understood that the whole idea at Orgreave was to 'take wind out us sails' and, as he told me, 'To be fair it worked.' Paul did not go picketing again until August; he just stayed away, because it had rattled him so much.

Around the same time as Paul was at home watching the evening news in disbelief, Kevin was being escorted out of the police station at Sheffield. As he was leaving, he walked past the other cells, which were covered in blood, urine and the remnants of broken bodies. In an interview, the solicitor Gareth Peirce recalled her horror at seeing similar scenes in the police cells over in Rotherham, with 'blood all over the place' and horribly injured men sat in custody, like the 'wounded survivors in wartime', who needed doctors rather than lawyers.[44]

Kevin was transferred to join these men in Rotherham,

where he was ushered into a big courtyard, like a quadrangle, in the middle of the new police station. There were many others there, men with 'broken arms, legs, wrists, and *loads* of head injuries, loads of head injuries, at the back of the head as well, as if, you know, they'd been caught running away'. No one appeared to have had medical attention. As a group, the men began helping each other out of their clothes, carefully lifting the bloodied garments over the damaged heads because, of course, as Kevin told me, every miner was trained in first aid, to help their own. One of his friends had suffered a broken skull and ended up being taken to Armley Prison Hospital. Others were 'patched up' and held into the night, before being ushered in front of the magistrates, ten to fifteen at a time, and given rules about where they could no longer go.

I wondered how Kevin must have felt in this moment. He had grown up in a mining community, a concrete canyon, an estate designed to, in his words, 'breed miners'. He remembered how it had been self-policing, as all the fathers worked side by side underground and drank together at the end of their shift. These older men kept an eye on what was going on. If somebody saw you doing something wrong, you would get a 'clip round the ear', and then the incident would be reported to your father, who would give you another one for good measure. It was like that, Kevin told me, 'not like today when you'd be up in front of the court'.

After being abandoned in Rotherham, Kevin eventually found his way back to the family home. He could remember his wife crying as he came through the door; she and his father had spent hours on the phone trying to track down his whereabouts. Later, his son told him his first impressions of his father being 'black and blue, cut up and everything'. I asked Kevin if he had returned to the picket lines after that incident and, perhaps unsurprisingly, he confirmed that he had. As he explained, 'It became a case of attrition, if you know what I mean, they're not going to tell me I can't picket.' I wondered whether his family had felt that both he and they had suffered enough.

In total, ninety-five miners were charged with having committed offences following events at Orgreave on the 18th of June. Amongst these, over fifty men were charged with riot, which, if proven, could carry a life sentence. Some of the accused may have been reminded of the bloody Peterloo Massacre of 1819, where the Riot Act had been read out before cavalry charged the crowd that had peacefully assembled to demand political reform, brutally injuring over 600 and killing 14 people.[45] Riot was a common-law offence, dating back to the Jacobite Rebellion and, until 1984, it had largely disappeared from court proceedings and faded into the annals of history.

Filmmaker Yvette Vanson interviewed some of the accused before their court appearance for her documentary *The Battle for Orgreave*.[46] Crouching in alleyways, leaning up against cars and rolling on the ground, men walked the viewer through the events of the 18th of June 1984, interspersed with photographs and footage from the day. The most incongruous account came from Welsh miner Bill Greenaway, a smartly dressed man in his fifties, who fell into the long grass as he recalled how he had been returning from Asda with cream buns in one hand and a can of shandy in the other, only to find himself struck across the back of the head, then across the wrist by a truncheon and charged with riot.[47]

Many families spent an anxious year awaiting their day of reckoning. Of the fifteen cases that eventually appeared in front of magistrates at Sheffield Crown Court in May 1985, all collapsed after almost fifty days of hearings.[48] Video evidence, recorded by independent monitors, contradicted the police version of events. Eyewitness accounts were riddled with errors, with claims of arrests made by officers who were not even there. Officers from Merseyside, Northumberland and South Yorkshire gave startlingly similar statements, with the same phrase repeated verbatim in multiple different accounts. Perhaps most disturbing were comments made by Tony Clement, who under cross-examination told the court how he would not have worried in 'the slightest' if a miner had been trampled by the horses that day.[49]

The remaining eighty accused miners were granted reprieve by the prosecution, who no doubt realised they would not win. In a confidential report written in September 1985, Peter Wright, then Chief Constable of South Yorkshire Police, admitted that the prosecution of the pickets was based on 'superficial evidence'.[50] Six years later, South Yorkshire Police paid £425,000 in compensation to thirty-nine of the miners who were arrested, over claims of assault, wrongful arrest, malicious prosecution and false imprisonment. The settlement was initially offered with a no-publicity clause. Not a single police officer was charged or even disciplined, either at the time or subsequently, following events at Orgreave.

In 2023, standing on the site once known as Orgreave, it is hard to imagine what happened here, especially as a sprawling new housing estate has sprouted up from the fields where bloodied police and pickets once ran. Passing 'Orgreave

Road' and 'Orgreave Lane', the familiar name disappeared as I turned into the new development overseen by the Harworth Group. Instead, I was met with a billboard proclaiming: 'We Are Waverley', with silhouettes of a family hand in hand beneath the slogan 'WORK. LIFE. BALANCED'; another, on the opposite side of the road read, 'WELCOME HOME'. I wondered whether the marketing team realised how the image echoed the mining families on the old banners, who once stood hand in hand heralding a better future under a nationalised mining industry.

The promotional video on the development's website was particularly jarring. It briefly alluded to the area's 'proud industrial past', with upbeat music thumping over scenes of fleeing pickets and riot police, but quickly transitioned to the 'bright new future' envisioned for over 3,000 new homes.[51] The many reminders of the new 'Waverley' brand around the site seem designed to hold the viewer in the present, to confound anyone hoping to find traces of the 'proud' past that lies beneath. Around the corner is the vast new 'Advanced Manufacturing Park', home to world-leading brands like Rolls-Royce, Boeing and McLaren as well as the University of Sheffield's Translational Energy Research Centre, which aims to advance low-carbon energy research. Such innovation is welcome, particularly as it will bring new opportunities to an area that has paid the high human cost of decades of industrial decline.

Despite the optimistic signage, I left Waverley feeling uncomfortable. I thought about the many other former mining communities I had visited, where pit wheels, coal tubs and memorials existed alongside new estates, as an impermeable reminder of what came before. In Waverley, the only vague nod to the area's industrial heritage comes in the form of the drystone walls at the entrance to the development, the dark line running through the middle suggesting the rich black seam buried underground. I remembered walking around genocide sites decades ago and how the custodians of these dutifully maintained them as evidence, so the past could not be denied. I feared that beyond the aspirational branding of the Harworth Group, there might be an insidious hope that changing a name and bulldozing the traces of Orgreave might also permit what happened here to slip from memory.

Deplorably, the veterans of Orgreave are still waiting for an official inquiry. Despite support from prominent public figures, their appeals have all too often fallen on deaf ears. In 2016, Amber Rudd, then Home Secretary, determined that as 'there were no deaths or wrongful convictions', the slate could be washed clean. However, the wife of one Conservative MP later claimed the probe was quashed following fears it could 'slur the memory of Thatcher'.[52] Whatever the reasons, the decision not to undertake an inquiry into the events of the 18th of June 1984 has been upheld like a baton silently passed on to each of Rudd's successors.

Every year, more people – like Tommy, whose story opened this chapter – who found their lives rocked by events at Orgreave, go to their graves without any answers, explanations or apologies. For many of those still living, the new Public Order Bill, which seeks to curb the right to protest, must send a shiver up their weary spines. Nonetheless, the Orgreave Truth and Justice Campaign remains steadfast in its fight for justice. You will see them each year on the anniversary, marching through Sheffield, banging their drums and flying a banner with Lesley Boulton's image, beneath the

Orgreave 35th Anniversary Rally, Orgreave, South Yorkshire.

lines 'No Justice, No Peace'. They will not be silenced and will never forgive, nor forget, until their dying breath. For the sake of men like Kevin, the two Pauls, and Huw, and countless others, I only hope justice is served and peace can be found before then.

8. The Rescuer

J: Have I ever given me dad a proper hug?
E: Have you?
J: Not really. That'd be when I were five year old for a hug before he went to work and he trod on me toe. But not, not when I were in me teens. So, I missed it and times have changed.

One of John's earliest memories was of moving to a new house in Castleford, West Yorkshire, a town equally renowned for its history in coal mining and rugby. He had no recollection of the building his family had left behind, but he could remember the novelty of reaching for the light switch in his new home. Although they enjoyed electricity, the terraces still did not have the luxury of indoor bathrooms and there were many frosty nocturnal journeys made outside when nature called. In those days, the family used newspaper squares in lieu of toilet paper, a frugality which meant John was better prepared than most to weather the supermarket shortages of the pandemic we were living through in 2020. John could remember the regular delivery of their coal allowance, the black fruits of his miner father's labours, and how even as a four-year-old he would help to carry it in. As a boy, he would imagine his father crawling through narrow tunnels underground, pick in hand, like one of the seven dwarves. It was not until many years later that John discovered the reality for himself.

John's first encounter with the cruelties of mining life had come much earlier, at the age of five, when his father accidentally trod on his toe, in his haste to leave for the night shift underground. At the time, John was in tears, but looking back he dwelled on the unspoken heartache his father must have felt, having to get to work on time and leave him behind. As his young son drifted off into forgetful sleep, his father was in a metal cage descending the pit shaft, to brood over his fraught departure in the darkness. This was the first and last time John could remember hugging his father, right up to the older man's death in 1982, when John was twenty-five years old.

John had often revisited this incident and the emotional distance he felt between himself and his father. It reminded me of a scene in the final episode of the BBC series *Our Friends in the North,* in which the character of Nicky confessed to his father how, as a child, all he wanted was to be loved, to be held and to be wanted as a son.[1] Just like John, Nicky got no resolution: by the time these words had found their way into the world, his once formidable father had already faded away, lost to the confusion of Alzheimer's. Other men carried memories of their own silent fathers, men who were on the threshold of the family and who had kept their sons at arm's length as, in John's words, 'You had to man up. That old thing about boys have got to be tough and all that, that's what it were like. It *really* was like that.'

Another memory John had from around the same time was of being roused from his sleep, in the room he shared with his brother, by a banging on the front door. Like many working-class families in the early 1960s, they could not afford the convenience of a home telephone and news, good and bad, had to be delivered in person, a far cry from the laptop screens we were now conversing over. The door banged again. It was still dark outside and the two boys did not understand why they were being made to leave the warmth of their beds, though they could see their mother was upset. They were rushed out of the house and off to their grandmother's, only later to learn that their father had been struck by a roof fall whilst working underground. Their father survived, but years later he still wore a deep blue scar across his forehead, which he would use to store his pencil in when he was betting on the horses.

Later, the pit's winding gear cast a dark shadow over John's school days. On 21 October 1966, when John was approaching his ninth birthday, news broke of the disaster that had occurred in the South Wales mining community of Aberfan. A suffocating torrent of coal slurry from an overlooking spoil tip had descended upon Pantglas Junior School at the start of the day's lessons, killing 116 children and 28 adults. South Wales had a formidable history of blood on the coal, but this accident was uniquely awful, as one miner described, 'these were children – not men, and that seems to make all the difference'.[2] The next day, newspapers printed bleak images of exhausted fathers digging with their bare hands through the ink black mound in the desperate hope of finding survivors. Aberfan was over 200 miles from Castleford, and a place John had never visited despite having Welsh cousins, but the incident sent shock waves across the British coalfields. In the weeks that followed, this young boy, like many other mining children, would stare fearfully out of the windows of his own classroom and imagine a black tidal wave pouring in.

Seven years on, a disaster closer to home played out on

the family's television set, when an inrush of water claimed the lives of seven miners at nearby Lofthouse Colliery. The incident, which occurred in the early hours of 21 March 1973, was caused by water breaking into new workings underground from an abandoned Victorian mine that was filled with 3 million gallons of filthy water. The Allerton Bywater Rescue Team, who attended the scene, was praised for following 'the glorious and unfailing tradition of the miner' in their willingness to risk everything – roof falls, further flooding, noxious gases – to free their imprisoned colleagues.[3]

Nonetheless, after six days of arduous and profoundly dangerous work, only the body of forty-nine-year-old face-worker Charles Cotton was recovered, a father working

A rescue crew waiting to make another attempt to free 7 miners trapped in the flooded Lofthouse Colliery, West Yorkshire, 23 March 1973.

alongside his son when the inrush occurred, and who had told his son to save himself. The mortal remains of the other missing men, Frederick Armitage (forty-one), Colin Barnaby (thirty-six), Frank Billingham (forty-eight), Sydney Brown (thirty-six), Edward Finnegan (forty) and Alan Haigh (thirty), were never brought into the daylight. Decades later, the rescuers continue to be haunted by the fact that they could not free their colleagues. As David Hagan, a colliery electrician and member of the Allerton Bywater Rescue team, commented on the fortieth anniversary of the disaster: 'Those six men were never put to rest. They're still down there. I still think about those men today.'[4] On the edge of Wrenthorpe village, a seven-sided obelisk now marks the spot where the men were lost, like a dark finger extending from the earth upwards into the sky, a reminder that they still lie beneath.

John was now fifteen, and he began to talk to his father about the accident and the brutal realities of life and death underground. A month later, the older man expressed his disgust because, though the events at Lofthouse had received daily coverage, when a group of Scottish miners were crushed and buried there were no updates on the outcome. News in the early 1970s was a world apart from the constantly refreshing stories we struggle to avert our eyes from today. Back then, John's family were reliant on the trusted word of the BBC, and its silence felt like a betrayal: those men were their brothers and yet they could not find out what had happened to them.

John took little more from his schooling than an appreciation of punctuality and the importance of following the rules. Most of the curriculum appeared to have little bearing on his daily life, and the archaic approach to teaching – copying from a blackboard – felt particularly futile. However, one lesson had lodged itself in his mind. It was English and the teacher, who had been a rear gunner in the Second World War, decided to read to the class, a prospect enthusiastically welcomed by the students, who were usually commanded to stand and recite themselves. Moments later, the man had the class hanging on his every word, as he described the plight of a group of miners trapped underground. The extract was from *The Stars Look Down* by A. J. Cronin, a story whose plot echoed – with unsettling similarity – the events that had occurred at Lofthouse, just a few short years before.[5]

Each child in that hushed classroom had a connection to the pit: they were the sons, daughters, nieces and nephews, brothers and sisters of men who worked underground; they lived under the slag heaps and, like John, spent the weekends playing on this blackened mountain range. Before the fate of the entombed miners was revealed to the expectant audience, the teacher slammed the book shut and abruptly told them: 'If you want to find out what happens you'd better go read it yourself.' On his fiftieth birthday, John had received his own copy and had finally discovered what happened to those trapped men who had haunted his imagination for over three decades.

When John left the familiar corridors of school for the final time, he was unsure which direction to take. His boyhood passion was skin-diving, and the prospect of a life at sea with the Navy held strong appeal (as it did for two of the other Johns in this book). However, as it turned out, he never really had much of a choice. Like the other boys, John was 'just herded' into the pit and offered little in the way of support or encouragement. Sadly, this story was a familiar one: mining sons up and down the country similarly described how they were given few alternatives but to join the production line of young blood channelled into the dark veins of the pit. It appeared some teachers saw slim chance of boys like John escaping a career underground, as he explained: 'For *them*, why would they not look at me and think, he's pit fodder.'

So, just like his father and so many other sons of the coalfields, it was to be a mining life for John. Within a radius of less than 10 miles, he could choose from over ten collieries. Ultimately, he decided not to go to Glasshoughton, his father's pit, compelled by the belief he should be his own man, and instead he joined Allerton Bywater Colliery. Reflecting on his decision not to follow his father, John felt the older man may have been happy – his nickname for his son was 'blithering idiot', so perhaps it was a relief from embarrassment. Or maybe he was glad not to have the weight of responsibility for his son's safety underground; his father never spoke to him about it.

John had the good fortune to join the industry in 1974, a time when miners' pay was the best it had ever been and new recruits were still being assured of 'a job for life', because 'people would always need coal'. The National Coal Board was offering four-year craft apprenticeships, through which young men would be trained up, paid some of the best rates going, and be guaranteed a job at the end. John chose to focus on the electrical side. He had already acquired an amateur proficiency, having bunked off school to help an older friend rewire local council houses, one of which his youngest son now happened to reside in. Having been held back 'like stallions' at school, John and his peers relished the world of work, the money and the new social connections they made.

Only later did John appreciate how once he joined the pit

he had also gained, in his words, 'a thousand dads'. Though these men were not all the best role models, and several were 'daft as brushes', they introduced the young incomers to the ways of the pit, gave them their first taste of chewing tobacco (which turned several sixteen-year-olds, including John, a queasy shade of green) and taught them a colourful new vocabulary. Crucially, these men also instilled their charges with common sense, which might prove life-saving later.

When the fresh-faced 'new bloods' were first ushered into the electricians' shop, the older men's opening enquiries were as to whether they had any sisters. Subsequently, each was allocated his own nickname: John was given 'ferkin hell', a play on his surname, which was a marginal step up from 'blithering idiot'. Compared to others, John had got off lightly. Another apprentice, who did not have a sister, but had both a lisp and a mother with large breasts, became known as 'titz'. Years later, when one man returned from Spain, which was beginning to tempt working-class holiday-makers away from the traditional resorts of Blackpool and Skegness, the pit embraced a new cosmopolitanism and everyone acquired an 'o' at the end of their nickname. John thus became known as 'ferk-o' from this point forward.

Overall, it appeared John enjoyed his work in a straightforward way, but it did not change who he was as a person. Rather, the most transformative move he made was joining the Mines Rescue Service, a decision inspired by both his memories of Lofthouse and the men who had saved his father many years earlier. With his skin-diving experience, which had become part of the training in the wake of the inrush at Lofthouse, John had a tick in the box and determined to go for an interview.

For as long as there had been mines there had been rescuers, though in the past they were more often men who received word of an accident underground and had come running. As time went on, blood spilled across the coalfields necessitated the formalised Mines Rescue Service, and rescue stations were a compulsory provision of the 1911 Coal Mines Act.[6] Early photographs of rescue teams in their archaic breathing apparatus may appear haunting today, but underground, this vision through the smoke offered salvation. Throughout the service's history, rescuers risked their own lives to help those in peril underground.

In September 1950, a disaster at Knockshinnoch Castle Colliery in Ayrshire, when a devastating inrush of liquid peat and moss engulfed the colliery, was widely hailed as the greatest rescue operation in the Scottish coalfields, if not the whole of Britain.[7] In an unprecedented operation, rescuers formed a human chain underground along the 800-metre roadway to guide the survivors out, equipped with breathing apparatus loaned from local fire services, to counter the presence of deadly fumes. Though the small Ayrshire community was left in mourning for the 13 men who died in the incident, as a result of the heroic efforts of the rescuers, 116 men were pulled back to life and light, after over two days entombed underground. Two years later, the episode was played out on screen in the film *The Brave Don't Cry*.[8]

At its peak, the Mines Rescue Service had forty-six rescue stations, standing by to come to the aid of over a million miners. The Mines Rescue Station in the village of Tankersley, near Barnsley in South Yorkshire, was the first of its kind to be built in Britain. Dating back to 1902, it is a proud redbrick building that still stands by the roadside today. The men who once resided within had a proud history of rescue work, as the *Sheffield Daily Telegraph* had observed the year it opened: 'The heroism of pit-men has been proved on too many occasions to doubt the sterling metal of which they are made, and nowhere more strikingly than in Yorkshire and the adjoining coalfields.'[9] However, other than a small plaque, there is little to denote the building's former life nor the lives its former occupants saved. Its latest reincarnation finds it dedicated to rescuing split ends, as the home of a popular local beauty salon.

Over in Lancashire, the Boothstown Mines Rescue Station, which was opened in 1933 on Ellenbrook Road in Salford, once represented the cutting-edge of mines rescue provision. It was designed by architects Bradshaw, Gass and Hope of Bolton on behalf of the Lancashire and Cheshire Coal Owners, and was delivered at a cost of £30,000 (today the equivalent of over £2 million).[10] Behind its sleek art deco façade and automatic garage doors, it housed training galleries and observation halls, gas and equipment testing facilities, kitchens, showers, offices, a boardroom and even an aviary for the resident canaries. Opening the station in November, the Earl of Crawford described how the occasion marked the fruition of twenty-five years of research, and would benefit from the indomitable courage of the Lancashire folk, which could not be excelled.[11]

Later, the Earl's comments were proved correct. In 1950, two members of the Boothstown team, forty-six-year-old Herbert Evitts and thirty-three-year-old William Seth Parr, who lived with their families behind the station, were awarded the British Empire Medal and George Medal respectively for gallantry below ground.[12] Early in the morning of 15 September 1949, the team had been called out to attend an explosion at the Lyme Pit in Haydock, during which two of them, Harold Clare and James Page, aged forty-seven and thirty-seven, were fatally overcome by gas. Having sent his exhausted colleagues back to fetch help, Parr remained underground by the side of an unconscious man, despite his own steadily depleting supply of oxygen. Evitts aided a stretcher bearer who had also collapsed during the episode, staying behind to revive him. Both men, who had worked at Boothstown since 1945, were characteristically modest about their bravery and the sacrifices they were willing to make to save their colleagues, or at least ensure they did not die alone in the darkness, jointly attesting, 'We only did our jobs.'[13]

After a spell as home to a hat manufacturing business, in 2016, the Boothstown station was 'sympathetically converted' and relaunched as the aspirational Orchard House, comprising fifteen contemporary and generously proportioned town houses and two apartments.[14] The sleek marketing materials featured images of the sooty-faced rescuers who used to call the building home; a stark contrast to the high-gloss kitchens, chrome downlights, soft-close toilet seats and luxury vinyl flooring detailed in the brochure. More lamentable was the fact that the surrounding land, once home to allotments, tennis courts, a children's playground and open space for recreation, has now also been consumed by housing.

Other buildings have managed to stay truer to their original purpose. In 2023, the rescue station at Houghton-le-Spring, Tyne and Wear, known locally as the Old Fire Station, celebrated its 110th anniversary. Today, it continues to offer confined-space training and supervision, firefighting and first-aid instruction across the North East of England. Whilst over in Mansfield, the rescue station that was purpose-built on Leeming Lane South in 1958 looks remarkably unchanged, though recently plans were approved to revitalise the building. Like the Old Fire Station, it has survived by transforming into a commercial enterprise, though today it is more likely to be called out to attend to problems of the post-coal era, like the recent removal of environmental protestors occupying a tunnel beneath London's Euston Station.[15]

When John spoke of the Mines Rescue Service, his voice broke under the weight of its noble history and his pride in the thirteen years he served as part of it. According to John, 'they could not pay you enough to do it', but nonetheless you did it, because 'it was your turn to step up to the mark and do the right thing for your mates'. This somewhat underplayed the sacrifices rescuers signed up to make for their colleagues. John emotionally recalled how on his first day of training, the superintendent had lined them up and told them, 'You're here for three weeks; you'll be men when you leave, you'll be better men.' In many ways, the service was the ultimate manifestation of miners' camaraderie, though perhaps for John, his membership was a means to exorcise the ghosts of his childhood: the blackened men who rescued his father, the human barrier preventing the imaginary torrent from engulfing his school and the trapped miners who haunted his memories.

In 1952, men were filmed training at the Wakefield Mines Rescue Station. In the event of an accident, the team was 'always together and away' in less than four minutes, equipped with enough oxygen to last two hours underground. Each man was qualified to give first aid, and their every move was checked and timed.[16] In Wakefield, they were particularly proud of their rocking stretcher, used across British coalfields, as it had been invented by the Rescue Service's own

William Riley, to aid men suffering from chest injury. However, though rescue techniques changed over the decades and technology improved men's abilities to save lives, the one thing that remained consistent was the challenging conditions the rescuers competed against in the dark warrens underground.

On holiday in Florida years after leaving the industry, John had been approached by a girl who had admired the tattoo on his arm. He explained that it represented the Mines Rescue Service, and in response the girl asked John the most scared he had ever been. He conceded that it was during the first three weeks of training, but that he had never been scared after that. Many of the trials John had to endure were later banned when more health and safety regulations were introduced. On one occasion, the trainees were sent into the mock pit under the old station in Wakefield, where the men had been filmed training two decades earlier. The team crawled through the narrow tunnels until they came to a dead end. Their kit was scraping the walls and it was really claustrophobic, particularly as they were all bunched up. Fortunately, the lad at the front figured out that they had to retreat backwards until they discovered another tunnel through which they could come out over the top. When they finally made it out, their relief was palpable, until the trainer told them they had to do the exercise again, but this time with the tunnels filled with acrid smoke. The second time, they got through by holding the foot of the man in front and keeping their distance, and in John's words, 'We did it, we all did it.'

Occasionally, training exercises simulated accidents that had happened just weeks ago. One day, there had been a serious incident at nearby Fryston Colliery: a man had been lifting a metal bar off a chain when it slipped and went straight through his body, impaling him. Everyone had heard about it: news of a gruesome accident at another local pit did not take long to circulate. The next time they turned up for training they were asked to attend to a man who was lying on the ground, with a bar through him, like a joke knife through the head. The mock casualty was indulging in histrionics with fake blood and guts spilling out onto the tunnel floor and the team struggled to agree whether to writhe it out of him, because there was no time to get a hacksaw. Of course, in a real disaster they could not discuss the matter. They would all be wearing mouthpieces and could only communicate by clicking their fingers. Lift a stretcher together. *Click*. Pull a bar out of an impaled colleague. *Click*.

Once John had done a drawing of what his life had been like in those days, before everything changed during the strike. It was a hole in the ground, a house, a rugby pitch and a club. In John's words, 'Got family. You'd work all the time. On a Sunday you'd go to the club. Saturday you were playing rugby and in the club. Sorted kids, went back down hole. Work for eight days a week.' You worked hard, you played hard, you had a good drink, you looked after your family.

Predictably, perhaps, given his strong commitment to the team, when the strike began in March 1984, John came out straightaway. By the end of May, he had been arrested whilst picketing at Orgreave and was later released on bail, after being badly beaten whilst in custody and charged with breach of the peace. The moment of John's arrest had been captured in a black and white photograph, in which he was shown being carried out of the crowd, head down and arms locked either side by two police officers. This image felt like an inversion of John's work as a rescuer: as opposed to being pulled from danger, he was being singled out in the crowd. However, this suffering bore little comparison to the hand life dealt John next. Just two weeks later, his daughter Nicola was taken ill, and it was discovered that she had an inoperable brain tumour. Nicola passed away on 13 June 1984, aged just three years and four months old.

No grief can compare to that of a parent who has lost a child, but John's family had further anguish to come. Unbeknownst to many, it transpired that the government had passed a law that meant that if you were on strike, you could not receive any financial help to bury your children. The legislation had been put in place a few years earlier, but it was believed that John's family were the first to be impacted. Later, when their case was heard by the European Parliament, there was widespread disgust as, in the words of the Labour MEP for Leeds Michael McGowan, 'Even in times of war we took time to bury our dead.'[17] It was only thanks to the benevolence of his colleagues who gave a day's picketing pay (the only income many had), the union and members of the surrounding community like the local undertaker Graham, who told him 'pay me when you can', that John was able to give his daughter a funeral with dignity.

As he told me this harrowing story, John pointed up to a portrait of a blonde-haired little girl on the wall above. This was the last picture of Nicola, taken long before a time everyone had a camera in their pocket. Nicola had been photographed when the family had attended a convention in Scarborough. When the photographer heard Nicola's story, she had sent the picture to them. For John, this was yet another example of how other people's kindness had lifted him from grief, 'It makes you strong, it makes you strong.'

Though at the time John wished nobody else would ever have to go through the pain of losing a child, as he got older, he realised that was never going to happen, as 'life isn't like *Little House on the Prairie*, where grandma gets older, silver hair, and the sun's setting, and her hand falls to the side, and all the family is there. It doesn't happen like that'. However, for John, cruelty was all man-made, and though Nicola would still have died, 'They didn't need to do what they did.'

The eventual return to work after the strike was an emotional affair as John walked behind the colliery banner, carrying his son on his shoulders. So many had lost so much during those long twelve months, but few had lost as much as John. In the end, the men of Allerton Bywater Colliery were split equally between those who had returned to work early and those who had upheld the strike directive. As a result, when everyone went back, tension permeated the atmosphere. Even the close bonds of the rescue team were eroded. That team, who had to rely on each other in the darkest of situations, who could communicate without words, who led each other blindly through stinging smoke and formed a human chain through the mire, was broken, fragmented and would never be the same again.

Allerton Bywater Colliery closed in March 1992, bringing an end to a local industry that had endured over a century, and through which its workers had wrestled almost 60 million tonnes of coal from the underbelly of the earth.[18] When I visited this former mining village, the air still carried the distinct aroma of coal fires. Aside from this familiar smell, there were scarce other echoes of Allerton Bywater's past industrial life. Over twenty years ago, John Prescott had announced that the former pit site would be home to the second 'Millennium Community', a multi-million-pound development intended to set the standard for future living in England, providing both housing and jobs.[19] Despite numerous delays owing to the impracticalities of the location – on a flood plain, adjacent to a chemical plant and over the top of gas ventilation shafts – by 2006, the first of the planned 500 new homes had been sold. Today, even the colliery's former spoil tip casts a surprisingly bucolic vision, providing a home to red deer, marsh harriers and cormorants.

The village's heritage has not been erased entirely. At the entrance to the new development stands a memorial to the former colliery and the lives lost there. Designed by local artist and former Fryston Colliery miner Harry Malkin, who like John was born in Castleford, it takes the form of a mining cage. Its carved sides carry scenes from the local history of the industry, a story of machinery, of Coal Not Dole, of community and camaraderie.[20] The stiff metal chains atop the cage extend into the sky, as if suspended in time, waiting to be reconnected and carried upwards into the heavens. A coal car stands nearby, spilling over with flowers, upon the side of which are detailed the names of the eighty-six men and boys whose lives had ended beneath the now verdant green, and a reminder of the living community that had been left searching for a new identity when the pit closed.

When he stepped off the cage at Allerton Bywater Colliery for the final time, John joined over a thousand men who found themselves without a job. Six years later, the village had an unemployment rate of over 10 per cent, twice the national average.[21] Alongside other industrial workers, who also found themselves cast onto the scrap heap, came men who had known nothing but coal all their lives and had been assured of a job for life. Across Yorkshire and elsewhere, Job Centres saw dozens of men looking for work in an ever-decreasing pool of opportunities. However, unlike the iconic scene in *The Full Monty*, filmed at the Job Centre on West Street in Sheffield, it is unlikely any men found themselves dancing in the queue.[22]

It was leaving the Mines Rescue Service that hurt John the most. He was not just leaving mining and his mates; when he left the rescue service, he felt he was leaving a part of himself behind and in John's words 'that really does, it did hurt a bit, loads to be honest'. Eventually, he found a newspaper advert seeking qualified electricians for a factory making dog biscuits. John was now thirty-five years old, with two young sons to support, and he launched into the job interview with his characteristic loquaciousness. Ultimately, the 1200 applicants who applied were whittled down to 12 successful candidates, and John was one.

During one shift, John had asked one of his new colleagues how he had ended up at the factory. The man described how he previously had 'the best job in the world', working for the specialist burns service at Pinderfields Hospital in Wakefield, which had been established in 1966 as the first NHS-funded facility of its kind in Britain. When someone had been badly burnt, his job was to set the bed up with pressure pads. This painstaking process could take up to two hours, but the man took great pride in getting it right, because he knew when he walked away from that bed, the patient was as comfortable as they could possibly be, under the circumstances. When John asked the man why he had left, his colleague replied simply, 'Because they pay me more to put dog biscuits in packets.'

Life at the factory was good, though it felt deeply unjust to be paid more for watching dog biscuits being pumped out onto a conveyor belt, where it was 'as safe as a cotton wool factory', than for toiling hundreds of feet underground as a coalface electrician. To John's disbelief, once fully trained, he was offered a 4 per cent pay rise, and Christmas came with a hamper and an extra week's wage. Not to mention that there was sick pay, additional pay for the hour gained when the clocks turned forward, and paid tea breaks. However, despite the perks of his new role and John's reticence to discuss personal matters at work, one manager observed that he was not coping, sent him home and advised him to see a counsellor. John was reluctant to do so but felt obliged, as they wouldn't let him return to work until he was 'right'; so he went.

Within fifteen minutes of his first appointment with the counsellor, John was in tears. He was crying about Nicola, he was crying because he felt he had to be strong and had never let go. He cried because 'it were all broken', that little photo with hole and house and club, 'it were all broken'. He cried in the way he had decades earlier, when his father had stepped on his toe, before he had learned the behaviour that was expected of men. In John's words, 'It all came out, it all came out, that macho-ness, I let it down.' Like joining the Mines Rescue Service years earlier, this moment marked another sea change in John's life. He subsequently decided to train as a counsellor himself, a move which saw all his experiences pulling in, as he found he could rescue people again, 'using me mind, not me body'.

Eventually, John became an accredited counsellor, with letters after his name and business cards, working in a jacket and tie at the local doctor's surgery, something that felt a million miles away from his former life. Despite this, he was still a miner, 'I still am, it's still in me, it's still, that's still in me.' John's success as a counsellor owed much to his refusal to elide his past identity. He didn't 'put a voice on, you get what you get', and his clients were both surprised and reassured by his directness. More than this, John was still a rescuer; though the close-knit team of which he had once been a member had long since disbanded and the pits had shut, he remained one of those rare individuals who would run towards a crisis, regardless of the risks. Where once he had hauled men out of the darkness of the pit, he became a link in a human chain pulling people out of the depths of addiction and depression.

John's father passed away long before his son evolved into the man I had spoken to. John was still a miner's son, but he was a son who had grown to realise that the version of manhood modelled by men like his father had left him with absences and ambivalences that punctuated his memories: silences that could now never be filled, unanswered questions hanging like smoke in the air. John shared his father's 'pearls of wisdom', which were 'always be true to yourself', and his own, which he passed on to me, 'be kind to your future self'. John still felt he would never be as good as men like his father, men whose life was one of constant hard work. But in my mind, John was a better man, through realising not only the parts of himself he must retain but how sometimes the only way forward was to let go.

9. Fathers, Sons and Picket Lines

It's like, if you were David Beckham's son playing football, like that was my problem, you were always going to be compared to him. I was always compared to me Dad.

As we have already heard, for many mining sons, their introduction to the pit came long before they ever set foot in the cage. It began with their father's blue scars, missing fingers and shortness of breath. Or the household routines of jam sandwiches pressed into snap tins and the monthly delivery of concessionary coal. Though countless family trades exist and more have come and gone in decades past, few industries could claim such intergenerationality as mining. For some, returning home wearing 'miner's mascara' after their first shift underground meant they could finally be looked upon as men.[1] For many others, taking the well-trodden path to the pit was not so much a choice as a necessity. For mining sons like Tony, whose words open this chapter, their fathers struck a figure very different to their own.

Born at the start of the swinging sixties, Tony was one of the youngest men I interviewed. He was raised in the Nottinghamshire village of Bestwood, where he lived in one of the regimented red-brick terraces built to house miners in 1876, and which were located 300 yards from the pit.[2] Both his childhood home on Park Road and the pit headstocks remain today. The Area Central Workshops, where mining machinery would be repaired, once stood at the back of his house. Tony compared his early experiences to those of the young protagonist in Ken Loach's film *Kes*, 'playing on the pit tips and everything'.[3]

One of the older collieries in the Nottinghamshire coalfield, production first started at Bestwood in 1876 and in time it became the first mine in the world to produce 1 million tons of coal in a year.[4] According to *COAL* magazine, after the industry was nationalised in 1947, Bestwood was a place where 'all the good things in life seem to have come at once'.[5] For forty years, the village had no proper roads or pavements but the Coal Board set about laying macadam roadways and modern pavements. A new sewer scheme was developed to provide modern sanitation and residents delighted in the improved electricity services on offer. Though housewives may still have dried their washing on lines crisscrossing the street, the Coal Board eased their burdens by suppling new line posts.

Tony was 'the son of an immigrant': his father had come over from Ireland in the 1950s to help rebuild Longbridge in Birmingham after the war.[6] When the job was complete, he travelled to Nottinghamshire and took a job in mining. Tony's father had started his mining career at Gedling Colliery, 'The Pit of Nations', so named due to the diversity of its workforce, which included a large number of black miners who had come over from the Caribbean as part of the Windrush generation.[7] Their contribution had been immortalised on the colliery banner, which portrays its racially diverse miners, above the line: 'Brothers Beneath the Surface'.

In Nottinghamshire, Tony's maternal grandmother used to host lodgers in the family's spare rooms, as people often did to supplement the household coffers, and Tony's father happened to be one of them. As a young girl, Tony's mother used to cook for their guests, and that is how she and his father first struck up a relationship out of which came six children, three girls and three boys, including Tony. Summoning forth the memory of his father, Tony struggled to reduce it to words: 'How can I describe him? He was a fighting man and all that like, very tough man, very tough.' Tony, on the other hand, 'didn't take any of his genes' and felt he was more like his mother, with a placid temperament that made him particularly well-suited to his later career as a driving instructor.

Tony was always aware that his father, Ron, was 'a bit of a legend' underground. He worked on development of the 'golden mile' tunnel that ran under Bestwood. His brother Bill, Tony's uncle, also lived in Bestwood and did the same. Ron was also a member of the Mines Rescue Service and during the 1950s he had helped clear up the aftermath of a fatality at Bestwood. As Tony explained, a man had been working on the face conveyor, the mechanical belt that transported cut coal away from the face, and 'it started up when it shouldn't have done'. It took off the man's leg, from the hip, and 'he died there and then'. The men had carried the body out of the pit, but 'the leg was still down there, nobody would go and fetch it'. In the end, Ron had to go back down, taking a large paper bag with him and placing the leg inside to bring it to the surface. Tony recalled how his father was walking across the pit yard, '"I had to do something", he says, "so I just says: 'does anybody want to buy a boot'", he said: "I felt awful", he says, "I just knew what I was carrying."' I had come to appreciate how miners used humour after an accident as the only way they felt they could carry on, making a joke instead of breaking their hearts.[8]

Ron had joined Linby Colliery in 1968, which was, by this point, the third colliery of his mining career. Founded around the same time as Bestwood Colliery, in the late 1950s Linby had been granted a new lease of life through mechanisation, including the installation of a single cable belt conveyor (believed to be the longest in Europe), a new skip winding system and pit-bottom circuits for loco haulage and man-riding, meaning men no longer had to walk 2 miles to reach their place of work underground.[9] According to the Area General Manager, after the renovations, Linby was the most highly mechanised pit in the area.[10]

Although a career in mining was being sold to young men as a 'good future now', just like many mining fathers before him, Ron did not want his sons to follow him underground.[11] Tony's eldest brother got a job with the Coal Board, working above ground, as a mechanic in the area workshop. Tony had tried to do the same but had failed his interview. As a result, he had applied to work underground. He could still remember his father's advice, 'If you need to go underground, go underground, but you're better off without.' Tony got the job, leaving secondary school on the Friday and starting his training on the Monday, at the age of sixteen. On reflection, he was pleased he had not been discouraged, as he told me: 'Just an *awesome* place the pit is, really awesome, I suppose everybody has said that to you.'

Tony's father left Linby in 1971, seven years before Tony arrived, moving to the nearby Blidworth Colliery. However, everyone at Linby remembered Ron, and underground he even had his own Butterley bunker named after him, ''cause he'd done it all'.[12] Though Tony felt proud of his father's reputation, the pressure it came with was hard to live up to, particularly as 'everybody always used to say, "you'll never be as good as him"'. Tony could still remember one interaction with a group of his father's friends: 'The guy I was with, he says, "Guess who this is Fergie?", to this big Irish man, and he says, "I have no idea", he says, "Ron's son", he says, "You never, that's not Ron's son, he's too skinny"', before they erupted into laughter. Tony took these comments in his stride, as 'just the way it was', aware that other people had experienced similar.

As elsewhere, at Linby the men would look after each other underground, particularly on face headings, which were especially dangerous due to the exposed roof. As Tony told me, at times, when you were engaged in work, your mates behind would throw a stone at you, 'to frighten you to death', but if anything was about to happen, you trusted them to watch your back. Fortunately, Tony had only visited hospital twice with injuries: once when a piece of steel had gone through his arm, piercing a nerve, and on another occasion when he had hit a girder, which, as he animatedly confessed, had resulted in a 'great scar'. Though Tony had never been on a rollercoaster, as he would be 'frightened to death', none of these accidents had ever made him think twice about going back underground, as he explained, 'I just felt proud of it all. It's *weird*, actually. You felt like you were something . . .'.

Tony had always enjoyed the social side of mining life. The eighteenth-century Red Lion pub, the oldest in Hucknall and the former rent house of the Byron family, was a particularly 'legendary' watering hole. When Linby men finished the day shift, they would be in the line at the bar from half past seven until half past ten at night. Later, the afternoon shift, who finished at ten to nine, would join them and the two groups would compare how much coal they had cut that day. If the pit talk became too much, beer mats would be placed over the top of pint glasses, with men announcing: 'I don't want no dust in there.'

On a Friday night, in days gone by, there was only one place to be: the Hucknall and Linby Miners' Welfare on Portland Road. Unveiled in May 1963 at a cost of £90,000, the three-storey building made of local stone and NCB facing bricks, boasted a concert hall large enough to hold 500 people with a wooden floor designed for dancing.[13] The new welfare had 5,000 members on its books before its doors had even opened.[14] As a child, Tony had attended the pit parties there but he returned as a young man for the discos, where people came to dance the night away and eye up the local talent amongst the sea of Chelsea collars, perms and pageboy haircuts in the Welbeck Suite. While big names like Judas Priest, The Exciters, Dr Feelgood and Slade played to sold-out audiences in the main hall, members who were 'getting on a bit' could afford to take things easier in the lounge with their wives. Along with its namesake collieries, the welfare closed in the late 1980s, and today an Aldi supermarket stands on its site.

Tony was still a schoolboy during the strikes of the early 1970s. I had come across a photo of his father Ron in the local newspaper, pictured smiling with his helmet lamp lighting up his ballot paper for the pit pay-offer vote, which had brought an end to the strike of 1972.[15] In both the strikes of 1972 and 1974, Nottinghamshire's men had followed the NUM's directive to come out, just like other areas. As Tony explained, whilst those disputes were over wages, as 'a postman was earning more than a man on the face', the strike of 1984–85 was an entirely different matter.

On the first day of the strike in 1984, Tony had arrived at

work, where he was met by some lads from Yorkshire, 'and I just handed them my snap and I went home'. Unsure of what was going to happen, he went back to the pit on the third day as there was no picket line, but speaking to his friends he realised the strike was still on and subsequently 'never went in again'. Tony upheld the strike for the whole year. Of course, as he reminded me, unlike Yorkshire who were 'solid', it was a very different picture in Nottinghamshire, where out of over 30,000 workers, only a quarter of men had joined the strike and less than 2,000 saw it through to the end.[16]

Of the 800 men employed at Linby, only 12 per cent remained on strike for the duration. As Tony explained, it caused 'a lot of ill feeling, it really did, 'cause our pit was regarded as Little Moscow many years ago'. As far back as 1900, Linby had been 'notorious in one direction or another' due to stoppages.[17] Men from neighbouring pits had told me of Linby's militancy, and how 'if the sun was shining, they'd find a grievance'. However, as Tony pointed out, during his eleven years there, he had only been on strike once. He contrasted it to the workforce of the British car industry, 'They were on strike every *week* they were.' I nodded thinking of my own grandfather, who had been on strike from Ford's Halewood plant in Liverpool during both the 1960s and 1970s.

I somewhat naively observed that the experience of being on strike must have been much more challenging in Nottinghamshire, which Tony conceded: 'Oh it was harder here, phwoar, every day of the week, watching them go by, was soul destroying, but . . . and my Dad went, he scabbed.' Though I had heard of families being divided by a picket line, I was not expecting this admission, assuming, incorrectly, father would be like son, in this instance at least. Tony recalled his father's position well: 'He says, "Why should I come out if there's young men going to work?"' The disagreement between father and son had caused a lot of hassle at home, and the pair had almost come to blows at Christmas. As a result, Tony avoided coming home as much as possible, instead staying with his girlfriend, to whom he has now been married for over thirty years. She was from Calverton, 'another scab pit', he conceded laughing, and had taken on extra work in a bar, in addition to her factory job, to support him during the strike.

As many have argued, both at the time and since, the strike was constitutional according to the NUM rule book.[18] Of course, Tony was well-versed in the other side of the argument, cited by 'a lot of people round here', that there should have been a national ballot over the strike action. Countless reasons have been cited for Nottinghamshire's disaffection, including the area's political moderation, weak local NUM leadership, cosmopolitanism, affluence, favourable geological conditions, refusal to be strong-armed by Yorkshire pickets and lack of a strong sense of 'community'.[19] Their refusal to follow the strike directive also summoned forth the spectre of Spencerism, which had haunted the coalfield since the 1926 lockout when the county's miners had returned to work and formed their own breakaway union.[20] With the formal establishment of the rival Union of Democratic Mineworkers in the autumn of 1985, the echoes of the past only grew louder.[21]

Holding a national pre-strike ballot would have removed the contention that hounded both the strike and its supporters.[22] However, regardless of any such vote, the sanctity of the picket line remained and as Tony confided, 'The principle of mining, through history, was never cross picket lines.'

As a relative youngster, who celebrated his twenty-third birthday whilst on strike, I wondered what had sustained Tony's commitment to that principle, particularly as he was watching his own father breach the picket line. He confessed that he had wavered after the big row with his father, and going into the New Year, when 'we *knew* we weren't going to win'; but in the end, it was the people he was standing alongside who had kept him going and kept morale high. Of course, it was demoralising 'watching people going by *every single day*', but Tony could not conceive crossing that picket line when 'they're all here, I've been with them all this time'.

Tony told me about Brian, a man who worked at Linby before Tony was born and another member of Nottinghamshire's striking minority. By the time I interviewed Brian, he was in his early eighties and enjoying a quieter life. However, he still had an energy about him and I could see how in decades past he would have been a man with few qualms about standing his ground. Brian was only at Linby for two years, starting at the age of fifteen in 1952 but coming out in 1954 to serve in the Army. Three years later he returned to work at Moorgreen, a different Nottinghamshire pit, first on pony ganging and later as a faceworker. When the strike began in 1984, Brian was 'flabbergasted' when blokes he had worked alongside 'for donkey's years', just went in to work, breaking 'that unwritten rule, never cross a picket line'.

Living in Hucknall, Brian was surrounded by working miners, and seeing their concessionary coal being delivered during that year used to eat at him: 'We're on strike to save their pits, and they're getting the coal and we've got to struggle.' He remembered marching through the town with his striking comrades in the early weeks of the strike, and how a woman with a pushchair had gone absolutely 'berserk' at them, screaming and shouting. Calling the memory forth, Brian reflected: 'I would imagine her boyfriend or husband was working.' I had seen an old photograph of Brian at a rally in Sheffield during the strike, face shaded by a cap covered in badges, as he carried a placard, signed by Arthur Scargill, which read 'NOTTINGHAM STRIKING MINERS ASK FOR THE EXPULSION OF ALL THE SCABS'.

During his twelve months on strike, Brian had picketed all over the place, including Dinnington, where he told me how the Nottinghamshire pickets had stopped Yorkshire men going back to work (the irony was not lost on me or him). However, it was hard not to think back to my conversation with John and Anne in Dinnington, and how much they had struggled and suffered. There were also many battles fought closer to home. On 1 May 1984, 7,000 working miners clashed with around half that number of striking miners at the NUM Area Offices at Berry Hill Park in Mansfield.[23] That summer, a group of striking miners, including both Brian and Tony, had occupied the offices overnight. The story appeared on the lunchtime news and seeing it Tony's father had confessed that he was proud of his son, as Tony explained: 'He *knew* I was right, he knew I was right, but he was a very stubborn man, very stubborn.'

Although they were in the minority locally, the Nottinghamshire striking miners used all means available to them to make their case heard. I met another Moorgreen striker, an electrician, who set an alarm to ensure my tea was brewed for the optimal length of time. He was a fascinating character and a self-described 'radio man', with a large aerial at the end of his garden. With a knowing look, he had told me about 'Radio Arthur', a pirate station that had successfully wiped

Nottingham's Radio Trent off the air on several occasions during the strike.

Starting in July 1984, for the next six months local news bulletins were spasmodically interrupted by the ominous sounds of Wagner's *Flight of the Valkyries*, Holst's *Mars* and the theme tune of *The World at War*, with the announcer theatrically declaring: 'You're listening to the voice of the striking miners.'[24] Transmissions described the army of miners, fighting 'for their very survival' against an 'insidious foe' in the form of 'geriatric hitman' Ian MacGregor and Margaret Thatcher, the 'iron maiden', who sought to place the country at the mercy of the oil barons. Going out to a potential audience of some 1.2 million, the pirate broadcasts sounded so professional that several listeners complained about the offensive content being aired by Radio Trent.[25] Despite the best efforts of investigators from the Department of Trade and Industry, they never managed to locate the source of the broadcasts, which remain a mystery to this day.[26]

When the strike ended in March 1985 and men returned to work, at pits across the British coalfields there were tensions between miners who had worked and those who had upheld the strike, particularly when a minority had deviated from the position taken by the local majority. Given the comparatively large number of Linby strikers, they stuck together as a group, though as Tony observed, in other pits, where there were only half a dozen lads on strike, 'it must have been so horrible'. Nonetheless, the atmosphere at Linby had soured. After his first shift back, Tony remembered taking 'the quietest shower' he'd ever had. Usually, the walls would reverberate with the sound of men shouting, laughing, screaming and swearing, 'but it was complete silence'.

Gradually, through sheer necessity, working together and

having to watch the backs of both strikers and scabs, life underground returned to a strained form of normality. Of course, above ground there were men who Tony had turned his back on. During the strike, when he was standing on the picket line, one of his close friends had been walking into work and when he saw Tony, he had turned away and kept going. Tony had not spoken to him since: 'If he didn't want to know me during that year, then . . .'. There were some strike-breakers that he did talk to because of his sense that 'deep down they know they were wrong'. Others, who had 'glorified in it', would not be forgiven until the day he died.

The government showed 'loyal' Nottinghamshire no leniency when it came to pit closures. Moorgreen Colliery closed in 1985, Hucknall Colliery closed in 1986 and in 1988, Linby Colliery ended production after 115 years. Though local councillors tried their best to bring new job opportunities to the area, they lamented that the closures had come so suddenly.[27] Tony's father had finished his career at Newstead Colliery in 1985, when he was fifty-three, because they were closing pits and 'getting rid of the older miners', so he opted to take the redundancy on offer. As opposed to drinking away his retirement in the pub, Ron decided to replace 'work with work', and became a volunteer ranger with Bestwood Country Park, patrolling right up until his death. At the age of sixty-four his photo had again appeared in the local newspaper, this time lifting his safety helmet into the air to celebrate the restoration of the Bestwood Colliery Winding Engine House, which had reopened as a visitor attraction.[28] Despite Ron's thirty-three years underground, Tony did not feel his father missed the pit as much as he did, having only done a third of this time: 'I probably didn't have my fussy out.'

Nottinghamshire may still be more famous for its mythical outlaw Robin Hood, who stole from the rich to give to the poor, but its less heroic past was never far from some minds. You need only listen to football fans from Yorkshire and Cardiff when their teams play Nottingham Forest to hear them chant: 'Oh scabby scabby, scabby scabby Nottingham.'[29] Sadly, the label has stuck over the last forty years. Tony, like many other Nottinghamshire strikers, still suffered when speaking to miners from outside of the area: 'As far as they're concerned, Nottinghamshire are scabs, but we're not all, there were men here that weren't that.' I remembered how Mick, a miner of Welsh descent, who had been on strike from Cotgrave Colliery in Nottinghamshire, banged his fists on the table in frustration during our interview, as he pointed out how few 'indigenous' Nottinghamshire miners existed: 'It wasn't the Notts miners that worked through the strike, it was the Welsh, the Scottish, the Newcastle, Sunderland, Yorkshire. They were the people who worked because the Notts miners were so few.'

There are still deep-seated divisions within Nottinghamshire's former mining communities, and many who would never forgive, or forget. For many years, the mining heritage of the county was silenced for fear of adding fuel to the glowing embers of the strike, though in the last two decades new memorials have appeared.[30] For Tony, as the years passed, anger had given way to sadness and disappointment that Nottinghamshire 'didn't follow the call'. As he reflected, 'We might be living in a different country now . . . they beat the strongest union in the world at the time, and we gave away *everything* they fought for, zero hours contracts things like that, privatised utilities, I don't think none of that would have happened if we'd have won.'

The Miners Memorial by Graham Ibbeson, unveiled in Hucknall, Nottinghamshire, in 2005.

Sat across his dining-room table, Tony modelled a gilet covered in strike badges and showed me a wooden plaque, one of his 'proud possessions'. On the front was an image of Linby Colliery with its dates, and on the other side were the words, '1 of 103, Loyal to the Last'. This number represented the 102 men and 1 woman, a canteen lady named Dot, who had remained solid throughout the strike at Linby. It was one of Tony's greatest achievements, as he observed: 'I've got three children, I'm proud of them, but to last that year, I feel so proud of it.'

As a group, the Linby strikers still meet up to reminisce about old times and swap stories of the lives they have lived subsequently. The Saturday following our interview Tony

Banner of the Nottinghamshire NUM Ex and Retired Miners Association, designed by Joan Craddock, David Jenkins, Bob Collier and Eric Eaton and made by Durham Bannermakers in 2012.

was going up to Barnsley for the annual pilgrimage in memory of David Jones, the twenty-four-year-old miner from Wakefield, who was killed whilst picketing in Ollerton, on 15 March 1984. In 2023, a new bench and plaque were installed in his memory, supported by the Nottinghamshire NUM Ex and Retired Miners Association.[31]

Brian had not seen some of his fellow Moorgreen strikers since their days on the picket lines and he rarely made it to the pub anymore. Though he missed the male companionship of the pit, in the last few years he had taken up his grandson's Sharpie pens to draw scenes from his former life. When I asked what had compelled him to do so, he explained how 'each bit I do is a memory'. With no formal training nor any practice since his schooldays, Brian was surprised at how good the resulting artworks were. In 2019, seventy of his pictures were exhibited at the Nottinghamshire Mining Museum in Mansfield. These brightly coloured vignettes breathed new life into a world long gone, of dads and uncles playing three-card brag on blankets in the fields, of pit ponies in chains underground, of roof falls and dour-faced stretcher bearers and men in bright orange uniforms lying prone as they rode the belts out of the pit. My particular favourite captured a miner smirking as he surreptitiously 'dropped a load' at snap time, unbeknownst to his colleagues sitting nearby.

Recently, I returned to Nottinghamshire with my children to visit the Mining Museum in Mansfield, where we were greeted by a wonderful team of volunteers in bright red T-shirts, and Eric, their Chairman, had kindly shown us around.

One of Brian Morley's artworks, inspired by his memories of life underground.

My son enjoyed catching rats underground, by virtue of the VR headsets, while my daughter eagerly pointed out the Welbeck Women's Action Group banner hung over the door. As we were leaving, both children were given a piece of coal. The following day we had crossed to the other side, to visit the Bilsthorpe Heritage Museum, where we were again enthusiastically welcomed by volunteers in blue jumpers. The majority of Bilsthorpe Colliery's men had remained working in 1984–85. I looked upwards at the UDM banners spanning the walls, while the children donned helmets and tried on overalls, marvelling at the weight of the lamp battery packs men used to carry underground. Once again, the children chose a piece of coal as a souvenir.

Each child left with two lumps of Nottinghamshire coal that looked no different regardless of which side you were on. The same was true of the passion with which the heritage of the mining industry was being kept alive by ex-miners and their communities from both sides of the strike. It made me think of Brian's incredible drawings and Tony's words as he had shown me his own collections relating to the strike, 'That was part of it, but obviously there's more to mining than that.' I felt extremely proud to have spent time in the company of the striking minority of Nottinghamshire, men who were brave enough to man the picket lines when friends and even family members passed on by. It was clear it was never the pay, the politics, nor the product, but the people that had made the pits what they were. More than anything else, in a place like Nottinghamshire, that is what needs to be remembered and passed on to future sons and daughters of this former coalfield.

10. Man of the People

Everybody knew who you were, what you were, or what you were doing, you know, and there's a sense of erm, not, not just camaraderie, or comradeship within that, there's, how do I put it, there's a sense of being, and it's like that, you know, you are, and the people around you are.

John told me he had a reputation for being rather talkative and on this he certainly did not disappoint. After it was typed up, our conversation ran across sixteen pages of A4, largely uninterrupted by my questions. That was in addition to the three-page synopsis John helpfully provided beforehand. Careful to adhere to chronology, John told me of his childhood in Ayrshire, his family's relocation to Warwickshire, his work as an underground electrician, his role in the National Union of Mineworkers and his long run as a local councillor above ground. He spoke animatedly of his participation in the strike of 1972, how as a 'young rebel' he had helped to bring down a government in 1974, something *he* never forgot 'and neither did they', and the painful divisions of 1984–85. But it was when John talked of community that something deeper stirred within him.

Though John uncharacteristically struggled to find the words to define what community meant to him, as in the quote above, his explanation was a moment of poetry amongst all the prose. Somehow, John had summed up that almost ineffable essence of mining villages, that though faded and battered over time you could still feel humming through the crowds on gala days or at the unveiling of a local memorial. In fleeting moments during our interview, when the public turned personal, John feared he was being too sensitive or 'daft', but he had always maintained that sense of interconnectedness, even after he was forced out of the pit.

John had lived in the Midlands market town of Bedworth, or 'Beduth' as it is known locally, for most of his life, though his broad Scots accent gave away his earlier origins. Over seventy years ago and 300 miles away, John was born at his grandmother's house in the mining community of Dalmellington, in Ayrshire's rugged Doon Valley. John's brother, as well as at least eight of his cousins, had also entered the world via the same nondescript semi-detached property on Park Crescent. Earnestly citing the well-worn proverb that 'it takes a village', John explained how such beginnings were quite usual in those days.

Dalmellington had a long history in mining, and in 1792 its coal was proclaimed both the 'cheapest and best' to be found in the West of Scotland.[1] As dusty diamonds kept being dug up nearby, the village had grown into a bustling town, with a railway in 1856, followed by a post office, a bank, hotels, a library and a public school, erected in 1875.[2] The Co-operative Society, opened in 1879, was still doing good business over seven decades later, with a membership of 1,455 and an annual turnover of £144,000.[3] As one resident recalled, the Co-op was a key fixture of local life, feeding, clothing and even burying the surrounding population.[4]

In their statistical study of 1951, Drs Strawhorn and Boyd found the Dalmellington miner to be 'less extreme in his views and habits' than most of his kind.[5] He voted Labour but was not 'an ardent politician', and off shift he was 'a collar and tie man'.[6] Echoing this spirit of moderation, the town had few 'social cleavages and little religious animosity'.[7] Though not many people could afford the luxury of books, other than a well-loved copy of Burns, Dalmellington's population were 'a reading people', with the local library much in use.[8] There was also a Burns Club, a well-attended Masonic Lodge, a curling club that played on the Ayr Ice Rink, an accomplished brass band, a gardening society and a junior football club with a keen following.[9] With more public drinking as the temperance movement waned in the wake of the Second World War, one resident feared that Dalmellington had 'turned almost as bad as Glasgow on a Saturday night'; but though there was more drinking, there was found to be little drunkenness.[10]

John had always felt safe in Dalmellington. While most men, like John's maternal grandfather and his brothers, were employed underground, the town's children had free reign of the world above, making their own fun in the surrounding fields and streams. As John recalled, everybody knew who you were because although they might not know you personally, they knew who you belonged to. It reminded me of how the great Scottish mining leader Abe Moffat described his own boyhood in the Fife coalfield, and his observation that you were 'never without friends in a mining village'.[11]

As a child, John's heroes were mostly footballers, including Ferenc Puskás the Hungarian striker and the Scottish 'King' Denis Law. However, after he badly twisted his left leg and had to wear a full leg caliper, John turned his attentions to the Soviet 'Black Panther', Lev Yashin, reasoning that goalkeeping was a more realistic aspiration. Another of John's idols, of the stage rather than the football pitch, was the African American singer, actor and activist Paul Robeson. This might have appeared an odd choice for a son of the Scottish coalfields, but Robeson had long been a champion of the miners' cause. In 1949, the *Mining Review* captured the occasion when the star dropped into the canteen at Woolmet Colliery on the outskirts of Edinburgh, filming the large figure of Robeson serenading the captivated audience within.[12] Watching the black and white footage, as Robeson's rich voice coaxed an executed labour activist back to life in the old American folk song 'I Dreamed I Saw Joe Hill Last Night', I wondered how it must have resonated with the onlooking miners.[13]

For a role model closer to home, John looked to his father, Samuel, who was an active trade unionist. Sammy, as he was better known, had started his career as a mechanic at Wallacetown Engineering, repairing mining equipment for collieries across Ayrshire. Subsequently, the family of four moved to Sanquhar in the Nith Valley, where Sammy worked in the small Tower Mine.[14] After a third child was born, another brother for John, the family relocated once more, to the coastal town of Ayr. Sammy took up a role at the 'spectacular' new Killoch Colliery, another of Egon Riss's modernist masterpieces, which had opened for fully mechanised production in 1960, absorbing men cast adrift by colliery closures in Ayrshire.[15]

Whilst Killoch's fortunes were reaching their peak, becoming the first Scottish pit to produce 1 million tons of coal in a year, John's family moved yet again in 1965.[16] As he told me, they were part of the biggest migration of people, volunteers from coalfields all over Britain, to lend their strength to the burgeoning mining industry of the English Midlands. In 1962, the Coal Board had introduced the Inter-Divisional

Transfer Scheme, with 6,000 men, largely from ailing collieries in Scotland, Northumberland, Durham and Cumberland, taking the opportunity to transfer in its first three years.[17] Miners were offered equivalent jobs in the more profitable coalfields of Yorkshire and the Midlands, and the Coal Board provided assistance with housing and removals.[18]

Settling in Warwickshire, Sammy became a mechanic at Daw Mill Colliery, and his family, now seven-strong following the arrival of two more children, took up residence on the Goodyers End estate in Bedworth, which had been purpose-built for incoming workers. In a well-meaning effort to make new tenants feel welcome, street names on the new estate took inspiration from the industry they had followed and the homelands they left behind. While John's family lived in a flat on Anderton Road (named after the inventor of the shearer loader), others took up residence on Dowty Avenue (after the mining equipment producer), Newcomen Road (after the inventor of the first steam engine used in mines), Humphrey Davy Road (after the inventor of the miner's safety lamp), and on neighbouring streets named after northern mining communities, like Ashington Road and Whitburn Road.[19]

Through the transfer scheme men were kept in employment by redistributing labour in the national mining industry. However, in Parliament, Margaret 'Peggy' Herbison, a miner's daughter and the MP for North Lanarkshire, criticised the 'almost enforced migration' of Scottish miners to the English coalfields.[20] She spoke of her horror upon discovering that some of the new Coal Board houses were being built in 'completely isolated communities', wholly incompatible with the 'kind of lives' that Scottish people wanted to live.[21]

The National Archives holds a photograph of the interior

of one of the new homes built to accommodate incoming miners and their families in Bedworth. On the surface, the domestic scene looks very comfortable. A middle-aged man sits in his armchair reading the *Daily Sketch* newspaper, with what appears to be a Pekingese dog on his lap, while in the background his wife, shown smiling in her apron, is laying the table. Yet, for many families, lured down to Warwickshire by the 'glossy-booklet promises' of the Coal Board, the new estate failed to live up to expectations.[22] In fact, according to the local MP, Leslie Huckfield, as far as the tenants of Goodyers End were concerned, the Coal Board was one of the worst landlords in the whole country.[23]

By August 1967, the level of dissatisfaction amongst residents was such that Lord Robens, Chairman of the Coal Board, deigned to pay Goodyers End a personal visit.[24] As

First house occupied by transferees in the newly built Goodyers End Estate in Bedworth, Warwickshire, 1965.

he sipped coffee in one local home, Robens heard of inadequate postal and telephone services, poor recreational facilities, infrequent street cleaning, and a lack of local school provision.[25] In addition to this, tenants complained of the stigma of living on the estate nicknamed 'little Scotland', and how they felt ostracised by the surrounding community.[26]

Fortunately for the residents of Goodyers End, Robens proved a good listener. Three months after his visit, a 'complaints caravan' was installed to process issues with homes and amenities.[27] The following March, Robens returned on happier terms to open a new community centre, which the Coal Board had provided at a cost of over £1,000.[28] Though telephone facilities were still nonexistent, other amenities were helping to improve local life, with a new supermarket and a fish and chip shop.[29] By 1971, another 150 houses were under construction to extend the estate, with the Coal Board hoping to entice men from the farming and holiday regions of East Anglia and Lincolnshire to make the move to mining.[30]

For over a decade, John's family lived on a building site, as houses were finished and more workers moved in, but he still recalled feeling safe and happy in Bedworth. He observed how incomers carried not only their possessions but their culture with them, with '*all that mining heritage*' from Scotland, the North East and Wales transplanted into the estate. When Hogmanay came around, they upheld the tradition of first footing, and if a light was on in a neighbouring house, they would help to bring in good luck for the year ahead. As John and his family toasted a new year in this new land, the familiar words of 'Auld Lang Syne', with its talk of old acquaintances and days long past, must have acquired new resonance.[31]

Although the local mining industry was crying out for new recruits, after leaving school, the first position John applied for was in the Army. He passed every test required to join the Royal Electrical and Mechanical Engineers, and all that remained was the medical. John dutifully stripped off, but the doctor overseeing proceedings took one look at the scars on his leg and told him, 'Sorry son, we cannae take the chance.'

After his 'dodgy left peg' thwarted his military ambitions, John endeavoured to find the best apprenticeship he could and, like many others, he found that the Coal Board offering was 'exceptional', providing the opportunity 'for you to go as far as you *wanted* to go'. On completing his training at nearby Birch Coppice Colliery, John opted to work at Daw Mill, like his father, as it was the newest colliery around. His decision was undoubtedly influenced by his father's oft-told stories of the older pits back home in Scotland, where everything was 'small like dinky toys', and he had to crawl up a 2-foot face with his tool bag tied to his leg.

As a young man, John was a bit of a rebel, who had no qualms about 'saying boo to a goose'; but such confidence was soon knocked out of him underground. One of the first instructions the training officer gave him was to clean up the aftermath of an accident: 'Here's a paintbrush and some paint', someone had been decapitated and John's job was to paint over the blood on the walls. John still had a photograph of all the apprentices in 1971 but, as he observed, within two years of it being taken 'there was only forty per cent of us left'. It came as no shock to hear some men had fled to the comparative comfort and safety of a factory. Somehow, John had remained unphased, as he told me: 'It's a job . . . I don't think you're *made* as a miner, you know, I think the environment makes you . . . if the people never liked the pits, they never *lasted very long*.'

*

Having acquired a stomach for the work, John enjoyed the atmosphere underground, where they were 'all in the same boat'. Reflecting on the relationship between pitmen, he drew a parallel with the Second World War, where 'nobody really talked about it because *they'd all been through it*, so there was an *understanding* there'. Nonetheless, if you showed a weakness, it would be exploited. John had once confided to a friend that his fingers were sensitive and later a trio of 'so-called mates' decided they would crush his hand, until 'it came to a point where I couldn't feel any more pain'. Underground, 'you sorted out your own problems', and once scores were settled, friendships were resumed, as John assured me, 'We never stared daggers at each other, you know, across canteen.'

Aside from injuries endured in the name of friendship, John had only suffered one bad accident across almost three decades underground. It happened as he was riding the moving conveyor belt when the side gave way and he was dragged, 'like a cork in a bottle, getting pulled along'. As John conceded, it would have been worse if he had been smaller, as he would have been dragged under the wheels. Eventually, when there was a gap, he had been flung violently into a bank of panels.

Having 'jiggered up' his neck and shoulders, John spent a couple of months at Higham Grange, a grand country mansion, which at that point was the local Miners Rehabilitation Centre. Back in 1947, the *Illustrated London News* had published a two-page feature showing injured miners enjoying the 'country house comforts' of the centre, rowing in the modern gymnasium, reading in the quiet room, trying their hand at loom-weaving and cycling through the wooded grounds.[32] Given such surroundings, it may have been a reluctant departure, but once he was deemed fit for work, John returned without argument. He was still paying the price of that accident forty years later, 'but it's part of the job, as they say'.

While John was an indentured apprentice, his ability to engage in workplace disputes was limited, as the training officer advised him, 'Your arse is mine until your indenture is finished.' At other times, when he 'tried to rebel a wee bit', his father gave him a 'rollicking' when he came home from work. However, when the ballot for a strike came around in 1972, John unwittingly found himself the self-appointed local spokesman for the dispute. On the eve of the ballot, he was drinking in the pub with a couple of mates when a reporter from the local newspaper came in looking for miners. Rarely lost for words, John ended up saying his piece on the strike. The following Monday, he was in the lamp room when he got a thump on the back from the senior overman, 'And it's the first time I heard the c-word, he says, "What the hell are you doing?", he says, "in that newspaper", he said, "Are you a communist?"'

When the ballot was passed, as John had predicted in print that it would be, the pit went on strike. He subsequently found himself languishing at home with his parents and siblings, 'all miners not working'. Not content with twiddling his thumbs, John went along to a union meeting where they were looking for volunteers to go to London, as flying pickets. Reasoning that he might as well get someone else to feed him, as opposed to further diminishing the family's scarce resources, John put his name down and he soon found himself in the ten-bus convoy destined for the capital.

Arriving at the imposing headquarters of the National Union of Mineworkers at 222 Euston Road, John was designated lodgings and provided with details of where pickets were needed. Along with a few other men, he volunteered to go to Battersea Power Station, where they successfully managed to turn around several lorries providing fuel. Another day, he and some fellow pickets received news that Derek Ezra, who had recently replaced Lord Robens as Chairman of the Coal Board, would be attending a meeting in a central London hotel. Accordingly, they 'toddled down' to find him, only to be told that Ezra had already made his escape out of the backdoor.

Before returning to headquarters, the pickets decided to take advantage of their surroundings, as none of them had been in London before and, in John's words, they were all 'like country mouses'. However, walking through the bustling crowds in Trafalgar Square, he became aware that they were being followed, 'So I held back a bit, and two coppers come up, and I said, "Are you following us?", he says, "Yeah". He said, "You're pickets, aren't you?"' John answered in the affirmative but was bemused as to how the policemen had managed to pick them out of the crowd, until one of them helpfully elucidated: 'He pointed to this guy, and he said, "We don't see many of them in London."' Laughing, John recalled how unbeknownst to him, one of their party was walking around in a donkey jacket with the unmistakable letters NCB across the back.

As an intrepid nineteen-year-old, John relished his time in London. Despite being shocked by their liberal use of profanities, he recalled how the Londoners he met 'were *absolutely* wonderful' and 'you *couldn't buy a pint*, as soon as they found out you were miners'.[33] Whilst picketing at a power station in Hackney, he formed a friendship with workers at the adjacent refuse depot, who were amongst the first out during the so-called dirty jobs strike two years earlier.[34] John told me how the refuse workers were 'absolutely brilliant', holding collections in support of the miners and throwing over pieces of wood to keep the fire going in their brazier. This was the only thing that had prevented them being frozen to the bone during those cold winter days and nights stood next to the River Lee Navigation.

Only one incident had soured John's time in London. In the early hours of one morning in February 1972, he and his fellow pickets were huddled around the brazier outside the power station when a guy in a black balaclava unexpectedly opened the gates and a lorry came hurtling through. When a second approached, John tried to stop it 'and like, just, just missed me by centimetres this lorry, and then the third lorry came and did exactly the same thing, scattered us all over the place'. After a hurried phone call to Euston Road, the cavalry arrived, along with the police, and John was allowed to confront the driver: 'I said "you nearly killed me", or words to that effect, and he smiled and he says, "Do you know, we get £50 a day for running through idiots like you."' John lodged a formal complaint, handing over details of the lorry's number plate to officers at the nearest police station. Later, he was advised that the registration marks were 'incorrectly recorded' and they were unable to pursue the matter further, which sadly came as no surprise at all.

Over the next few years, John became more active in the union, 'taking on the old boys', including his own father, and joining the NUM branch committee, the consultative committee, the safety committee and the colliery's firefighting team. At the time, one colleague accused him of being 'addicted to committees', though John was quick to point out that the more committees he joined, the less time he had to spend 'doon the bloody pit'. Though he chuckled as he remembered his reply, John's demeanour shifted when he spoke of the good work they had done, like on the retired miners' committee, which paid for all the old miners and their wives to have an annual evening out, free of charge.

By March 1984, John was both a seasoned striker and an established union man, but he was still shocked by the way events unfolded that year. Trying to find the right word, he concluded that in the Midlands, 'it's not too much to say that it was a civil war'. In the first weeks of the strike, 500 police had arrived in riot gear to confront just four unarmed pickets outside Daw Mill Colliery in a stand-off, which, according to a letter from one Goodyers End resident, 'looked more menacing than anything in Big Brother's 1984'.[35] By the time of the annual Bedworth carnival in June, community relations had deteriorated so badly that the Church Silver Band were spat at during the procession, as onlooking strikers thought they were the Daw Mill Colliery Band, who had pulled out of the event at the last minute after receiving 'threats of violence'.[36]

As members of a 'showpiece colliery', Daw Mill's miners were confident they would avoid the sword of Damocles hanging over other collieries, and as a result the majority of them worked during the strike.[37] As John told me with a deep sigh, this included several of his family members. The few who chose to follow the union's directive were shunned by their colleagues. One twenty-four-year-old striker reported his disgust at workmates roaring past the picket lines, waving £20 notes and dropping their trousers, as 'they thought it was a big laugh'.[38]

After coming out on strike at the beginning, even John

was persuaded to return to work for three weeks on the grounds of not having had a ballot. The repercussions of his return were awful: 'All the names I was called, because I'd been on strike, and *oh God* it was blinking horrible.' Later, he did another volte-face after seeing a group of Kent pickets forcefully arrested in front of him: 'I said, "This ain't bloody right", I said, "These lads have not done anything bloody wrong", "Well, go and *fucking* join them then."' John decided he would, though as an elected union representative he felt he had to respect the wishes of the men at his pit. Instead of manning the picket line outside his colliery, he went to Birmingham to argue the striking miners' case in factories and on the streets.

Unlike other pits, where the return to work in March 1985 was accompanied by banners and brass bands, John recalled how Daw Mill's striking minority 'went back like thieves in the night'. After collecting their pit checks, they were instructed to go into the canteen, where they were sent to see management, 'like naughty schoolboys'. Though he kept his job, the personnel officer advised John they would be 'keeping an eye' on him. From this point forward, he was never allowed back on the coalface and was instead kept 'outbye', working alone.[39]

In the meantime, while other collieries around the country were closing, everything was still coming up roses at Daw Mill, which achieved a record output at the end of June 1985.[40] John maintained his role in the union, attending branch meetings and even appearing on the BBC's *Breakfast Time* at Pebble Mill Studios, where he told presenter Selina Scott the reasons why Daw Mill miners should stay in the NUM. Nonetheless, in November, it was announced that following a 75 per cent turnout Daw Mill's workers had voted

861 to 276 in favour of joining the new Union of Democratic Miners, which they felt better represented their interests.[41]

John did his best to champion the minority at Daw Mill who remained loyal to the NUM, though, by this point, the atmosphere underground 'was absolutely blinking *terrible*'. He felt he could not put a foot out of place and gradually he was frozen out of his responsibilities, including the retired miners' committee, which felt particularly vindictive. One evening in 1994, John found himself sitting alone in the dark colliery carpark, thinking, 'What the hell am I doing here, why do I have to go through all of this.' Fearing that the pit was going to be privatised, which would have been anathema to him, John decided to cut his losses and took redundancy, driving through the red brick entrance of Daw Mill for the final time a week later. As he told me, 'It felt *horrible, horrible, horrible*' that it had ended that way, after so many good days and years.

Later owned by the private mining company UK Coal, Daw Mill remained one of the last deep coal mines operating in the UK. As the only pit left in Warwickshire, it was something of an anachronism in the twenty-first century, as one of its workers described how no one realised they were still there.[42] Daw Mill eventually went down in flames in 2013, victim of the worst fire at a British coal mine in over thirty years, which blazed underground for over a month and expedited the loss of 650 livelihoods, though thankfully no lives.[43] As John reflected, King Coal was dead and though it was 'so, so, so, sad', in the end 'it is what it is'.

Alongside pit work, John had been a local councillor since 1984 and after leaving Daw Mill, he decided to return to education, hoping to improve his employment prospects. He enrolled on a humanities access course and managed to get enough 'brownie points' to go to university in 1996. As he explained with both pride and amusement, he went to '*the* Birmingham University', the one in Edgbaston, where he completed a social policy degree, graduating three years later with new letters after his name.

In May 1996, the same year as he started his degree, John was appointed Mayor of Nuneaton and Bedworth. During his term in office, John enjoyed a packed diary of civic duties as well as presenting local schoolchildren with their road safety awards, attending the ever popular teddy bears' picnic at Bramcote Barracks and switching on Nuneaton's Christmas illuminations.[44] However, his proudest achievement was his work with the Life Education Centre, a charity which educated children, between the ages of three and fifteen years, about the dangers of drug and alcohol abuse. In October 1996, John's beaming mustached face appeared in the local paper alongside the headline 'Dream Comes True for Drugs Battle', after his civic appeal in support of the charity resulted in a 'huge cash boost'.[45]

The following year, John was in the papers again, complete in his golden regalia, accepting giant cheques from supporters and joyfully taking a hammer to a collection bottle at the local Italian restaurant.[46] In the *Heartland Evening News* he described his dream to do something for the community, and how thanks to local support one of the most ambitious mayoral appeals ever had been successful.[47] The celebratory press conference was attended by Paul and Janet Betts, whose eighteen-year-old daughter Leah had died fifteen months earlier after taking a single ecstasy pill and whose childlike image, comatose and connected to a ventilator, was burnt into the public consciousness.[48] In an article on the appeal,

Leah's father Paul was quoted as saying: 'You have all done exceedingly well. I understand you are a small community, but this shows you care.'[49]

Early the following year, while it was parked outside the now-closed Hob Lane School in Bedworth, the Life Education Centre's mobile classroom was raided by thieves, who stole all the equipment inside and rendered it useless.[50] Undeterred, the charity found a substitute, and the show was soon back on the road again. John defiantly told the local paper: 'We were never going to just sit back after these knocks, we are going to give the kids a positive message and get back out there. These people will never stop us.'[51]

Across its lifetime, John and his colleagues raised almost a million pounds for the Life Education Centre and hundreds of local schoolchildren benefitted from its services. In 2009, funding for the charity was cut by the local council and despite John's best efforts to save the project, it was axed.[52] As of 2023, the borough of Nuneaton and Bedworth has the highest number of referrals for issues with substance misuse in Warwickshire, including two children who needed professional help for addiction to alcohol and cocaine.[53]

Reflecting on the end of his mayoral term back in 1997, John had been quoted in the local paper, as saying: 'Bedworth is my home, I grew up there and so did my children, but at the end of the day I am Scottish and proud of it.'[54] Other men who had left their homelands behind them told me they felt they also had to abandon their culture in order to fit in elsewhere. Yet, somehow, John had managed to carry both the accent and values of a small Ayrshire mining community into the new estates of Warwickshire. Now, after twenty-eight years as a miner and thirty-five as a local councillor, John has reluctantly removed his red rosette and retired from public service, his hand forced by ill-health.

During my travels, I met many former union men, 'old Labour' types who spoke through me rather than to me, sermonising on the agreed narrative of past events. As I listened, a captive but admittedly not always a captivated audience, I conjured images of them in blazer and tie, rapping their fists on the table of some smoke-filled meeting room. Just like these rooms, now long forgotten or repurposed, these men were of a different time. Their social conservatism, what one man referred to as 'Blue Labour', was never fashionable, though now it seemed almost extinct.[55] For as long as there had been mining communities, it was these men who were behind the reassuring knock on the door of the house hushed in mourning, whose hoary face appeared at the end of the hospital bed with promises of compensation, who pulled the strings needed to reconnect the electricity and bring a family back into the light. It was their arms, like weather-beaten rope, that firmly held the community together. These men seemed oddly out of place in the quiet domesticity where I found them now.

Like the other union men, John had kept a sober steer on public issues throughout our conversation, only occasionally offering up snippets of his inner world. As a result, towards the end of our interview, I was taken aback by the sincerity of his quiet observation that the Life Education charity was 'one of my best things that's ever happened to me in life, that'. More than anything else, this statement summed up the measure of the man, who had steadfastly maintained his village mentality and had done the best he could for his adopted community. As I bade John farewell, my mind drifted to the words of Ayrshire's most famous son.

A Prince can mak a belted knight,
A marquis, duke, an' a' that!
But an honest man's aboon his might –
Guid faith, he mauna fa' that!
For a' that, an' a' that,
Their dignities, an' a' that,
The pith o' Sense an' pride o' Worth
Are higher rank than a' that.

Then let us pray that come it may,
As come it will for a' that,
That Sense and Worth, o'er a' the earth
Shall bear the gree an' a' that.
For a' that, an' a' that,
It's comin yet for a' that,
That Man to Man the warld o'er
Shall brithers be for a' that.[56]

11. The Men of Kent

There was one young lad picked a lump of coal up and he said, 'What's that mister?', and I looked at him and thought are you serious? [. . .] That's why you are here, that's why your dad and your grandad and your great-grandad, that's why you're here in Aylesham.

When thinking of the British coalfields of the past, do you imagine yourself traversing the pit paths of the North East, like Ted, George and Stephen and those flat-cap-wearing men immortalised in the art of Norman Cornish or that of his fellow pitmen painters? Others may think of the legendary South Wales coalfield, the black mountains Raymond Williams wrote about and the deep green valleys that Richard Llewellyn's novel mourned.[1] Perhaps you think of Scotland, the Ayrshire mining village where John began his life or the once mighty Lanarkshire coalfield, birthplace of Keir Hardie, the founding father of the Labour Party. Or do you know of the pit-brow lasses of Lancashire, their scarf-covered heads, men's breeches, long aprons and clogs, sooty from sorting the coal? If you lived through the year-long strike, you may remember the pickets of the so-called People's Republic of South Yorkshire, or the much-contested coalfields of the Midlands.

Few people would picture themselves on the Kent coast. Indeed, many would be surprised to hear that Kent even had its own miners, let alone its own coalfield. Still, there is something compelling about Kent, the youngest of Britain's coalfields, which extends far beyond its geographical incongruity, sitting as it does at the easterly limits of a county far better known as the Garden of England than for its grimy industrial past. Maybe it is the way in which Kent, more than any other area, was a microcosm of the industry, made up of mining immigrants from across the country. It could be the area's renowned militancy, a throwback to the blacklisted incomers who arrived after the General Strike of 1926, and the fact its punch far outweighed its diminutive size in the strikes of the later twentieth century. Or perhaps it is the pride Kent's miners have in the area's industrial past and the communities it produced; men like Philip, whose words open this chapter.

When I first met Philip, I was struck by his accent, which sounded more like he was from my native South Yorkshire than East Kent. Despite often being mistaken as a 'northerner', Philip was born in Canterbury Hospital in 1948 and, in his own words, 'You can't get more south than that.' I soon learned that the Aylesham vernacular was a unique phenomenon emanating from the array of accents that the miners carried with them to Kent's first colliery community in the early twentieth century. Philip recalled a friend's explanation of the village's unique composition: 'He lived in this street, and he said, "Go over to meet some friends and they'll talk in Scottish, went over to next door it was real, hard Geordie, and then Welsh."' In recent years, the Aylesham accent had sparked considerable interest from academics at the nearby university.[2]

Similarly unusual was the village itself, which better matched the accent than its surroundings. I remembered my first visits to Aylesham over a decade ago, accompanying my future husband as he travelled the county as a locksmith in a temperamental white van. Even at the time, Aylesham had felt strangely familiar. Later, I realised this was because it bore greater similarity to the northern communities of my childhood than any of the other Kentish towns and villages we visited, which were an assorted chocolate box of oast houses, weatherboarded cottages and Georgian country homes.

Unlike most of Britain's coalfields, which were developed feverishly in the nineteenth century, coal was not discovered in Kent until relatively late. Black gold was first struck near Dover in 1890, following investigations into the geological underpinning of the east of the county, after early plans to build a Channel Tunnel were abandoned. The resulting Shakespeare Colliery, the first of its kind in Kent, lasted only twenty-two years before it was sold for scrap. During this period, the peace of the Kentish countryside was continually disturbed by the 'busy hum of men' as dozens more bore holes were drilled.[3] Owing to the chalky Kentish subterrain, many collieries came and went before coal extraction became a viable business. Ultimately, the new coalfield had four surviving collieries within the triangle of Canterbury, Dover, and Deal: Tilmanstone, begun in 1906; Snowdown, where the first sod was turned in 1907; Chislet, commenced in 1914; and finally Betteshanger, which opened in 1924.

As Philip and his wife Kay explained, the Kent mining companies 'wanted more or less anybody'. As a result, after the General Strike of 1926, increasing numbers of miners left behind both their loved ones and blacklisted identities in declining coalfields for the promise of brighter days down south. Philip's father had made the journey down from

Yorkshire, and Kay's father had moved from Penrhiwceiber in South Wales in the early 1930s. Many men hitch-hiked, biked and walked the long miles to Kent from their far-flung homelands, with some arriving so exhausted they were unable to work. More harrowing stories are told of men dropping dead on arrival.

For some, like twenty-seven-year-old Albert Victor Romeling, the so-called Sunshine Corner Coalfield would be their final destination. Albert had been unemployed in South Shields for six months before he borrowed the money needed to venture to Kent.[4] Early one May morning in 1934, Albert left his South Tyneside home and travelled over 270 miles by bus to London. From there, he boarded a train bound for Canterbury, where he arrived shortly after midnight. Alighting in Kent's cathedral city, Albert applied for a night's lodging at the local police station but being turned away, he walked to Barham Crossroads, a journey of around 8 miles. He sat at the crossroads 'for some time' until a passing cyclist directed him to Snowdown Colliery, over 2 miles further on.[5]

When Albert applied for work at Snowdown, after over a day travelling and an evening by the roadside, the colliery manager observed that he looked tired, but the candidate confirmed he was fit. Albert's enthusiasm was noted by onlookers, who described how he appeared 'happy as a lark' to be back in employment.[6] His first and only shift at Snowdown began at ten o'clock in the evening, during which time he worked as a loader, pushing empty tubs to the underground conveyor. The job was not considered 'heavy' by the standards of the pit, but a co-worker later reported that his new colleague had appeared 'weak on his feet'.[7] After pushing twelve tubs up the incline, Albert sat down and did not get up again. An autopsy would later conclude that Albert had suffered from acute tubercular pneumonia, a chronic form of consumption that may have been lying dormant but had suddenly flared up, no doubt exacerbated by his hours tramping through the darkness in search of work.

Though men may have sought a new beginning in Kent, existing residents were often resistant to newcomers taking up their seats on the seafront or lodgings in their homes. Whilst enterprising butchers sold cheap cuts of 'miners' bacon' on the high street, local hostility was increasingly manifested in housing adverts designating properties 'not suitable' for miners.[8] Before moving to Aylesham, Kay's father found lodgings in Dover, where in 1931 one resident wrote of the housing difficulties faced by men like him, who were 'unfortunate enough to earn our livelihood in the bowels of the earth', and who were treated 'as some weird subterranean creature only to be tolerated when he has money to spend and shunned like the very devil on all other occasions'.[9] Other miners attempted to conceal their occupation from inquisitive landladies, only for it to be discovered later, at which time both they and their belongings were promptly turned out onto the street.

One solution to address the issue of miners' lodgings was to build new communities like Aylesham, which was designed by the monocled architect Patrick Abercrombie in the 1920s. As the founder of the Council for the Preservation of Rural England, Abercrombie was more aware than most of the importance of keeping 'England's front door' presentable and preventing it emulating 'one of those northern areas dimly apprehended through a mist of smoke whose very names can infallibly be used to raise a laugh on a London revue stage'.[10] Instead, inspiration was drawn from the aspirational new Garden Cities of Letchworth and Welwyn. Planners varied the style and regularity of properties using setbacks and tree planting to avoid the monotony of existing 'dreary industrial communities'.[11]

It was anticipated that the finished settlement in Aylesham would accommodate 15,000 residents across 3,000 dwellings as well as provide amenities like shops, banks, schools, and places of worship and amusement. However, in the wake of the economic depression that gripped the country over subsequent years and the changing fortunes of coal, only around a fifth of the properties planned and few communal facilities were built. At least the homes that were completed were comfortable, benefitting from modern conveniences like electricity and indoor bathrooms, a vast improvement on what incoming miners had left behind. While Aylesham housed the miners of Snowdown, other communities were formed to supply Kent's other collieries: at Mill Hill for the workers of Betteshanger, at Elvington for the workers at Tilmanstone and at Hersden for the workers of Chislet.

In the *Westminster Gazette*, the amenities of the new coalfield were proclaimed a 'Paradise for Miners', with colliery owners pledging to do 'everything in their power' to encourage the social and recreational lives of new residents.[12] Despite the optimistic rhetoric, life was no idyll for those who endeavoured to make their homes in the new mining settlements. While men joined a fellowship of newcomers underground, things were more challenging for their wives, who left behind family and friends and found themselves in isolated communities several miles from the nearest high street. The *Dover Express* was especially critical of the new settlements, which it felt were little more than a 'compound', with residents left to endure 'a very lonely country life'.[13]

Gone were the marketplaces of home; instead, given the meagre supply of provisions locally, residents were forced to rely on high-priced wares touted by itinerant traders or commute to larger towns. Some women were reluctant to leave the house at all, as there was simply nowhere to go.[14] It was small wonder that some compelled their husbands to leave Aylesham, the so-called 'City of the Lost', to return to more familiar lands.[15]

As well as suffering from the transient behaviour of its homesick residents, Philip recalled how in its early years Aylesham was made out to be like the Klondike, with fights between different factions of men seeking to establish whether the Geordie, Welsh or Yorkshire miner was superior. Philip had witnessed such altercations himself and was aware of people in the neighbouring towns of Canterbury and Dover who feared coming to Aylesham, and perhaps they still did. The dubious reputation the community acquired was encapsulated in a news story in August 1930, which appeared under the headline 'Would Mayor's Gold Chain Be Safe at Aylesham?', after a joke made by the Police Chairman at the village's expense.[16]

The incoming miners were less deferential than the indigenous Kent population and, it appeared, had little hesitation in picking apples and poaching on private land.[17] Their attitude towards the bounties of the Kent countryside was captured in farcical headlines like 'Miner and Cabbages', after a man was summonsed for stealing four cabbages in 1930, or the 'Miners' Broccoli Raid', committed by three Aylesham residents in 1933.[18] In one case of 'Poaching Miners', the prosecutor summed up the bemusement of the local population: 'The miners apparently had no idea of what belonged to others and they thought they could go into other people's woods and do exactly what they like.'[19] Perhaps this behaviour should have been viewed as an overhang from the backdrop of poverty from which many had fled.

A decade later, during the Second World War, more newcomers entered the Kent coalfield. These young men were not miners but were among 48,000 optants and ballotees for whom the Second World War would be fought at the bottom of a pit shaft. These conscripts were known as 'Bevin Boys', named after Ernest Bevin, the Minister of Labour who launched the scheme in December 1943 to boost the dwindling numbers in the pit.[20] Kent's new mining recruits came from all walks of life, from manual labourers and hospitality workers to those whose private education would usually have seen them ascending the ranks of British society as opposed to descending into the bowels of the earth. While some took lodgings in local hostels, in other instances, mining families opened their homes to the recruits.

Some Bevin Boys found established miners hostile to their presence.[21] However, others recalled the warmth with which they were welcomed into their homes, and the generosity shown to them underground, despite their obvious naivety. One 1945 film told the story of Albert and Richard, two eighteen-year-olds whose studies were interrupted by call-up papers directing them to Chislet Colliery.[22] Billeted to the home of Mr and Mrs Lavery, the friends apparently passed 'their evenings in homely comfort, as accepted members of a typical mining family'.[23] Future playwright Anthony Shaffer and his twin brother Peter had left the prestigious corridors of St Paul's School to take up places at Chislet in 1945. As Anthony observed in his autobiography, though it was 'three years of unrelieved hell', the miners he worked alongside did not resent him 'as they might have', but were 'helpful and sympathetic', and endeavoured to make life easier.[24] Though such experiences were dependent on the individuals whose stewardship the new recruits were placed under, similar remarks were made by Bevin Boys at the other Kent collieries.[25] Perhaps the welcome extended in Kent was in part due to the fact miners there could remember the way in which they had been treated by the native Kent population not long before.

Over time, the county could finally claim its own indigenous miners, as sons born in Kent, like Philip, began to follow their fathers into the pit. Philip left school at the age of fifteen after receiving a less than adequate education, with only the basics of reading and writing and no qualifications to speak of. The employment officer had come round, 'said "hands up all the boys that want to go to the pit" and it was a foregone conclusion, so we all put our hands up'. Girls were offered cleaner work at the nearby shirt factory. In Philip's class, there were only a few children deemed to be 'smarter than the average kid', who were 'sorted with some sort of career'. Fortunately, Philip was quite content to follow his father and two older brothers to Snowdown.

Other men had fallen into pit life through entirely different circumstances. London-born Gary, another Snowdown miner, had started his working life at T. Wall & Sons, dealing in bacon and sausages. However, after coming down to Kent for a school friend's wedding, Gary met his future wife, Barbara. Not wanting to part from her, Gary moved to Kent, and after trying and failing to get a job, Barbara's father, who was a mechanical engineer at Snowdown, suggested that he could find a job there. Gary's own father was a salesman with Findus, a frozen foods company, and his mother worked part-time at the record factory in Hayes. I asked Gary how they felt about their son's choice to go 'down pit', and he described how like 'anybody who lived in West London, if their son said: "I'm going to go and work down the mine", they'd probably think what on earth for.'

After passing the medical exam to check they were fit for work underground, both Philip and Gary followed the same route to Betteshanger Colliery, albeit years apart, which was the main training centre for the area. By the time Gary joined in the early 1970s, the turnover of personnel was very high. He recalled how several recruits dropped out after seeing the realities of life underground and decided to go and work in pastures greener, on the factory floor. Undeterred, both Philip and Gary stuck it out and once their training was complete, made their way to Snowdown.

Despite working at Snowdown for almost twenty-five years, Philip never got used to riding in the cage, with three decks of twenty men, plunging a mile down in just three minutes. Some men took this in their stride, like a religious bloke at Betteshanger who had said he was not bothered if they died as he would be going straight to heaven, to which his colleagues had replied, 'Not with all of us hanging on your feet you won't.' Later, when Philip was the Chairman of the Snowdown branch of the NUM, there were occasions when he was called up from the pit on union business, but he was never comfortable riding the cage alone. He shared the tale of a man at Tilmanstone: he was put on the bottom of the cage by himself and the bell was rung to lift the cage; but when it arrived at the top, the bottom deck was empty. They never knew whether the man fell or jumped out, but he was no more. That story always played on Philip's mind for the few minutes he was alone in the darkness.

Known locally as 'Dante's Inferno', Snowdown was one

of the deepest pits in the country, where the mercury in the summer easily exceeded 30 degrees Celsius. On the coalface, it was usual for workers to wear little more than pants, helmet and boots. Some men opted to work naked, and an announcement would be made over the tannoy in the event of visitors, to warn them to cover up. Philip recalled seeing men 'sweat like mad', pouring pints of perspiration out of their boots. It was not uncommon for Snowdown miners to drink as much as twenty-four pints of water across one eight-hour shift, refilling their Dudley bottle several times. Other unfortunates ended up being carried out suffering from heat stroke or debilitating stomach cramps, a consequence of severe dehydration.

Despite the conditions, by the time both Gary and Philip had entered the pit, it was mechanised, with a machine cutting the coal and hydraulic supports keeping up the roof. I discerned a glimmer of sadness when Philip described how the 'hard graft' undertaken by men like his father, who worked the coal with nothing more than a pick and shovel, had been 'taken away' by the time he came of age. Philip compared the dogged stamina of such men to footballers today, who after playing a game for ninety minutes needed a few days' rest. 'There was no rest for the miners, once you started on a Monday, you done that physical work for eight hours, and then you'd have to start again doing it all over again the next day.'

Though he did not share the mining pedigree of others at Snowdown, Gary adapted easily to life underground. He worked as a ropeman, a role that entailed splicing metal ropes together, which were used for haulage of equipment as well as for the paddy train, which transported men from the pit bottom towards the coalface. Gary took satisfaction in seeing

Snowdown Colliery miners coming off a shift, *c.* December 1976.

the output of his labours, extending the haulage as the face progressed and ensuring that the materials were in place for other men. Though he had started out in a gang of four, as time went by, numbers dwindled as men either retired or took redundancy. By the end, Gary was the only ropeman remaining and had to rely on other workers to help him with the pulling, the dragging and everything else that came along.

Fortunately for Gary, one thing that remained unchanged underground was the camaraderie between men. In a community like Aylesham, these relationships easily extended above ground. Consequently, workmates were well versed in the comings and goings of each other's lives, as Philip described: 'You knew when they were courting, when they got married, you knew about their kids.' It was a general rule that when they were down the pit, men talked about girlfriends, wives, 'and all that sort of malarky', whereas in the club the reverse was true, with conversation centred on the shift you'd had and the conditions you could expect underground the following day. When it was dusty underground, water would be sprayed to suppress it, and if there was too much pit talk in the club, somebody was sure to shout, 'Put the sprays on!' Gary, on the other hand, was by his own admission more of a loner and was less keen to 'talk shop' in the club after leaving work.

The Kent coalfield had a reputation for militancy. However, none of the miners I spoke to seemed particularly inclined to incite a rebellion, rather the concept that came up time and again was of 'fair play'. For some, the area's militancy harked back to its early blacklisted settlers. Writing of the seven-week long strike of 1972, Malcolm Pitt, President of the Kent NUM, described how it had marked the reinvigoration of a culture that had been dormant since 1926: 'A tradition which, outside the pit lodges, had become the preserve of nostalgic socialists and folksong addicts, took on flesh and muscle.'[26]

Following his father's directive to always go to the union meetings, the 1972 strike was the first time Philip became actively involved. He was twenty-four and 'all in favour of it', picketing the power stations across London. In the end, some 3,500 Kent miners took on responsibility for 150 miles of coastline, twenty-one power stations and several major coal depots.[27] Philip described how back then people were more unionised and would not cross a picket line, so you soon had 'the place sewn up'. He developed a taste for trade unionism and when the 1974 strike began, he was on the strike committee, later becoming Vice-Chairman and eventually Chairman of the Snowdown branch of the NUM.

Kay's activism easily matched that of her husband, and her reputation had preceded our first meeting. I knew she was the author of the poem 'Coal Not Dole', which became an anthem of the 1984 strike, and has since been performed by artists from Norma Waterson to Chumbawamba.[28] During the strikes of the 1970s, Kay had been part of the Aylesham Ladies Action group, a title that now made her wince, as 'we wouldn't call ourselves ladies anymore'. Neither Kay nor her fellow miners' wives saw themselves as political figures, and at this point, the group mostly provided social support, hosting visitors from other trade unions.

The 1984 strike was to prove a very different dispute to those of the previous decade, although when he first came out on strike, Philip thought it would follow the usual trajectory, 'in six weeks people will realise, the country will realise'. Nobody ever envisaged it would take a year, or a year and a week in Kent. This time, instead of fighting for wages, the Snowdown men were fighting for their futures, particularly as theirs was one of the pits earmarked for closure.[29] Knowing the intertwined fates of pit and village, Kay had approached the NUM to ask if they could reform a women's support group, and they agreed. Subsequently, Kay and a few other wives had called a meeting in the local working men's club, expecting anything from ten to twenty women to turn up, so they were surprised when the numbers rose to over fifty.

Though, according to Kay, some of the men in the village initially had the attitude that 'you should be looking after things at home, you shouldn't be doing that', as the strike evolved, they came on side. Initially, the women's efforts focused on the basics, like providing blankets for flying pickets who often found themselves sleeping wherever they could. Later, as strikers were being prevented from travelling through the Dartford Tunnel, the women changed course: 'Why can't *we* get a bus and we'll go up and support them, so that's what we did.' Collecting women from the surrounding mining communities, the bus drove on to Coalville in Leicestershire, where the Kent women ended up processioning through the streets. Under the headline 'Boos and Jeers for Pit Wives', the *Leicester Mercury* covered the events of that day in March 1984. In the story, Kay had been quoted: 'We are prepared to suffer. We will fight on until we win.'[30]

Philip was also picketing in Leicester and did not return home for a month. During this time, one pit broke a European record for coal production while they were picketing outside, 'and they put a big European flag up on the headgear to sort of rub your nose in it'. Subsequently, the Kent strikers had concentrated their attention closer to home, and Philip found himself at the Wivenhoe docks in Essex, where imported coal was being unloaded, with the privately-owned port cooperating with lorry drivers willing to cross the picket lines.[31] He was arrested and jailed there, with bail conditions that stipulated he could not go near Wivenhoe or anywhere else coal was being brought in.

On the day of Philip's arrest, Kay was attending a women's meeting at the club. Back then, they would dress up as if they were going somewhere nice for the evening, 'heels on and everything'. Afterwards, a group of them decided to borrow a dormobile and go to Wivenhoe to find out what was happening, still dressed as they were, and 'to do a protest'. When they arrived, they ended up being asked to move by police, who told them if they put one foot onto the road, they would be arrested for stepping on the Queen's highway.

Kay was working in an office in Canterbury and the couple had three daughters, all of school age. Family life during that period was a constant juggling act, in which they were supported by Kay's mother and sister-in-law. The children were fed at the soup kitchen and the welfare club, and the striking miners would help collect them from school and bring them to the club for dinner. Their eldest daughter would wear a 'Support the Miners' badge at school, but was told to take it off, which she refused to do as there were other children wearing badges in support of the Army and the Scouts, and she couldn't see the difference, especially as she was supporting her own parents. Though the children were looked after well and got to meet a lot of people from other areas, Kay conceded that it must have been hard for them, 'There wasn't a home life, for a long time.'

Of course, as a family they were luckier than others who had no income, and as Philip conceded 'people like them did struggle'. One friend, a fellow striking miner, had five children but according to Philip, 'he never ever thought of going, scabbing'. Philip's definition of a scab was broad, encompassing those who had found work elsewhere, to make ends meet. When he found out about a lad who was working in the fields during the strike, his initial reaction had been to chuck him out of the union, though the area secretary, a man who used 'his brain before his heart', determined that it was better for this man to be in the fields than down the pit. Several of the strikers I had spoken to had worked in different fields during that long year, trading scrap metal, collecting empties at the working men's club or helping friends with odd jobs. None of them would ever have considered this activity scabbing, especially considering a strike of unparalleled duration, and where families had no other way of making ends meet.

Like Philip, Gary had also been on strike from Snowdown Colliery. Facing a situation where they had almost no money coming in and 'savings were going out the door quicker than anything else', Gary and his wife had visited the social services office in Dover. Though he dutifully signed a statement confirming he was not receiving any strike pay, which was 'the whole truth, nothing but the truth', they received no support from the state for the whole twelve months. As a result, Gary had reluctantly gone picketing, because the £10 it paid each week was a lifeline they could not do without.

Picketing did not come easily to Gary. He recalled finding it particularly unnatural to stand there shouting at fellow miners as they returned to work. Nonetheless, he never once considered breaking the strike. In his own words, maybe this was because he 'didn't have the bottle to go back'. One man who lived nearby had been struggling to survive and bit the bullet, returning to work, which in Gary's mind 'took a lot more courage than staying out did, knowing what the repercussions were going to be, at a later date'.

Ten miles away in Dover I had spoken to Gareth*, a former Kent miner, who was the most unrepentant of all the strike-breakers I interviewed.[32] Gareth's decision to return to work had not stemmed from any bitterness towards the mining community, rather he clearly never felt part of it. At the start of our conversation, he shared a story from his childhood, about how he had once been a keen supporter of Everton Football Club; but one weekend they lost six–nil and he decided he'd had enough, looked up who had won that week and moved his allegiances accordingly. Gareth seemed oblivious of the pertinence of this anecdote, and how this behaviour had repeated itself in later life, though the stakes had been much higher.

Having neither grown up in a mining family or community, Gareth was first attracted to the industry by virtue of the apprenticeships offered by the Coal Board, when he left school in the mid-1970s. Though he had not realised he would have to go underground, Gareth found mining life satisfactory, and he spent the next four years training as an underground fitter. When the strike had been called in March 1984, he had come out, albeit 'unwillingly', and maintained the status quo for the first six months, until he decided he no longer wanted to be part of it. Although he never regretted his decision, he did feel misled by the 'return to work brigade' about the encouraging response they were having from local miners. Only later did Gareth find out that he was one of only twenty-five miners returning, out of a thousand.

Gareth told me of bricks flying through his windows and paint thrown at his home, but he realised that even this was negligible compared to what would have happened if he was living in one of the mining villages. Thankfully, he was a member of a local biker group, a fact that had made his decision to return to work easier, that and the weaponry he kept behind the front door. Today, he felt no connection to the industry and although he had fond memories of people he used to work alongside, he kept himself in the shadows, for fear that if he were to shine too bright a light on himself, someone would still want to 'have a little go'.

When the strike officially ended on 3 March 1985, the Kent men remained out. They did so to protest on behalf of around 1,000 miners who had been sacked during the dispute, including over forty Kent men, like those who had conducted a sit-in at Betteshanger Colliery.[33] They travelled to Wales and other places that had been 'a hundred per cent supportive', where Philip recalled how fellow striking miners were brought to tears over having to cross a picket line. Given the level of distress being caused, they eventually called it off, with Betteshanger the last pit in the country to return to work on 11 March 1985.

When the Snowdown miners returned to work, Gary recalled how some met together at the working men's club and marched back to the colliery accompanied by the band, with their heads held high. Others, like Gary, avoided the pageantry, returning quietly, as he 'didn't feel that there was anything to celebrate'. According to Philip, the manager at Snowdown had been 'brilliant' during the strike, pointing out unguarded piles of coal and turning a blind eye to those taking from it. However, after the men returned, the first thing the Coal Board did was switch things around. Snowdown's manager went to Tilmanstone, the Tilmanstone manager was sent to Betteshanger, and Snowdown ended up being managed by someone from Betteshanger.

While he did not welcome the merry-go-round of management, at least Philip did not have to work alongside scabs. He referred to a photo that had been taken of him standing in front of a list of Snowdown men's names, 'scab names' as Kay had pointed out. Later, I had found this image online. There in black and white stands Philip in his pit helmet, smiling into the camera; on the board behind him is a special notice from the branch secretary of the union. Handwritten in capital letters, with underlining for further emphasis, it listed the thirty-one Snowdown men SUSPENDED (triple underlined) from the union for gross misconduct, as a result of STRIKE BREAKING. I wondered how these men had fared underground after they had been publicly named and shamed. Gary used to receive calls from a ropeman he knew from Snowdown who had broken the strike and transferred to Betteshanger once it was over, 'He used to phone me up and we'd have a chat. Most blokes wouldn't talk to him.'

Despite the Kent mining community's Herculean efforts to defend their coalfield, the death knell tolled for Tilmanstone in 1986 and Snowdown closed the following year, on the grounds of financial viability. In his capacity as Chairman of the Snowdown branch of the NUM, Philip held a mass meeting, which was attended by most of the 160 NUM members at the pit. He recommended that people vote against British Coal's plans to shut Snowdown completely, but they lost in a show of hands, with two to one in favour of accepting the decision.[34] Although saddened, Philip could understand why people had voted the way they did: 'They'd had enough, they'd been worn down.' The Chairman of Aylesham Parish Council, Percy Wilson, who worked at Snowdown for over forty years, described the closure as a 'tragedy', with collective morale in Aylesham 'absolutely devastated'.[35]

The former fitter and blacksmith's workshop at Snowdown Colliery, abandoned and being reclaimed by nature, *c.* 2020.

Snowdown's miners were given a choice between transferring to nearby Betteshanger, the one remaining pit in Kent, or taking voluntary redundancy. Philip decided against moving to Betteshanger. Despite visiting twice, he couldn't get the feel for the place, plus they would not guarantee that he would be able to retire there in thirty years' time, and he could not face going through it all again. By the time he came out of the pit for good, Philip had given Snowdown twenty-four of his thirty-nine years on earth.

Just as Philip feared, though men had been assured of a place at Betteshanger, such promises proved to be short-lived when it followed its forebears and closed at the end of August 1989, with the loss of 600 jobs. One miner's wife, who was born in sight of Betteshanger and had worked in its canteen for thirty years, described her anger that her son and so many others like him had been 'reduced to the dole queue'.[36] The local news featured a portrait of a 'bewildered' Betteshanger miner, a fifty-eight-year-old electrician, who feared he and his colleagues would be 'thrown on the scrap heap', with little hope of finding employment.[37]

The closure of Kent's last pit was just one of a succession of tragedies to affect the local population, including the Zeebrugge ferry disaster two years earlier and the IRA bombing of Deal Barracks a few weeks later.[38] At the time, the local vicar, the Reverend George Lings, told the *East Kent Mercury* how, since his arrival in Deal four years earlier, no part of the town remained untouched by tragedy. Yet, Lings felt the community would survive and suggested its tenacity was at least in part the result of its imported culture: 'I don't believe it will destroy us. We have the resilience and grit of a northern town but with a southern accent.'[39]

In an instance of life's strange circularity, many of Kent's former miners found employment at the Channel Tunnel, which had begun development in 1988. Several of Philip's friends worked there and the pay was good, but after applying and being turned down three times, Philip concluded that he had been blacklisted because of his union activities. In the end, he found a job at a local factory, but though he was happy there 'it wasn't the same' as the pit. He started a union, along with some mates who had also made the transition from the coalface to the factory floor, but this placed them at odds with colleagues who were not interested in being part of their group. 'I think their idea of getting on was "well, if I butter up the manager, as an individual, I'll get on better than sticking with them lot."'

Other Snowdown men followed the industry to Yorkshire and the Midlands, with a couple even descending the gold-mines of South Africa, something that never really crossed Gary's mind. Leaving Snowdown after sixteen years, he ended up in a fairly well-paid job with an electric distribution company, where he stayed until he retired with a decent pension. Characteristically magnanimous, Gary could recognise that in his shoes it had turned out alright, but that was probably not the same for everybody.

Though Gary did not wear his mining past 'as a badge of honour', nor was it 'a chip on his shoulder', and he felt no shame in having been a miner. The pit was still inside him, in the background, 'floating around in the memory cells somewhere, and sometimes something just clicks, and it will just come out'. On holiday in Salisbury a little while ago, he had been chatting to the lady on the hotel's reception about general things, of which Brexit was one. The receptionist told him that all the country needed was Maggie Thatcher back, and he was swift to disclose his former identity and advise her: 'Don't mention Maggie.'

In 2003, a bronze sculpture by local artist Stephen Melton had been erected in Aylesham to commemorate Snowdown Colliery and its families. A miner stands in his pit gear, lifting his young son upon his shoulders and ushering forward his smartly dressed daughter, who carries his lamp. The accompanying plaque observes how in the school holidays mining children would accompany their fathers for dinner in the pit canteen and bring his weekly pay home to mother. It seemed a fitting reminder of the many local lives, men and women, young and old, that were once shaped by the fortunes of the pit. It stands near the old Aylesham Secondary School, which closed three years after the pit and was, in the words of one former student and miner, yet another 'great ship' that had been 'scuttled ignominiously, almost without trace'.[40]

Just like its residents, over time Kent's former mining communities have changed. In Aylesham, the final phase of

Payday at Snowdown Colliery by Stephen Melton, unveiled in Aylesham, Kent, in 2003.

building is underway as part of a project that will see the delivery of over 1,000 new homes. Entrepreneurial developers have branded the estate 'Aylesham Garden Village', harking back to Abercrombie's vision. A recent news story decried how the once close-knit community was turning into a 'village of strangers'.[41] Residents, including Philip, had raised valid concerns regarding the loss of green space, the affordability of the housing and the lack of local infrastructure (the secondary school is yet to be replaced). However, knowing Aylesham, it seems likely that in time the new residents, living on roads like 'Canary Grove', 'Pithead Drive', 'Lamplight Gardens' and 'Davy Street', would be embraced by the old.

Today, Philip is one of the directors of the Aylesham Heritage Centre. Spurred on by the fact that local schoolchildren had visited and failed to recognise a lump of coal, he remains committed to ensuring people understand how the village began. Gary had visited the centre and was pleased to meet former colleagues who he hadn't seen since he left the pit. Though they had a good chat, he was surprised to find that 'they still lived it. Like they were still miners'. Aside from its appearance in his dreams, Gary did not hang on to the pit in the same way, 'maybe because I wasn't brought up with it, it wasn't in my blood, if that's the right word to say, it didn't feel the same to me, I moved on'.

Elvington and Eythorne also has its own volunteer-run heritage centre and, after some delays, in 2022 Kent finally opened a museum dedicated to the county's mining past. The ceremonial ribbon was cut by representatives of Kent's four collieries and the opening was marked by performances of the Betteshanger Colliery Welfare Band and the Snowdown Colliery Welfare Male Voice Choir. The museum is small but perfectly formed, and tells the story of the many families who journeyed south in search of black gold and brighter futures. It is located on the former site of Betteshanger Colliery, which is now a bustling country park frequented by packs of Lycra-clad cyclists and energetic children.

The Waiting Miner statue by sculptor Harry Phillips sits near the entrance to the park, overlooking the roundabout on the A258 Deal to Sandwich road. First installed outside Richborough Power Station in 1966, when this was decommissioned in 1997, the statue was moved to Dover seafront. Following a campaign by local miners, it was transferred to its current location in 2010. Standing next to this silent crouching figure, I was reminded of Albert Victor Romeling, who once sat at a crossroads not far from here, and who later sat down underground, never to get up again.

The Waiting Miner by H. Phillips, first unveiled in 1966. Statue photographed in its present location at the entrance of Betteshanger Country Park, 2022.

Like the miners he remembers, it seems the statue may be forced to move again, and there has been recent furore over plans to rehome him inside Betteshanger Park. Given that many old miners chose to have their ashes scattered at the site, the concern from the community is understandable. Regardless of the eventual decision, what is certain is that Kent's former mining communities remain fiercely committed to their heritage, and where some areas might slip into nostalgia, they will not be going down without a fight. Though, as the coalfield's surviving veterans die out, Kay's prediction of forty years ago, has perhaps never felt so prescient:

What will become of this pit yard
Where men once trampled, faces hard?
Tired and weary, their shift done,
Never having seen the sun.

Will it become a sacred ground?
Foreign tourists gazing round
Asking if men once worked here,
Way beneath this pithead gear.[42]

12. The Price of Coal

They didn't last long, the miners didn't last long at all. The village was always full of sick men, that's all you were seeing was sick men, because their lungs had basically concreted over, with the dust, so they couldn't breathe very well, they could only walk about twenty yards and then stop and get a second breath and move on, and you'd see that all over the village. And you don't see that now.

Unlike Philip, Keith could not look back at the mining industry fondly. When he heard other miners romancing about the pit, his thoughts returned to his father who, after serving fifty-three years underground, spent his short retirement 'coughing his guts up' whilst attached to an oxygen tank. Throughout the twentieth century, countless newspapers sold the sensational stories of the big mining disasters, the details of a moment's tragedy drawn out in print across many weeks. Memorials old and new were erected to remember those ill-fated dates when explosions burned through generations of men and dark waters swept away lives. Individual miners had told me of a hundred smaller tragedies they witnessed whilst working underground. However, much less was said of the legions who had withered away gradually, with sunken eyes and a cyanotic tinge, gasping for their next rattling breath. Men like Keith's father, who succumbed to 'the dust'.

Like Philip and Kay, Keith also lived in Aylesham. Our

conversation took place in the house in which he was born in 1958, the same house he called home over six decades later. Like most of Kent's mining population, Keith's family were incomers: his father found his way to Snowdown Colliery from Lancashire and his mother came from South Wales. As far as Keith was aware, once settled in Kent, his parents had not pined for their distant homelands – conditions in Aylesham were far superior to those they had left behind, where, in his words, 'Things were really bad.' Though Keith's father was consigned to working in a deep hot pit, the countryside above provided a more wholesome backdrop against which to raise a family.

Though new to the Kent coalfield, Keith's family had deep roots in mining that reached back over 200 years. Once upon a time, they had owned a seam of coal, though, as he explained, the land above probably 'belonged to Lady Muck, Lord this and that'. When Keith's father was a child, his family worked as blacksmiths and owned their own home, which, as Keith reminded me, was rare for working-class people back then. They hammered out a reasonable existence and his father received a decent education, but the family's fortunes were decided by the First World War, when 'they all died'. As Keith starkly concluded, 'The money must have gone away in that time.' Consequently, his father began a lifetime of hard work at the tender age of thirteen.

After decades in the darkness, Keith's father was a 'proper miner', and he had the scars to prove it. As Keith told me, it was as if a tattooist had drawn sweeping lines all over his father's back – like one of Jackson Pollock's canvases, 'he was covered'. I remembered how George Orwell described some of the old miners he had encountered, men who were 'veined like Roquefort cheeses'.[1] According to Keith, his father was unbothered by the marks, 'He didn't care, no, he didn't care about anything.' Other ways in which the pit permeated miners' bodily landscapes were obscured from public view, like the coal dust in their lungs, only coming to the surface later in life.

The risks of silicosis, a lung disease caused by stone dust, were known from the mid-eighteenth century. However, in the first few decades of the twentieth century, it was still thought that inhaling coal dust was harmless or even therapeutic.[2] It was not until further investigation by the Medical Research Council that the harms of coal dust were acknowledged. In 1943, a new compensation scheme for 'pneumoconiosis', a condition whose name derived from the Greek words for breath and dust, was introduced for certified sufferers of lung diseases caused by both rock and coal dust.[3]

Greater knowledge of this 'modern Black Death' and compensation for those already afflicted did little to assuage rising concerns, particularly amongst prospective miners.[4] In March 1946, during an inquest into the death of a sixty-three-year-old miner who suffered 'total disablement' due to silicosis, the Kent Mineworkers' Association highlighted how dust diseases were acting as a deterrent to young men who might have sought work underground.[5] This was especially concerning as since the start of the Second World War manpower in the industry had fallen significantly.

As nationalisation of the mining industry loomed, in 1945 a Pneumoconiosis Research Unit was built, supported by 4,000 steel girders donated by the Coal Board.[6] Two years later, a three-page article in *COAL* magazine praised the unit's scientists who were 'waging war' against coal dust and reducing the scourge of lung disease.[7] Inside the new unit, based at Llandough Hospital near Cardiff, technology was developed to monitor dust levels underground, and miners were studied with X-rays and new spirometers to estimate lung volume.[8] Alongside treatments like breathing exercises, patients suffering from fibrosis of the lungs were recommended good food, rest and relaxation. As the article in *COAL* blithely observed, many sufferers were 'not as ill' as they thought, and all they needed was a renewed spirit of confidence to get back on their feet.[9] By 1952, the *Western Mail* triumphantly announced that miners' dust disease was being 'overcome', with modern research steadily reducing both the incidence and severity of the disease.[10]

Nevertheless, the plight of those already afflicted gave less cause for celebration. Between 1931 and mid-1948, over 20,000 men left Britain's pits after developing pneumoconiosis, the vast majority of whom lived in South Wales.[11] In 1953, some 50,000 miners and their families led a demonstration in Cardiff's Sophia Gardens to protest against the introduction of a 'means test' for disabled men receiving

Members of the Great Mountain Lodge protesting at Sophia Gardens, Cardiff, 1953.

extended unemployment benefit.[12] A black and white photograph in the Glamorgan Archives shows members of the Gwendraeth Valley's Great Mountain Lodge walking together beneath a gigantic banner decrying the sorry fate of hundreds of miners, who had been left disabled, in one Welsh village.[13] The banner was used as a backdrop for the speakers at the rally, and the local newspaper reprinted its bitter slogan: 'They toiled to dig the nation's coal, / And breathed the deadly dust; / Betrayed once more, denied the dole, / By those who held their trust.'[14]

Despite his own experiences, Keith's father had not dissuaded either of his sons from following him into the pit, and Keith duly signed up after leaving school, 'because it was easy to go there'. He recalled his first day underground and how they had stopped on the pit bottom, which was 'where all the old, sick, broken men worked'. That was where his father had ended up, engaged in lighter work, like uncoupling mine cars, because 'he couldn't really do much else'. It was, in Keith's words, 'God's waiting room'. It struck me as a strange introduction to a 'job for life', to be confronted by these damaged figures, a living memento mori, resembling a future you might well share in time.

As the industry evolved in the later twentieth century, health and safety improved significantly. After fatal fires occurred at several collieries, self-rescuers to protect miners from gas were trialled and by the 1970s they became mandatory equipment.[15] These life-saving inventions, encased in steel and worn on a miner's belt, contained a chemical compound to convert lethal carbon monoxide into breathable carbon dioxide. If the worst happened, according to the step-by-step instructions, all miners needed to do was break the seal on the canister, insert the mouthpiece, affix the nose clip, and place the harness over their head to hold the device in place.[16] They were then advised to walk at a steady pace towards fresh air, as rushing or running would only make breathing more difficult.

When Keith first entered Snowdown Colliery, self-rescuers only lasted around half an hour. Half an hour in the dark confines of a tunnel that was full of smoke. As he dryly observed, it was not like the London Underground, where you could follow the wall, 'it's not like that at all', and half an hour did not give you much time to get somewhere safe. The longest journey he knew men to make, from coalface to the surface, took about two hours. As technology improved, self-rescuers were able to last an hour and a half, which provided some relief to Keith and his colleagues; as he explained: 'I thought gah this is good, at least you've got a bit of a chance with this.'

Modernisation also reduced other threats that once lurked underground. As ponies left British pits, so did the number of rats, thus decreasing the prevalence of Weil's disease.[17] Better lighting underground shrank cases of nystagmus, which had left so many miners wild-eyed and blinded in decades past.[18] The shift away from 'hand-got' coal and the use of antibiotics reduced incidences of 'beat' conditions (chronic inflammation caused by repetitive motions or pressure from prolonged squatting and kneeling on a hard surface).[19]

Progress also had its price. As ever more powerful machinery roared through the pit, the miners began to suffer new ailments, like occupational deafness and vibration white finger, which left sufferers with numb, blanched hands. Man's fragility was increasingly apparent, and as Keith told me, it was 'quite easy to get injured, quite seriously injured'. One chap he knew had 'all the back of his head smashed open, you know, you could see his brain and stuff'. Other accidents were closer to home: Keith's brother lost his leg in the pit aged just nineteen. As Keith reflected, 'If it happened, it happened pretty bad.'

Keith had carried eight stretchers out of the pit during his time at Snowdown. Four men carrying the stretcher, others carrying clothes and water bottles, periodically swapping places as their arms grew tired, two hours journeying out of the pit, dodging obstructions, 'If you're on a stretcher you've got a problem, you know, if you're right in there.' Putting things into layman's terms once more, Keith explained how it was not like a car crash on the motorway, when 'pretty soon they'll have an ambulance to you'. In the pit, they had to look after themselves. Earlier that day, I had been sat in a pub in Dover, where a Tilmanstone miner, who once held a key to the morphia safe, animatedly told me how if someone lost an arm or a leg you would use 'superglue', with morphine in it, 'and go whack', as he slammed the fictive needle into the pub table.

As well as heightening the severity of accidents, mechanisation also aggravated the long-standing problem of dust, as more particles were thrown into the air by coal cutters and conveyors.[20] The installation of more powerful ventilation systems could add to the issue, circulating dust from areas of high concentration and exposing more miners' lungs to it in the process.[21] Keith recalled how the dust was ubiquitous underground, 'It's there all the time', and though usually it was in the background, at times you could 'hardly see your hand in front of you'. By the end of his annual three-week holiday from the pit, he would still be pulling black bogeys out of his nose, as the coal dust worked its way through his body.

Water was consistently viewed as the key to preventing the dust underground from becoming airborne. As one Yorkshire miner told me, 'Wherever you went, you had to have water. Water, keep that fucking dust down.' Roadways were dampened, water-infusion was used on coalfaces and sprays were fitted to cutting machines and conveyor heads.[22] However, despite widespread awareness of the risks, it appeared dust prevention was not always at the forefront of workers' minds.

In 1951, the great Welsh miner-author Bert Coombes attempted to be the canary in the coal mine, writing into the *Porthcawl Guardian* to lambast miners' apparent indifference to dust disease.[23] Having witnessed the desperate endings of three victims of the dust, Coombes was puzzled as to why miners appeared unconcerned, with some even cutting pipes conveying water to dampen the dust and intentionally breaking off sprays. One young miner, who he had found working in a 'cloud of dust', exhibited an especially 'devil-may-care' attitude, telling Coombes he had no time to check the dust and confiding that 'a short life and a merry one' was his motto.[24]

Pressures on production in the later twentieth century continued to override the necessity to protect against industrial injury and disease.[25] A letter from Dave Douglass, the NUM Branch Delegate for Hatfield Colliery, that was published in *Coal News* in 1976, summed up the issue at hand, as he asked: 'When will you people realise that safety and production are two contradictory elements under the present capitalist system?'[26] Of course, such accusations were refuted by the Coal Board's Chief Safety Engineer, John Collinson, who claimed in response that safety and production were 'not mutually exclusive'.[27]

Notwithstanding official protestations to the contrary, it appeared dust was often a secondary concern in the face of production. Men told me how water sprays on coal cutters were prone to break off or get clogged, and while some machines would not start without working sprays, on other occasions, when the sprays failed, production was prioritised. I spoke to one man who worked at the state-of-the-art Selby mine complex in North Yorkshire in the early 1990s. When he finished work each day, he would take three showers, and even then, he needed to change his bedclothes constantly as the dust was still coming out of his ears and nostrils. This was strange as the dust readings taken underground were always clear. It later transpired that some of the safety team had been cheating the system, wrapping a Tesco carrier bag over the equipment used to take gravimetric samples. As he explained, this was just one example of what people would do to keep producing coal when the conditions breached regulations.

In the later twentieth century, the Coal Board provided respirators to protect against dust. These were a vast improvement on improvised solutions of bygone years, which had even included wearing women's hosiery about the mouth and nose.[28] However, several men confessed that they had avoided wearing masks underground. Some complained of the discomfort of wearing such restrictive equipment in hot enclosed environments. This was something I had new empathy for, particularly after seeing the painful indentations on NHS workers' faces after long shifts spent working on hospital wards during the recent pandemic. Other men chose not to wear a mask as it prevented them spitting out the juice from the tobacco they chewed underground.

Keith's father had always maintained the view that he could breathe better down the pit. At the time, Keith argued that this was because he did not have a fag hanging out of his mouth underground, but 'he couldn't quite work that one out, me old man'. Later, the fact miners smoked above ground would be used against them in compensation claims for lung disease though, as Keith told me, 'you didn't get like that through smoking'.[29]

His father's ailing health had cast a shadow upon Keith's final years of childhood: 'I was living with it, because my dad was here and he was on oxygen bottles, and I could see what it had done.' The daily realities of miners' suffering was something Keith remembered all too well, as he told me, 'You think about how desperate that must be, you're trying to breathe and you can't breathe', 'that's what I grew up with'. While Keith and his father never had a 'proper' father and son relationship, 'because he was so sick', Keith's older sisters could remember their father when he was still a fit man. After years honing his strength shovelling coal, he could walk about on his hands, 'up the stairs and everything'. However, these playful memories clouded over as Keith reflected on his father's fate: 'But when your lungs are full of coal dust and you can't breathe, even the powerfullest of men will succumb to that.'

After Keith's father gave the bulk of his life to the pit, it still could not help claiming his remaining years: 'He was dead in 1975, so he was only out of the pit about eighteen months from when he retired at sixty-five.' Keith's uncles suffered similarly for their time underground, though as he observed, 'They weren't as bad as my Dad.' Over a decade later, the *East Kent Mercury* reported on the inquest into the death of another Snowdown Colliery miner, who after his retirement was diagnosed as '100 per cent disabled' by pneumoconiosis and had remained bedridden until his death, at the age of just sixty-nine.[30]

As more miners developed dust disease, the issue of

compensation rumbled on. In 1971, the Kent Area of the NUM published an advert in local newspapers inviting members and ex-members who were certified as suffering from pneumoconiosis to make a claim for damages against the Coal Board.[31] Following the successful conclusion of the 1974 strike, a new compensation scheme for pneumoconiosis was agreed upon by the government at a cost of £110 million.[32] Over in County Durham, miners' union officials found themselves swamped with applications from people wanting to claim, with an estimated 2,000 pneumoconiosis sufferers in the local area.[33]

As a chronic disease with a long latency period, pneumoconiosis was typically diagnosed in older men, though this made it no less pitiful. I imagined all those miners who had done their time underground, the lucky ones who left with limbs and lives intact, who hung their long-service certificate on the living-room wall above the oxygen tank they now needed as their contribution to the industry belatedly took its toll. Like the bronchi in their dust-darkened lungs, pneumoconiosis branched outwards from the dark veins of the coalfields, stalking men into retirement or redundancy. Year after year, small notices in local papers printed the names of pitmen all over Great Britain discovered to have died from 'the dust'.

A sixty-three-year-old miner from Ramsgate in 1946; a fifty-one-year-old miner from Abertillery in 1955; a fifty-six-year-old miner from Leicester in 1961; a seventy-five-year-old First World War veteran and miner from Amersham in 1965; an eighty-two-year-old miner from Rugeley in 1974; a fifty-eight-year-old miner and a sixty-five-year-old miner, both from North Staffordshire in 1990; a seventy-seven-year-old miner from Worksop in 1999; a seventy-two-year-old

Gwendraeth Valley miner in 1999; an eighty-six-year-old Rhondda Valley miner who died in Suffolk in 1999.[34] Some had succumbed to the dust as many as six decades after leaving the pit. Often their cause of death was only known through a post-mortem.

In life, too many miners were told they were not sick enough or did not have sufficient dust in their lungs to warrant compensation, despite being unable to work or walk more than 50 yards without becoming breathless.[35] In 1994, the *South Wales Echo* accused the government of cheating former miners out of benefits for chest diseases. Only 534 out of 5,683 Welsh applicants aged over seventy had been successful in applying for the benefit, after the rules were apparently made intentionally strict to limit the number of claims.[36] Many men and their families spent years fighting for compensation, appealing time and time again after being turned down.[37] Of those who were successful, many were dead by the time compensation was paid out. Others, suffering with chronic bronchitis and emphysema, believed to have impacted 15,000 former pitmen in the North of England alone, were overlooked entirely.[38]

Towards the end of our interview, Keith reflected on the demise of the British mining industry. Though, like others, he missed the craic of working underground, at the same time it was a 'crap' job and he never forgot that 'there's a price for coal, it comes at a price to some families'. More than anything, he felt sorry for his father, a man who he felt could have done something better with his life, 'but if that's what's in your blood, that's what's in your blood'.

The most recent report of the Health and Safety Executive on coal workers' pneumoconiosis noted that available sources were likely to 'substantially underestimate the annual incidence' of the disease.[39] As I totted up the faceless numbers of those lost to the dust, listed in small font on an official spreadsheet, the total was galling: over a thousand deaths in Great Britain between 2013 and 2021.[40] Over a thousand private tragedies, over a thousand empty armchairs haunting family homes, the smiling faces of over a thousand fathers and grandfathers conspicuously absent from family photographs. I could find no stone memorial to this mining disaster.

Flicking through the second edition of *Ballads and Songs of the Coalfields*, diligently compiled by A. L. Lloyd back in 1978, I came across the song 'Ah Cud Hew'. It was written by Ed Pickford, the so-called Noel Coward of the Coalfields.[41] When I tracked down Ed, he told me how the song was inspired by memories of his own father, a miner from the age of thirteen and later a compensation secretary, who fought on behalf of those with pneumoconiosis. As a child, Ed's household resounded with talk of sick men, and it was this atmosphere which gave birth to the song. Ed recalled how one of the best moments he ever had was when an old miner later chided him, upon hearing the song, 'Yer bugger – that's just how Ah feel.'

Searching Spotify, I found a recent rendition of Ed's song recorded by Jim Ghedi, a young folk singer from my native Sheffield.[42] At the Durham Big Meeting in 2023 I saw it performed by Jack Drum Arts, a vibrant group of singers, drummers and dancers based in Crook, County Durham.[43] A song passed down the decades: perhaps this was the memorial I had been seeking for all those lives lost to the dust. Slowly passing my finger over the printed score, I did my best to sing the lyrics in tune, and as the story unfolded my mind drifted to Keith's father.

When Ah was young and in me prime
Ee aye Ah cud hew
Ah was hewin' aal the time
Noo me hewin' days are throo, throo,
Noo me hewin' days are through.

At the face the dust did flee
Ee aye Ah cud hew
But now that dust is killin' me
Noo me hewin' days are throo, throo
Noo me hewin' days are through.

Ah've lain down flat and shovelled coal
Ee aye Ah cud hew
Me eyes did smart in the dust filled hole
Noo me hewin' days are throo, throo
Noo me hewin' days are through.

It's soon that pit nee mair Ah'll see
Ee aye Ah cud hew
But Ah'll carry it round inside of me
Noo me hewin' days are throo, throo
Noo me hewin' days are through.[44]

13. Fight Like Hell for the Living

It's a working man I am and I've been down underground
And I swear to God if I ever see the sun
Over any length of time, I can hold it in my mind
I never again will go down underground.[1]

On the first Sunday in April, they gathered on the old colliery football ground in the village of Moorends, South Yorkshire. The marching band led the procession, the spring sunshine bouncing off their jaunty emerald and black uniforms, the plumes of their tall hats dancing in the wind. The youngest marchers were born after the last lump of coal had been wrestled from beneath British soil. Next came the banners, faded flags of industry carried aloft by grey-haired men, championing pits long since closed and whispering the values of a past era to the sky above. The pipers followed on, with green kilts and blue feathered caps, their highland songs reverberating between the tightly packed rows of council houses. As they proceeded, more followed: men in leather jackets with Coal Not Dole badges on beanie hats; daughters and sons pushing wheelchair-bound parents; babies in prams and older children holding grandparents' hands whilst skipping in time to the beat. They walked through the streets where young families, pyjama-clad, stood in doorways to watch, children averting their eyes from the television to gaze at the spectacle before them. Teenagers hung out of upper-floor windows with their mobile phones fixed on proceedings.

They congregated in front of the new Moorends Family Hub, elderly women seated at the front while older men held themselves up on walking sticks behind, the crowds spilling into the road. Speeches came from local councillors, men of God in puffer jackets and Catholic regalia, and union representatives. A band played 'The Miners' Hymn' and the 'Concierto de Aranjuez', better known in these parts as 'Orange Juice'.[2] One silver-haired man stood alone and sang an a cappella rendition of 'Working Man', that was both a song of defiance and resignation.

At the end, the new monument was unveiled, the design chosen by the community and sculpted by Graham Ibbeson to represent the circle of life: the winding gear that was once a familiar landmark; the coal from which the community grew; the miner and his family; the lamp that provided safety and comfort in the eternal blackness. Adjacent a memory wall: each brick dedicated to a life spent underground. All this was in recognition of a colliery that operated for just thirty years, and which closed in 1956, long before the bitter exodus from the industry later that century.

On the last Sunday of the following April, different crowds stood in the marketplace in Shirebrook, a place nicknamed the 'Belfast of England' during the 1984–85 strike.[3] Masses now flocked to this Derbyshire town to see the unveiling of a new memorial for the colliery which was closed thirty years ago to the day. During the ceremony, Alan Gascoyne, a former union leader and now secretary of the Shirebrook Miners' Welfare, spoke of how the pit had been the mother of the community: she provided work for her children and when they were injured, she did not throw them onto the scrap heap, she took them back and found them jobs to suit their capabilities. As I listened, I remembered how I had been told that *everyone* was found a role at the pit, how apprentices were taught both the basics of mining and life and how some gained 'a thousand dads'. When the pits were closed, it brought an end to all these unconventional families.

Similar scenes have been repeated across Britain's former coalfields. Local communities have united to erect memorials and restore banners, from Aylesham in Kent to Allanton in North Lanarkshire, from Ffynnongroyw in the North of Wales to Abertillery in the South. After years of planning, in 2021 a National Miners' Memorial was unveiled at the National Memorial Arboretum. Made from light Derbyshire stone, a bronze frieze zigzagging like a dark seam through its sides, the memorial tells the story of those who once worked Britain's mines. As I followed their journey, each vignette framed by sculpted pit props, I saw mothers and daughters in clogs and shawls, sisters pulling heavy tubs wearing girdle and chain, fathers and sons working together, the tunnellers of the First World War and the Bevin Boys of the Second. Their history could now be brought to life via a QR code on a nearby plinth. Though deep-pit mining in Britain ended in 2015, the memory of the industry not only lingers but is resurgent. *They were here, they should not be forgotten.*

I finished my own journey in the same place it had started five years ago, among the throngs lining the medieval streets of Durham for the annual Gala, watching fallen fathers of trade unionism resurrected as their portraits sailed through the crowds. It was heartening to see how after a hiatus during the pandemic it had risen phoenix-like. The streets were packed but weaving through the crowds was a surprisingly congenial affair, as was queuing up to buy a cold lager from

Procession of banners at Durham Miners' Gala, 8 July 2023.

the on-street bar. What I noticed this year, more than ever, was the number of children involved in proceedings. There were girls and boys holding the strings of the banners, which their fathers held aloft. Young children were eating snacks whilst sat on the wall alongside their grandparents, or dancing at the side. There were new banners for the next generation 'standing on the shoulders of giants'.

I lost count of the number of T-shirts reminding me who still hated Thatcher. As one teenager strolled past, I noticed he was wearing a shirt upon which the usual Ralph Lauren logo had morphed into the image of a baton-wielding policeman on horseback. In this year of strikes, everything felt charged with a new dynamism, and the crowds erupted in loud applause as the Royal College of Midwives processed through, and then again for the teachers' union.

The next day, I visited the Mining Art Gallery in Bishop

Auckland – an immaculate new space showcasing mining art, finally given the prominence it deserves against gallery walls of deep grey and blue. On the way home, I reflected on a quote I had seen painted on the ceiling of the Spanish Gallery next door, attributed to Sir Thomas More: 'Tradition is not the worship of ashes, but the preservation of fire.' At Durham, the fire was still alive, it burned in the arms of everyone carrying a banner aloft or banging a drum, on the palms of those clapping from the sidelines and in the voices of those addressing the crowds on the Racecourse. *We are still here, we will not be forgotten.*

I remember my apprehension at the start of my journey into Britain's mining past, my concerns over where my enquiries might lead, whether the hypermasculine men I imagined the miners to be would grant me safe passage into their history. How it felt when I first walked nervously through the heavy doors of the NUM headquarters in Barnsley and the warm welcome I received inside. The subsequent afternoons spent flicking through the weighty catalogues of the *Yorkshire Miner* and eating slices of cold black pudding left over from buffets earlier that day. On my final visit, Paul told me that the archives would soon be taken to a new home at the University of Warwick. Though I was pleased that the collection would be preserved for posterity, I felt sad that future researchers would not get to look through the yellowing documents surrounded by banners in the Miners' Hall, reminding them of what it had all meant.

I thought of all the people I had spoken to over the last five years, all the homes I had been welcomed into and the pride with which people had shared their mining heritage. There were men for whom the destruction of the industry had felt like a loss of identity, and others, who despite working underground, never really understood themselves as miners, but who had still played their part in this story. All the strong women like Anne and Kay, who had steered their families through such uncertain times with their heads held high. There were those who had spent the last forty years living with the memory of the strike, like a thorn in their side or a lump in the throat that would not pass. I wondered whether Huw, Kevin and the two Pauls would finally see justice for Orgreave in their lifetime or whether the issue would keep getting swept under the carpet, with the revolving door of Home Secretaries kicking the notion of an inquiry further down the road.

And what of Britain's former coalfields? Those places blackened with industry, then hollowed out. In the Horden Welfare Park in County Durham, surrounded by benches of canoodling teenagers, I had stood at the weathered feet of Ray Lonsdale's 'Marra' sculpture, a 9-foot steel miner with his heart torn out, erected in 2015. This solitary figure was an emblem of the loss still mourned by many former mining communities. Into the cavity had crept addiction, poverty, apathy, social disorder and some of the highest male suicide rates in Britain.[4] We should not be surprised that some of these same communities were drawn to the chance to 'Take Back Control' in the Brexit vote, or to Boris Johnson's promise to 'make Britain great again' in 2019.[5] Over in Dinnington, South Yorkshire, I had spoken to the new vicar who told me how the loss of the 1984–85 strike and the death of the mining industry could still be felt around every corner, in every household, and how this had become part of her story too. I hope that one day when we remember the strike, we can look beyond scenes of warring police and pickets, of divided communities and loss, and celebrate the way in which coalfield communities bravely took on the might of the government to preserve their way of life.

When I think of the miners now, I no longer imagine the faceless vanguard of the working class. I think of Ted's pride as he strutted over Durham's Elvet Bridge, and young George's despair at working deep underground when his family and friends were tucked up in bed. I can see Stephen and his pony Colin walking together through the dark tunnels, and Stewart kicking in the canteen doors and declaring himself the Daddy. I smile when I think of the lying competitions during snap time at Wolstanton, and raucous Friday nights in the Hucknall and Linby Miners' Welfare. I can appreciate what it meant to be in the Mines Rescue Team and the lengths men would go to in aid of their colleagues. I think of Scottish families first footing on a new housing estate in Bedworth, and the prejudice faced by Kent's mining immigrants. I remember the great price Keith's father, like so many others, paid for their work underground. Just like coal, which on first look may appear little more than a dark rock but when burnt emits all the colours of the rainbow, amongst the miners I had found the full spectrum of humanity. They were not all saints, far from it, and some of the things that happened underground made me wince, but they were rightly proud of their service to this country, working in conditions few would tolerate today.

On a banner made for the Barnsley Miners Wives Action Group, there is a large portrait of the great Irish-born American trade union organiser Mother Jones, with her immortal instruction to 'pray for the dead and fight like hell for the living'.[6] Miners are quite literally a dying breed in Britain, whether through the dreaded dust caught in their lungs or just its passage through life's hourglass. Whilst memorials are

Daughters of Mother Jones banner, designed by Joan Heath and first unveiled in 2014. Photographed in the NUM Miners' Hall, Barnsley, 2019.

important to acknowledge what has already been lost, we owe it to them to ensure that their contribution to the country, the culture and communities they built, and the families they left behind, are not forgotten. When we are asked who made Britain great, alongside a history of kings and queens, colonisation and subjugation, and wars that wiped out generations, we should remember the miners. Ordinary workers who educated and organised themselves, provided for their families and the nation, looked out for each other, who continually strove to improve working conditions and ensure life would be better for their sons and daughters. Think of all that ordinary workers have lost in the decades since the pit wheels stopped turning. The embers are still there, it is left to us to *'rage, rage, against the dying of the light'*.[7]

Notes

Preface

1 Department for Energy Security and Net Zero and Department for Business, Energy & Industrial Strategy, Historical Coal Data: Coal Production 1853 to 2022, Availability and Consumption, Statistical Data Set (22 Jan. 2013, updated 27 Jul. 2023), www.gov.uk/government/statistical-data-sets/historical-coal-data-coal-production-availability-and-consumption, accessed 29 Aug. 2023; *People Will Always Need Coal* [online video], UK, NCB, 1975, player.bfi.org.uk/free/film/watch-people-will-always-need-coal-1975-online, accessed 29 Aug. 2023.

2 Department of Energy and Climate Change, *60th Anniversary Digest of United Kingdom Energy Statistics*, 30 Jul. 2009, 8.

3 'Opening of the Miners' Offices at Barnsley', *Sheffield Daily Telegraph*, 3 Nov. 1874, 3.

4 'Opening of the South Yorkshire Miners' Association Offices at Barnsley', *Barnsley Times and South Yorkshire Gazette,* 7 Nov. 1874, 6.

5 Department for Energy Security and Net Zero and Department for Business, Energy & Industrial Strategy, Historical Coal Data: Coal Production 1853 to 2022, Availability and Consumption, Statistical Data Set (22 Jan. 2013, updated 27 Jul. 2023), www.gov.uk/government/statistical-data-sets/historical-coal-data-coal-production-availability-and-consumption, accessed 29 Aug. 2023; Our World in Data,

'Share of the Workforce Employed in the Coal Industry, United Kingdom', ourworldindata.org/grapher/share-of-the-workforce-employed-in-the-coal-industry-united-kingdom, n.d., accessed 15 Sep. 2023; B. Supple, *The History of British Coal*, Vol. 4, *1913–1946: The Political Economy of Decline* (Oxford, 1987), 5.

6 Letter from W. Fisher to his cousin C. Mason, 11 Nov. 1913, Aber Valley Heritage Museum.

7 A water jack was a tin container miners used to transport water or cold tea underground; see: J. H. Brown, *The Valley of the Shadow*, 2nd edn. (Port Talbot, 2009), 102; J. Llywelyn, *Remember Senghenydd: The Colliery Disaster of 1913* (Llanrwst, 2013), 62.

8 W. Benton, 'Welsh Pit Disaster. A Street in Senghenydd. A Victim in Every House', 1913, photograph, Amgueddfa Cymru – Museum Wales, 87.166I/93.

9 A. F. B., 'Senghenydd. An Impression', *The Labour Leader*, 43/10, 23 Oct. 1913, 2.

10 'A National Sorrow', *The Times*, 17 Oct. 1913, 9.

11 This sculpture by Dai Edwards was inspired by a photograph taken after the disaster; see: W. Benton, 'Welsh Pit Disaster. A Little Mother Waiting for News', 1913, photograph, Amgueddfa Cymru – Museum Wales, 66.489/20.

12 A. Plater, *Close the Coalhouse Door*, rev. edn. (Newcastle, 2000), 27.

13 B. Wilson, 'Trapped in Time', n.d., unpublished memoir.

14 See: E. Peirson-Webber, 'Mining Men: Reflections on Masculinity and Oral History during the Coronavirus Pandemic', *History Workshop Journal*, 92 (2021), 242–50.

15 See, for example: R. A. S. Redmayne, *The British Coal-Mining Industry During the War* (Oxford, 1923); F. Zweig, *Men in the Pits* (London, 1948); N. Dennis, F. Henriques and C. Slaughter, *Coal Is Our Life: An Analysis of a Yorkshire Mining Community*

(London, 1956; 2nd edn, London, 1969); R. Page Arnot, *The Miners in Crisis and War: A History of the Miners' Federation of Great Britain (From 1930 onwards)* (London, 1961); W. R. Garside, *The Durham Miners, 1919–1960* (London, 1971); R. Moore, *Pit-Men, Preachers and Politics: The Effects of Methodism in a Durham Mining Community* (London, 1974); A. Burton, *The Miners* (London, 1976); M. Benney, [Henry Ernest Degras], *Charity Main: A Coalfield Chronicle* (Wakefield, 1978); V. L. Allen, *The Militancy of British Miners* (Shipley, 1981); H. Francis and D. Smith, *The Fed: A History of the South Wales Miners in the Twentieth Century* (London, 1981); M. Pollard, *The Hardest Work Under Heaven: The Life and Death of the British Coal Miner* (London, 1984); W. Ashworth, *The History of the British Coal Industry*, Vol. 5, *1946–1982: The Nationalized Industry* (Oxford, 1986); B. Supple, *The History of the British Coal Industry*, Vol. 4, *1913–1946: The Political Economy of Decline* (Oxford, 1987); D. Howell, *The Politics of the NUM: A Lancashire View* (Manchester, 1989); D. Waddington, M. Wykes and C. Critcher, *Split at the Seams? Community, Continuity and Change after the 1984–5 Coal Dispute* (Buckingham, 1991); J. Owens, ed., *Miners 1984–1994: A Decade of Endurance* (Edinburgh, 1994); R. Church and Q. Outram, *Strikes and Solidarity: Coalfield Conflict in Britain, 1889–1966* (Cambridge, 1998); R. Turner, *Coal Was Our Life: An Essay on Life in a Yorkshire Pit Town* (Sheffield, 2000); K. Gildart, *North Wales Miners: A Fragile Unity, 1945–1996* (Cardiff, 2001); T. Strangleman, 'Networks, Place and Identities in Post-Industrial Mining Communities', *International Journal of Urban and Regional Research*, 25/2 (2001), 253–67; B. Curtis, *The South Wales Miners, 1964–1985* (Cardiff, 2013); E. Gibbs, *Coal Country: The Meaning and Memory of Deindustrialization in Postwar Scotland* (London, 2021); H. Beynon and R. Hudson, *The Shadow of the Mine: Coal and the End of Industrial Britain* (London, 2021).

16 J. Lawson, *A Man's Life*, rev. edn. (London, 1944); B. L. Coombes, *These Poor Hands: The Autobiography of a Miner Working in South Wales* (London, 1939); A. Moffat, *My Life with the Miners* (London, 1965); W. Paynter, *My Generation* (London, 1972); J. Bullock, *Them and Us* (London, 1972); J. Gormley, *Battered Cherub* (London, 1982); M. Pitt, *The World on Our Backs: The Kent Miners and the 1972 Miners' Strike* (London, 1979); D. Douglass and J. Krieger, *A Miner's Life* (London, 1983); D. Douglass, *Pit Sense versus the State: A History of Militant Miners in the Doncaster Area* (London, 1994); D. Douglass, *The Wheel's Still in Spin* (Hastings, 2009); D. Defoe, *A Tour thro' the Whole Island of Great Britain. Divided into Circuits or Journeys*, Vol. 4, 3rd edn. (London, 1742), hdl.handle.net/2027/gri.ark:/13960/t5r815v7s; B. Disraeli, *Sybil: Or the Two Nations*, ed. S. Smith (Oxford, 1998); J. B. Priestley, *English Journey* (London, 1935), archive.org/details/in.ernet.dli.2015.175896/page/n11/mode/2up, accessed 5 Mar. 2024; G. Orwell, *The Road to Wigan Pier* (London, 1937; new edn, London, 2001).

17 D. H. Lawrence, *Sons and Lovers* (London, 1913; new edn, London, 2006); J. C. Grant, *The Back-To-Backs* (London, 1930); L. Jones, *Cwmardy: The Story of a Welsh Mining Village* (London, 1937; new edn, London, 1978); T. Hague, *Totley Tom: Tales of a Yorkshire Miner* (Kineton, 1976); A. J. Cronin, *The Stars Look Down* (London, 1935); L. Thomas, *The Deep of the Earth* (London, 1956).

18 W. Maurice, ed., *A Pitman's Anthology* (London, 2004); A. L. Lloyd, *Come All Ye Bold Miners: Ballads & Songs of the Coalfields*, rev. edn. (London, 1978).

19 W. A. Moyes, *The Banner Book: A Study of the Banners of the Lodges of Durham Miners' Association* (Newcastle upon Tyne, 1974); J. Gorman, *Banner Bright: An Illustrated History of Trade Union Banners* (London, 1976; new edn, Buckhurst Hill, 1986); N. Emery, *Banners of the Durham Coalfield* (Stroud, 1998).

20 C. Oldham, *In Loving Memory of Work: A Visual Record of the UK Miners' Strike 1984–85* (Manchester, 2016).
21 A. Bryan, 'The Most Real Man', *COAL*, Jan. 1952, 12.

Introduction: A Brief Journey Through Coal

1 W. Owen, 'Miners' (1918).
2 It was not until 2005 that coal output from opencast mining overtook that of deep mining in the UK, see: Department for Energy Security and Net Zero and Department for Business, Energy & Industrial Strategy, Historical Coal Data: Coal Production 1853 to 2022, Availability and Consumption, Statistical Data Set (22 Jan. 2013, updated 27 Jul. 2023), www.gov.uk/government/statistical-data-sets/historical-coal-data-coal-production-availability-and-consumption, accessed 29 Aug. 2023.
3 In 1842, the Mines and Collieries Act was passed banning all women and girls of any age, as well as all boys under the age of ten, from working underground. The Act followed a Royal Commission of Inquiry into working conditions in Britain's mines led by Lord Ashley, following a fatal accident at Huskar Pit in Silkstone, South Yorkshire, in 1838, in which twenty-six children were killed. See: R. Turnbull, *Shaftesbury: The Great Reformer* (Oxford, 2010), 89–90. Women maintained a presence above ground at British collieries – most notably the 'pit brow lasses', who helped sort, load and move the coal. The last two pit brow lasses were made redundant at Harrington No. 10 Pit, in Lowca, Cumberland in 1972, see: D. Lane, *Pit Brow Lasses* (Lulu.com, 2007), 6. For further discussion of women's employment in the mining industry, see: A. V. John, *By the Sweat of Their Brow: Women Workers at Victorian Coal Mines*

(London, 1984); also: D. Bates, *Pit Lasses: Women and Girls in Coalmining, c.1880–1914* (Barnsley, 2012).

4 B. Supple, *The History of the British Coal Industry*, Vol. 4, *1913–1946: The Political Economy of Decline* (Oxford, 1987), 6.

5 Letter from Wilfred Owen to Susan Owen, 19 Jun. 1916, in: W. Owen, *Collected Letters*, ed. H. Owen and J. Bell (London 1967), 395.

6 'Bantam battalions' were comprised of men who fell below the Army's regulation minimum height of 5ft 3in (160cm). 'Bantam Battalion', *South of England Advertiser*, 3 Dec. 1914, 5; 'The Rosebery Bantam Battalion', *Midlothian Journal*, 5 Feb. 1915, front page; '"The Bantams" Medical Praise of the Little Man', *Liverpool Echo*, 27 Nov. 1914, 5.

7 M. Mellor et al., ed., *A Nation's Tribute* (Chase Arts for Public Spaces, 2021), 24.

8 'Mine Disaster', *The People*, 20 Jan. 1918, 7. The disaster is said to have provided the inspiration for Wilfred Owen's poem 'Miners' (1918).

9 F. Leigh, 'North Staffordshire's Worst Pit Disaster Took Place 100 Years Ago', *Stoke-on-Trent Live*, 3 Jan. 2018, www.stokesentinel.co.uk/news/history/north-staffordshires-worst-pit-disaster-1004603, accessed 7 Sep. 2023.

10 'Terrible Pit Explosion', *Liverpool Daily Post*, 14 Jan. 1918, 4.

11 'Accident This Morning', *Staffordshire Sentinel*, 12 Jan. 1918, 3; 'Bodies Recovered at the Minnie Pit', *Sunderland Daily Echo*, 14 Jan. 1918, 4.

12 These were the words of Arthur J. Cook the General Secretary of the Miners' Federation of Great Britain, which became an anthem for the strike. The General Strike began on 4 May 1926 and involved over 1.5 million people.

13 B. L. Johns, 'Nationalisation of the Coal-Mining Industry: The Lessons of British Experience', *Australian Quarterly*, 30/3 (1958), 71–81, 71.

14 A. J. Taylor, 'The Miners and Nationalisation, 1931–36', *International Review of Social History*, 28/2 (1983), 176–99.

15 For a discussion of perceptions of the industrial militancy of miners, see: D. Geary, 'The Myth of the Radical Miner', in: S. Berger, A. Croll and N. LaPorte, eds, *Towards a Comparative History of Coalfield Societies* (Aldershot, 2005; rep. Abingdon, 2016), 43-64; also: R. Church and Q. Outram, *Strikes and Solidarity: Coalfield Conflict in Britain, 1889–1966* (Cambridge, 1998), 1–2.

16 C. R. Attlee, 'A Message from the Prime Minister', 1 Jan. 1947, front page of Vesting Day leaflet announcing the nationalisation of coal, The National Archives, CAB 21/2207.

17 Johns, 'Nationalisation of the Coal-mining Industry', 74; see also: F. Zweig, *Men in the Pits* (London, 1948), 10–11, 158–59; A. Moffat, *My Life with the Miners* (London, 1965), 87, 90, 313; J. Bullock, *Them and Us* (London, 1972), 138.

18 Ministry of Power, *Fuel for the Future* (London, HMSO, 1967).

19 'Rothes: Resentment Storm Building Up', *Edinburgh Evening News*, 14 Mar. 1962, 10.

20 *New Day*, Templar Film Studios, 1959, movingimage.nls.uk/film/0307, accessed 12 Oct. 2023.

21 Ibid.

22 'N.C.B. Death Sentence', *Leven Mail*, 14 Mar. 1962, 10.

23 'And the Winner of the Most Dismal Town in Scotland Is . . . Glenrothes', *Scotsman*, 29 Jan. 2009, www.scotsman.com/news/and-the-winner-of-the-most-dismal-town-in-scotland-is-glenrothes-2452659, accessed 31 Aug. 2023.

24 KnowFife, *Glenrothes Area Profile* (18 Oct. 2022), Fife Council Research Team for KnowFife Hub, know.fife.scot/__data/assets/pdf_file/0027/408384/Glenrothes-Area-Profile.pdf; KnowFife, *Children in Low Income Families – 2021/2022 Local Area Statistics* (24 Mar. 2023), Fife Council Research Team for

KnowFife Hub, know.fife.scot/__data/assets/pdf_file/0021/462108/Fife-Findings-Children-in-low-income-families-2022.pdf.

25 A. Merat, 'Making a Killing: Inside the Scottish Town Built on the Arms Trade', *Prospect*, 3 Mar. 2020, www.prospectmagazine.co.uk/essays/39896/making-a-killing-inside-the-scottish-town-built-on-the-arms-trade, accessed 31 Aug. 2023; B. Briggs, 'US Arms Manufacturer with Factory in Glenrothes Develops 'Lethal' Missile Steering System Similar to One Used in Yemen Bombing', *Daily Record*, 10 Apr. 2016, www.dailyrecord.co.uk/news/uk-world-news/arms-manufacturer-factory-glenrothes-develops-7726745, accessed 31 Aug. 2023.

26 W. Ashworth, *The History of the British Coal Industry*, Vol. 5, *1946–1982: The Nationalized Industry* (Oxford, 1986), 256, 'Table 6.1 Number of Colliery Closures, 1958 to 1972–3'. By 1960 the workforce had shrunk to 600,000, half the number of those employed forty years earlier.

27 'Bryn Colliery Closure: Inevitable and in the Best Interests', *Port Talbot Guardian*, 5 April 1963, 12.

28 W. Paynter, *My Generation* (London, 1972), 144.

29 The suffocation of British cities by King Coal's toxic fog was portrayed in John Tenniel's cartoon 'Old King Coal and the Fog Demon', which appeared in *Punch* magazine 13 Nov. 1880, see: The Victorian Web, 'Old King Coal and the Fog Demon', 10 Jul. 2020, victorianweb.org/periodicals/punch/publichealth/5.html, accessed 13 Oct. 2023.

30 M. Pitt, *The World on Our Backs: The Kent Miners and the 1972 Miners' Strike* (London, 1979), 17.

31 A. E. H., 'Position of a Miner's Wife', Letters to the Editor, *Coleshill Chronicle*, 11 Feb. 1972, 4.

32 'The Miners' Strike', Letters to the Editor, *Coleshill Chronicle,* 11 Feb. 1972, 4.

33 The exact number of miners and supporters who amassed in Saltley on 10 February 1972 is disputed: Bunyan estimated the number as 22,000, whereas Ashworth gives the smaller figure of 12,000. See: T. Bunyan, 'From Saltley to Orgreave via Brixton', *Journal of Law and Society,* 12/3 (1985), 293–303, 294; also: W. Ashworth, *The History of the British Coal Industry,* Vol. 5, *1946–1982: The Nationalized Industry* (Oxford, 1986), 609. Later Margaret Thatcher argued that the events at Saltley had demonstrated the 'struggle to bring trade unions properly within the law', in: M. Thatcher, *The Path to Power* (London, 1995), 218.

34 BBC News, 'Arthur Scargill: Battle of Saltley Gate a Lesson in Solidarity', 10 Feb. 2022, www.bbc.co.uk/news/uk-england-south-yorkshire-60290283, accessed 5 Mar. 2024.

35 S. Schofield quoted in: '"Forget Past – Build Future"', *Coal News,* 128, N. Yorks and other edns, Mar. 1972, 2.

36 K. Jefferys, *Finest and Darkest Hours: The Decisive Events in British Politics from Churchill to Blair* (London, 2002), 219.

37 The Energy Minister Patrick Jenkin caused outrage after he advised the British public to clean their teeth in the dark to save electricity. It would later emerge that the minister used an electric toothbrush and left most of his lights on at home. See: M. Davies, 'So . . . Clean Your Teeth in the Dark', *Daily Mirror,* 16 Jan. 1974, 5.

38 L. Baston, 'Who Governs?', *Guardian,* 4 Apr. 2005, www.theguardian.com/politics/2005/apr/04/electionspast.past9, accessed 6 Sep. 2023.

39 K. Jefferys, *Finest and Darkest Hours: The Decisive Events in British Politics from Churchill to Blair* (London, 2002), 236.

40 A. Shuster, 'Miners in Britain End Their Strike; Get Raise of 35%', *New York Times*, 7 Mar. 1974, front page.

41 W. Ashworth, *The History of the British Coal Industry*, Vol. 5, *1946–1982: The Nationalized Industry* (Oxford, 1986), 608.

42 See: B. Towers, 'Running the Gauntlet: British Trade Unions under Thatcher, 1979–1988', *Industrial and Labor Relations Review*, 42/2 (1989), 163–88. The 1980 Coal Industry Act called for an end to government subsidies to the industry by 1984, see: J. Tomlinson, 'Deindustrialisation and "Thatcherism": Moral Economy and Unintended Consequences', *Contemporary British History*, 35/4 (2021), 620–42, 631.

43 Hansard, HC Deb, 9 May 1984, Vol. 59, Col.1059; D. Kelliher, *Making Cultures of Solidarity: London and the 1984–5 Miners' Strike* (Abingdon, 2021), 2–3.

44 NUM President Arthur Scargill claimed the list of pits earmarked for closure was significantly more extensive, with over seventy pits implicated.

45 F. Beckett and D. Hencke, *Marching to the Fault Line: The 1984 Miners' Strike and the Death of Industrial Britain* (London, 2009), 51.

46 Office for National Statistics, 'The History of Strikes in the UK' 21 Sep. 2015, www.ons.gov.uk/employmentandlabourmarket/peopleinwork/employmentandemployeetypes/articles/thehistoryofstrikesintheuk/2015-09-21, accessed 5 Mar. 2024.

47 A. Travis, 'Battle of Orgreave: More Unreleased Police Files Uncovered', *Guardian*, 1 Mar. 2018, www.theguardian.com/politics/2018/mar/01/battle-of-orgreave-more-unreleased-police-files-uncovered, accessed 27 Sep. 2023; R. East, H. Power and P. A. Thomas, 'The Death of Mass Picketing', *Journal of Law and Society*, 12/3 (1985), 305–19, 309. The Orgreave Truth and Justice Campaign is still campaigning for

an official government inquiry into the events of June 1984, see: Orgreave Truth and Justice Campaign, 'About', n.d., otjc.org.uk, accessed 26 Sep. 2023.

48 D. Skinner quoted in: A. J. Richards, *Miners on Strike: Class Solidarity and Division in Britain* (Oxford, 1996), 84.

49 M. Adeney and J. Lloyd, *The Miners' Strike, 1984–5: Loss Without Limit* (London, 1988), 164.

50 F. Sutcliffe-Braithwaite and N. Thomlinson, 'National Women against Pit Closures: Gender, Trade Unionism and Community Activism in the Miners' Strike, 1984–5', *Contemporary British History*, 32/1 (2018), 78–100, 78.

51 A. Law, 'The Bitter End', *Daily Mirror,* 4 Mar. 1985, front page.

52 *Brassed Off,* dir. Mark Herman, 1996.

53 *Billy Elliot,* dir. Stephen Daldry, 2000; *Pride,* dir. Matthew Warchus, 2014.

1. Jack the Lad

1 'Making Army Service a Career for Men', *Newcastle Evening Chronicle*, 10 Aug. 1937, front page.

2 *Newcastle Evening Chronicle*, 9 Aug. 1937, front page.

3 Durham City Council, 'Conservation Area Appraisal: Burnopfield', Dec. 2009, 10, www.durham.gov.uk/media/3545/Burnopfield-Conservation-Area-Map-Character-Appraisal/pdf/BurnhopefieldConservationAreaCharacterAppraisal.pdf?m=636736391190930000.

4 *Triple Cross*, dir. Terence Young, 1966.

5 W. Scott, *Marmion: A Tale of Flodden Field* (London, 1888), hdl.handle.net/2027/uiug.30112066382711; Joseph Mallord William Turner, *Norham Castle, Sunrise*, *c.*1845, Tate, London.

6 *Newcastle Evening Chronicle*, 7 Dec. 1990, 30.

7 M. Engel, 'From Greatness to Self-Destruction: Colin Milburn's Story to Take Centre Stage', *Guardian*, 21 Oct. 2016, www.theguardian.com/sport/blog/2016/oct/21/colin-milburn-play-when-the-eye-has-gone, accessed 8 Apr. 2023.

8 F. Keating, 'Remember Colin Milburn among the Many Marks of May', *The Guardian*, 12 May 2009, www.theguardian.com/sport/blog/2009/may/12/frank-keating-colin-milburn-may-anniversaries, accessed 8 Apr. 2022.

9 Engel, 'From Greatness to Self-Destruction'.

10 *Sunderland Daily Echo*, 19 Apr. 1909, 3; Durham Aged Mineworkers' Homes Association, *Residents Handbook* (2019), 1, www.durhamhomes.org.uk/wp-content/uploads/2021/10/V2-DAMHA-2019-Residents-Handbook.pdf.

11 Durham Aged Mineworkers' Homes Association, *Residents Handbook* (2019), 1, www.durhamhomes.org.uk/wp-content/uploads/2021/10/V2-DAMHA-2019-Residents-Handbook.pdf.

12 'Obituary, Lord Joicey's Career in Industry', *Yorkshire Post and Leeds Intelligencer*, 23 Nov. 1936, 7; *Newcastle Journal*, 20 Oct. 1913, 10.

13 R. C. Bell, 'A Brief History of the Plastic Surgery Unit Based on Shotley Bridge General Hospital', *British Journal of Plastic Surgery*, 39/3 (1986), 422–31.

14 Billy Jones, *Peggy O'Neil* [Edison Disc], USA, Edison Records, 50792, 1921.

15 J. Meyer, *Men of War: Masculinity and the First World War in Britain* (Basingstoke, 2009), 127.

16 S. Chaplin, 'Saturday Saga', in S. Chaplin, *The Leaping Lad and Other Stories* (London, 1946; new edn, Harlow, 1970), 77–90.

17 Advert, 'Jackson, the Tailor', *Croydon Advertiser and East Surrey Reporter*, 17 Oct. 1958, 11.

18 'Men Who Matter: Mr. Lionel Jacobson', *Investors Chronicle,* 15 Jul. 1960, 233.

19 Advert, 'Jackson, the Tailor', *Morpeth Herald*, 27 Jun. 1952, 8; Advert, 'Jackson, the Tailor', *Morpeth Herald*, 26 Sep. 1952, 8.

20 Mark Benney [Henry Ernest Degras], *Charity Main: A Coalfield Chronicle* (Wakefield, 1978), 24, 101. Benney was posted to the North East of England during the Second World War and *Charity Main* was written based on his experiences of the mining industry at this time. See: R. M. Lee, '"The Man Who Committed a Hundred Burglaries": Mark Benney's Strange and Eventful Sociological Career', *Journal of the History of the Behavioral Sciences*, 51/4 (2015), 409–33.

21 *Newcastle Journal,* 12 July 1958, 5.

22 S. Sterck, 'Spare a Thought for These Men . . . on the Fish Quay Patrol in the Icy Winter Rain', *Newcastle Journal*, 24 Dec. 1964, 6.

23 'Police Tackle Drivers' Bad Habits', *Newcastle Journal*, 10 February 1965, 9; 'Tynemouth Police Get Social Club', *Newcastle Evening Chronicle*, 4 Feb. 1965, 9.

2. The Miner Who Went to Fleet Street

1 Spanish City, 'The History of Spanish City', n.d., spanishcity.co.uk/about-us/history, accessed 22 May 2023; 'Whitley Bay Not "Down and Out", Resort Will Rise to Greater Heights', *Shields Daily News*, 29 Mar. 1943, 3.

2 'Tynemouth Borrowed Buses for Holiday Traffic', *Shields Daily News*, 18 Aug. 1947, 5.

3 Advert, 'Spanish City', *Newcastle Journal*, 23 Aug. 1946, 3.

4 R. A. Hart and M. Moro, 'Grammar Schools Have a Long History of Being Dominated by Middle-Class Children', *The Conversation*, 8 Sep. 2016, theconversation.com/grammar-schools-have-a-long-history-of-being-dominated-by-middle-class-children-64198, accessed 17 May 2023.

5 B. Jackson and D. Marsden, *Education and the Working Class* (London, 1962; rev. edn, Harmondsworth, 1966), 109.

6 'Scholarship Exams. Fair and Impartial', *Northern Daily Mail*, 17 Jun. 1948, 2.

7 See, for example, the study of working-class children who attended grammar schools in Huddersfield in: Jackson and Marsden, *Education and the Working Class*.

8 'Scholarship Exams. Fair and Impartial', *Northern Daily Mail*, 17 Jun. 1948, 2.

9 See, for example: C. Horrie, 'Grammar Schools: Back to the Bad Old Days of Inequality', *Guardian*, 4 May 2017, www.theguardian.com/news/2017/may/04/grammar-schools-secondary-modern-11-plus-theresa-may, accessed 17 May 2023.

10 D. Broadley and K. J. McElwee, 'A "Hair-Raising" History of Alopecia Areata', *Experimental Dermatology*, 29/3 (2020), 208–22.

11 Ibid.

12 See, for example: Advert, 'Falling Hair', *Newcastle Journal*, 12 May 1952, 5.

13 In the 1950s such 'sun ray therapy', where patients would sit in underwear and goggles in front of a UV lamp, was used to treat a wide range of ailments, including chest infections, anaemia and ringworm. A number of those who received this treatment as children subsequently developed skin cancer. See: L. Atkinson, 'For Years Doctors Prescribed It for Everything from Sore Throats to Childhood Acne: How "Sunray Therapy" with Ultra Violet Lamps Has Put a Generation at Risk of Cancer', *Mail Online*, 22 May 2014,

www.dailymail.co.uk/femail/article-2635599/For-years-doctors-prescribed-sore-throats-childhood-acne-How-sunray-therapy-ultra-violet-lamps-generation-risk-cancer.html, accessed 19 May 2023.

14 Broadley and McElwee, 'A "Hair-Raising" History of Alopecia Areata'; 'Today's Crossword', *Shields Daily News*, 10 Jan. 1950, 4.

15 J. Elliot, *Jowl and Listen Lad* [sound recording], c.1960–65, Reg Hall Archive, British Library Collection, sounds.bl.uk/World-and-traditional-music/Reg-Hall-Archive/025M-C0903X0006XX-0800V0, accessed 9 Dec. 2020.

16 See, for example, concerns voiced in the House of Commons in 1929: Hansard, HC Deb, 25 Feb. 1929, Vol. 225, Col. 63. In some later reports, steel supports were said to have been reducing mine accidents; see, for example: 'Use of Steel Props Is Reducing Mine Accidents', *Derby Evening Telegraph*, 4 Feb. 1950, 4; 'Owed Life to Two Steel Pit Props, Says Survivor', *Nottingham Evening Post*, 25 Jan. 1951, 1.

17 'Pits Buy German Props', *Daily Mirror*, 28 Apr. 1952, 4.

18 Unlike the most common deep mines, in which the coal was accessed via a vertical shaft, drift mines reached the coal seam horizontally, above water level, usually through the side of a hill or mountain.

19 By 1960, the number of workers employed at Barcus Close Colliery had risen to 263, thereafter falling until its closure in 1966. Durham Mining Museum, 'Barcus Close Colliery, NCB Employment', n.d., www.dmm.org.uk/ncb/b032.htm, accessed 17 May 2023.

20 The Durham Mining Museum website does not list any names of those who had been killed at Barcus Close Colliery, compared to nineteen names listed for the Burnopfield Colliery (Hobson Pit), twelve names listed for Byermoor Colliery,

twenty-eight names listed for Lintz Colliery, and thirty-seven names listed for Garesfield Colliery. In my own research, I found a report of the death of William Scott Thompson, aged fifty-eight, who was killed after being crushed by a fall of coal and timber at Barcus Close on 9 November 1961; see: 'Opinions Clash at Inquest on Miner', *Newcastle Journal*, 8 Dec. 1961, 11.

21 'A Thank You for "Happy" Pitmen', *Sunday Sun*, 4 Sep. 1955, 5.

22 'Pit Without Disputes', *Yorkshire Post*, 5 Sep. 1955, 5.

23 It seemed the condition was particularly prevalent amongst workers in drift mines; see, for example, the study into occurrence among workers in Wales and Scotland: T. H. Jenkins and W. C. Sharp, 'Weil's Disease: Occurrence amongst Workers in Welsh and Scottish Coal-Mines', *British Medical Journal*, 1/4453 (1946), 714–17. See also: W. Ashworth, *The History of the British Coal Industry*, Vol. 5, *1946–1982: The Nationalized Industry* (Oxford, 1986), 561.

24 It was the equivalent of around £30 today.

25 '£12,900 Theft at Colliery', *Northern Daily Mail*, 16 Sep. 1949, front page.

26 'Thieves Take Wages of 1,700 Miners', *Evening News and Southern Daily Mail*, 16 Sep. 1949, 12.

27 Whickham and District Local History Group, 'Unsolved Crime at Marley Hill', 19 Feb. 2013, whickhamdistrictmemories.co.uk/listings/unsolved-crime-at-marley-hill, accessed 23 May 2023.

28 G. Campbell, 'Riddle of the Pit Robbery', *Newcastle Evening Chronicle*, 29 Apr. 2003.

29 The National Service Act was passed by Parliament in 1947, and came into force in 1949, for all physically fit men between the ages of seventeen and twenty-one, requiring them to serve in a branch of the armed forces for an eighteen-month period.

In 1950, a further National Service Act extended the period of service to two years. National Service ended in 1960, with the last servicemen discharged in 1963.

30 G. Campbell, 'Who Shot the Quiet Stationmaster?', *Sunday Sun,* 3 May 1964, 8.

31 'Lintz Green Murder Recalled', *Sunday Sun*, 26 Nov. 1933, 11; 'Stationmaster Shot Dead by a Mysterious Assassin', *Illustrated Police News*, 14 Oct. 1911, 4.

32 Ibid.

33 'The Lintz Green Murder', *Northern Daily Mail*, 26 Oct. 1911, 6; 'The Lintz Green Murder', *Yorkshire Evening Post,* 9 Nov. 1911, 6.

34 'Wild Man of the Woods Was Never Captured', *Gateshead Post*, 18 Jan. 1979, 13.

35 J. Graham, *Ink* (London, 2017).

36 A. E. Housman, 'Blue Remembered Hills', in *A Shropshire Lad* (London, 1898), 57.

37 G. Campbell, 'Black Remembered Hills', a parody of A. E. Housman's *A Shropshire Lad*, undated.

3. The Dark Horse

1 'Colliery Explosion', *Newcastle Guardian*, 10 Mar. 1860, supplement.

2 'The Explosion in Burradon Pit', *The Times*, 6 Mar. 1860, 9.

3 'Alan Carr Unveils Burradon Pit Disaster Artwork', *Chronicle Live*, 1 Nov. 2011, www.chroniclelive.co.uk/news/north-east-news/alan-carr-unveils-burradon-pit-1406509, accessed 11 May 2023.

4 A. Carr, *Alanatomy: The Inside Story* (London, 2017), 110.

5 'School Teas at Burradon', *Morpeth Herald,* 14 May 1937, 8.

6 'Treat Fund', *Morpeth Herald,* 12 Feb. 1937, 10.

7 'Burradon', *Morpeth Herald,* 1 Oct. 1937, 11; 'Burradon Presentation', *Morpeth Herald,* 22 Oct. 1937, 3.

8 'Burradon Man Bound Over', *Morpeth Herald,* 28 May 1937, 3.

9 'Burradon', *Newcastle Weekly Chronicle,* 25 Nov. 1939, 5.

10 Many working-class homes in the North East had proggy mats or rag mats, homemade rugs made from old sacks and scraps of fabric, a cheaper alternative to carpets. The dense and often chewy texture of the bread cakes referred to here, traditionally made from leftover dough, gave them the name 'stottie', from 'to stott', which in the Geordie dialect meant 'to make bounce'. See: S. Seddon, 'What Is a Stottie Cake? The Life and Times of a North East Delicacy', *Chronicle Live,* 19 Sep. 2017, www.chroniclelive.co.uk/news/north-east-news/stottie-cake-life-times-north-13645034, accessed 5 Mar. 2024.

11 Another person I spoke to told me that as Sunday was a day of rest, there was less industrial smog in the air to blacken drying clothes the following day.

12 Many POW camps remained in use until 1948, with Germans contained at the camp in nearby Ponteland. See: R. J. C. Thomas, *Twentieth Century Military Recording Project: Prisoner of War Camps (1939–1948),* English Heritage (2003), historicengland.org.uk/images-books/publications/prisoner-of-war-camps/prisoner-of-war-camps.

13 All women and girls, as well as boys under the age of ten, were barred from working underground in the Mines and Collieries Act of 1842.

14 'The Pit Pony', *Sheffield Daily Independent,* 17 Aug. 1908, 8.

15 'Nine Ponies Burnt to Death', *Sunderland Daily Echo*, 8 Nov. 1883, 3.

16 N. Emery, *Banners of the Durham Coalfield* (Stroud, 1998), 155.

17 The banner was recreated by Durham Bannermakers in 2013. See: Coxhoe Parish Council, 'Quarrington Hill Banner', *Hill Talk*, newsletter, Sep. 2013, 1, coxhoeparishcouncil.gov.uk/wp-content/uploads/sites/4/2016/05/Hill-Talk-September-2013.pdf.

18 The National Equine Defence League was first established by Francis Cox in 1909 to improve the lives of 72,000 ponies in British mines.

19 'The Pit Pony', *Falkirk Herald*, 3 Jan. 1906, 8.

20 E. Zola, *Germinal*, trans. P. Collier (Oxford, 2008), 186, 433.

21 See, for example: 'Fight with Bare Fists', *Western Daily Press*, 28 Mar. 1922, 8; 'Bare Fist Fight', *Wishaw Press and Advertiser*, 28 Nov. 1930, 2; 'Miner in Bare Fist Fight Sequel to Wager Dispute', *Blyth News*, 10 Jul. 1939, 6.

22 Images of boxers appeared on the cover of *COAL* seven times across its run from 1949 through to mid-1960.

23 *COAL*, May 1949, 3..

24 'Pitmen's Champion Who Kept His Feet on the Ground', *Northern Echo*, 4 Dec. 2001, www.thenorthernecho.co.uk/news/7091201.pitmens-champion-kept-feet-ground, accessed 14 May 2023. Apparently, Durham was the hardest place the fairground boxing booth visited, due to the miners' appetite to have a go, with the boxers having up to twenty fights a day; see: R. Gray, '"I Started in Fairground Boxing Booths at 16, No Headguards, Small Gloves and I'd Get a Pound a Fight." The Life and Times of Big Ron Gray', *Boxing News*, 9 Aug. 2019, www.boxingnewsonline.net/i-started-in-fairground-boxing-booths-at-16-no-headguards-small-gloves-id-get-a-

pound-a-fight-the-life-and-times-of-big-ron-gray, accessed 14 May 2023.

25 R. Wills, 'Sportlight', *Daily Mirror*, 18 Dec. 1967, 16.

26 R. Conner-Hill, 'Sculpture to Honour Champion Boxer Maurice Cullen Unveiled', *Northern Echo*, 7 Apr. 2018, www.thenorthernecho.co.uk/news/16144206.sculpture-honour-champion-boxer-maurice-cullen-unveiled, accessed 14 May 2023.

27 'Pitmen's Champion Who Kept His Feet on the Ground', *Northern Echo*, 4 Dec. 2001, www.thenorthernecho.co.uk/news/7091201.pitmens-champion-kept-feet-ground, accessed 14 May 2023.

28 'Pit Dies – but the Village Lives On', *Newcastle Evening Chronicle*, 21 Nov. 1975, 19.

29 J. Kay, 'Pitmen Shun "Pick and Shovel" Mines', *Newcastle Journal*, 12 May 1973, 10.

30 'Pit Dies – but the Village Lives On', *Newcastle Evening Chronicle.*

31 Ibid.

32 'Coal Cutting Starts', *Newcastle Evening Chronicle*, 8 Feb. 1985, front page.

33 'End of the Line for Brenkley', *Newcastle Evening Chronicle*, 25 Oct. 1985, 2.

34 N. Thompson, 'Axe falls on Pit', *Newcastle Journal*, 26 Jun. 1985, front page.

35 'Clear Obligation', *Newcastle Journal*, 22 Oct. 1985, 6.

36 'End of the Line for Brenkley', *Newcastle Evening Chronicle.*

37 Ibid.

4. Last of the Big Hitters

1 N. Dennis, F. Henriques and C. Slaughter, *Coal Is Our Life: An Analysis of a Yorkshire Mining Community*, 2nd edn (London, 1969), 176.

2 B. Taylor, '"Their Only Words of English Were 'Thank You'": Rights, Gratitude and "Deserving" Hungarian Refugees to Britain in 1956', *Journal of British Studies*, 55/1 (2016), 120–44, 141.

3 Ibid.

4 *People Will Always Need Coal* [online video], UK, NCB, 1975, player.bfi.org.uk/free/film/watch-people-will-always-need-coal-1975-online, accessed 29 Aug. 2023.

5 Department for Employment, *Report of Court of Inquiry into a Dispute between the National Coal Board and the National Union of Mineworkers under the Chairmanship of the Rt. Hon. Lord Wilberforce* (HMSO, London, 1972), Cmnd. 4903.

6 V. L. Allen, *The Militancy of British Miners* (Shipley, 1981), 94.

7 *The Miners' Film,* dir. Cinema Action, 1975.

8 D. Defoe, *A Tour thro' the Whole Island of Great Britain. Divided into Circuits or Journeys*, Vol. 4, 3rd edn (London, 1742), 160, hdl.handle.net/2027/gri.ark:/13960/t5r815v7s; B. Disraeli, *Sybil: Or the Two Nations*, (Oxford, 1998), 139; R. H. Horne, 'The True Story of a Coal Fire', in: C. Dickens, ed., *Household Words,* 1/3 (1850), 72, hdl.handle.net/2027/gri.ark:/13960/t5r815v7s.

9 G. Orwell, *The Road to Wigan Pier* (London, 2001), 18–19.

10 A. Barney Seale, *Ideal Miner*, sculpture, 1947, Amgueddfa Cymru – Museum Wales, 2001.1/42.

11 '"Giant" George Points Way to Top Jobs', *Coal News,* 111, HQ & Kent edn, Jul. 1971, 7.

12 E. MacColl, C. Parker and P. Seeger, *The Big Hewer (On Coal Miners), The Big Hewer (A Radio Ballad)* [CD], rec. 1961, UK, Topic Records, B0000JG3W, 2008.

13 J. Dean, *Big Bad John* [CD], rec. 1962, UK, Jasmine Records, B01BWXNE74, 2016.
14 C. Coffey, 'When Bold Rob Earned His Name', *St Helens Star*, 31 Jan. 2013.
15 H. A. Freeth, 'Pit Profile No. 1: Griffith Thomas', *COAL,* May 1947, 9.
16 H. A. Freeth, 'Pit Profile No. 21: John Jones', *COAL,* Jan. 1949, 9
17 H. A. Freeth, 'Pit Profile No. 23: James A. Henderson', *COAL,* Mar. 1949, 9; H. A. Freeth, 'Pit Profile No. 37: Morgan Morgans', *COAL,* May 1950, 15.
18 T. Wadsworth, 'Strong Man', *COAL,* Nov. 1959, 6.
19 L. Quibell, 'Giant Dave Earns a World-Class Rating', *Coal News*, 122, N. Yorks. and other edns, Aug. 1971, 15; M. Weiss, 'Gee, He's a Hit', *Coal News,* 175, S. Notts. and other edns, Feb. 1976, 19.
20 *New Power in Their Hands,* dir. Alun Falconer, 1959.
21 'From Aircraft Factory Back to Mining', *Birmingham Daily Gazette,* 24 Jan. 1948, 3; *Daily Mirror,* 22 Jan. 1948, 7.
22 G. Goodman, 'The Miracle in Jim's Pit', *Daily Herald*, 17 Dec. 1957, 4.
23 'Pit Monster Digs a Bold New World for Mining', *Western Mail*, 14 May 1957, 4.
24 Ibid.
25 'New 125 HP Anderton Shearer-Loader', advert, *COAL*, Sep. 1959, 15; see also: H. A. Longden, 'Mining Today – And Tomorrow', *COAL*, Sep. 1959, 10–16; 'Mechanisation Speed-up in Cumberland Pits', *COAL*, Sep. 1959, 24; 'New Technical Devices', *COAL,* Sep. 1959, 27.
26 'Pit Monster Digs a Bold New World for Mining', *Western Mail.*
27 'Richard Burton Interview', *The Dick Cavett Show* [online video], 1980, uploaded 19 Jan. 2013, www.youtube.com/watch?v=NFnra54Yk44, accessed 25 Sep. 2023.

28 F. A. Canning, cartoon from back cover of *COAL*, Sep. 1959.
29 *Liverpool Echo*, 29 Oct. 1965, 9.
30 Local Darby and Joan Clubs provided social activities and support for elderly people.
31 'Miners' Ride of Terror', *Liverpool Echo*, 27 Apr. 1985, 9.
32 H. Dean, 'Miners in Battle to Rescue Pit', *Liverpool Echo*, 10 Oct. 1985, 2.
33 C. Lenton quoted in: Dean, 'Miners in Battle to Rescue Pit'.
34 H. Dean, 'History Takes a Big Crash!', *Liverpool Echo*, 27 Mar. 1987, 8.
35 D. Bates quoted in: Dean, 'History Takes a Big Crash!'.
36 'Whoompf!', *Liverpool Echo*, 26 Mar. 1987, 4.
37 *Bold Moss* [online video], The Groundwork Trust, 1993, uploaded 1 Feb. 2017, www.youtube.com/watch?v=SzNdX2MIPnY, accessed 25 Sep. 2023.
38 J. Molyneux, 'Kids with "Crates of Beer" Being Dropped Off by Parents at "Blue Lagoon"', *Liverpool Echo* online, 19 Jun. 2021, www.liverpoolecho.co.uk/news/liverpool-news/kids-crates-beer-being-dropped-20830689, accessed 25 Sep. 2023.
39 NCB Western Area, 'Bickershaw Colliery 1877–1977, Centenary Brochure', pamphlet produced for the Centenary Open Day, 12 Jun. 1977, Coal and Community website, www.coalandcommunity.org.uk/bickerhsawbrochure, accessed 25 Sep. 2023.
40 Neil Rigby interview with Keith Gildart, 6 Dec. 2018, Coal and Community website, www.coalandcommunity.org.uk/transcripts, accessed 25 Sep. 2023.
41 'March Marks End of an Era', *Liverpool Echo*, 27 Mar. 1992, 28.
42 '"Black Friday" on Jobs Front', *Aberdeen Press and Journal*, 1 Feb. 1992, 7.
43 G. Henderson, 'Cement City', *Liverpool Echo*, 5 Feb. 1992, 6.
44 'Cotgrave Fears for Its Beauty', *Nottingham Guardian*, 23 Jan. 1960, 3.

45 '"Integration of Different Types Will Be Disaster to Cotgrave," Inquiry Told', *Grantham Journal*, 29 Jan. 1960, 4.

46 BBC News, 'Sports Direct Staff "Not Treated as Humans", Says MPs' Report', 22 Jul. 2016, www.bbc.co.uk/news/uk-england-derbyshire-36855374, accessed 21 Jan. 2022.

47 BBC News, 'Boys-Only Wall of Fame at Shirebrook Academy "A Gimmick"', 21 Mar. 2019, www.bbc.co.uk/news/uk-england-derbyshire-47643986, accessed 20 Oct. 2021.

48 V. Woan, 'Monument a Reminder of Town's Coal-Mining Heritage', *Liverpool Echo*, 23 Feb. 1996, 18.

49 'The *Dream* Concept', Dream St Helens website, n.d., www.dreamsthelens.com/the-story-of-dream/the-dream-concept/, accessed 12 Jan. 2023.

50 J. Plensa quoted in: 'The *Dream* Concept'.

51 'Ex Terra Lucem Restored as Motto of St Helens', *St Helens Star*, 18 Apr. 2013, www.sthelensstar.co.uk/news/10363386.ex-terra-lucem-restored-as-motto-of-st-helens, accessed 20 Oct. 2021.

5. You've Just Got to Laugh

1 Dating back to the 1890s, Birchenwood Colliery closed in 1932. It continued producing coke and other by-products with coal from other collieries into the later twentieth century.

2 BBC News, 'Potters Club Reopens for Fine Dining after Makeover', 20 Jan. 2011, news.bbc.co.uk/local/stoke/hi/people_and_places/history/newsid_9365000/9365261.stm, accessed 20 Jun. 2023.

3 *Black Snow*, dir. Stephen Linstead, 2017. Barnsley-born sculptor Graham Ibbeson lost a relative in the disaster; see: Oaks

Colliery Disaster website, n.d., www.oaks1866.com, accessed 21 Jun. 2023.

4 'Stoke City's New Player', *Staffordshire Sentinel*, 17 Sep. 1926, 6; 'Man of the Moment', *Football Gazette (South Shields)*, 8 Oct. 1932, 3.

5 'Stoke City's New Player', *Staffordshire Sentinel*.

6 'Man of the Moment', *Football Gazette*.

7 'Local Wedding', *Staffordshire Sentinel*, 22 Oct. 1929, 10.

8 'Deaths', *Staffordshire Sentinel*, 28 Feb. 1934, 3.

9 'Funeral of Mrs A. Beachill', *Staffordshire Sentinel*, 5 Mar. 1934, 4.

10 Navy Recruitment advert, *c.*1970, Advertising Archives, 30525271.

11 R. Jenkins, 'From School to the Coal Mine', unpublished memoir, 2019, 1.

12 P. Haxby and D. Parkes, 'Apprenticeship in the United Kingdom: From ITBs to YTS', *European Journal of Education*, 24/2 (1989), 167–81, 167; L. Unwin 'Employer-Led Realities: Apprenticeship Past and Present', *Journal of Vocational Education and Training*, 48/1 (1996), 57–68, 62.

13 See: Haxby and Parkes, 'Apprenticeship in the United Kingdom', 32–44.

14 *Name changed to preserve anonymity. It is possible that he had arrived on the *SS Ormonde*, which brought Caribbean migrants to Liverpool in March 1947, a year before the more famous *Empire Windrush* arrived at Tilbury Docks in Essex.

15 For example, writing of the mining industry in South Wales in the early twentieth century, Michael Lieven observed that there would be 'frightening initiation rites and humiliating practical jokes', see: M. Lieven, *Senghennydd: The Universal Pit Village 1890–1930* (Llandysul, 1994), 166.

16 K. Gildart, 'Mining Memories: Reading Coalfield Autobiographies', *Labor History*, 50/2 (2009), 139–61, 146.
17 D. Moseley, b.1948, 'The Pit Years', unpublished memoir, 11 Oct. 2019, 5.
18 Break time in the pit, where miners would eat their 'snap' – the food they had brought down with them.
19 'Safety Award', *Birmingham Daily Post*, 9 Apr. 1979, 7.
20 'Miners Call for Thermal Clothing', *Staffordshire Sentinel*, 19 Apr. 1983, 14.
21 'Last Stand Pit Now Back in Production', *Staffordshire Newsletter*, 12 Oct. 1984, 7.
22 'Bullied Miner Took His Own Life', *Daily Mirror*, 21 Jul. 1984, 9.
23 J. Worgan, 'A History of Wolstanton Colliery', Apedale Heritage Centre, n.d., nsmg.apedale.co.uk/collieries/w1.htm, accessed 20 Jun. 2023; C. Black, '£70,000 Pay Off for Miners', *Sandwell Evening Mail*, 12 Oct. 1985, 5.
24 Black, '£70,000 Pay Off for Miners'.
25 'Brothers to Blow Up Pit', *Staffordshire Sentinel*, 30 Dec. 1987, cover.
26 'Plaque Unveiled', *Staffordshire Sentinel*, 1 Feb. 1989, 10.
27 Black, '£70,000 Pay Off for Miners'.
28 I. Ladyman, 'Ten Miners Chase Each New Pit Job', *Staffordshire Sentinel*, 26 Apr. 1994, 5.
29 P. Holmes, 'Former Energy Secretary Keeps a Promise as Hem Heath Colliery Re-Opens', *Staffordshire Sentinel*, 27 Sep. 1994, 9; 'MP's Hem Heath Plea', *Potteries Advertiser*, 16 May 1996, 5; M. Corish, 'Buy-Out Saves 700 Pit Jobs', *Birmingham Mail*, 10 Jun. 1996, 15.
30 Vibration white finger was usually caused by the prolonged use of vibrating tools. In 1999, miners suffering from the condition

won a significant compensation claim, see: S. Milne, 'Miners Awarded £500m for "White Finger" Misery', *Guardian,* 23 Jan. 1999, www.theguardian.com/uk/1999/jan/23/2, accessed 25 Sep. 2023.

6. The Meaning of Camaraderie

1 See: M. Jones, *South Yorkshire Mining Villages: A History of the Region's Former Coal Mining Communities* (Barnsley, 2017), 154.
2 St Leonard's Church Dinnington, n.d., 'The History of St Leonard's Church Dinnington', www.stleonardsdinningtonsheffield.co.uk/history.html, accessed 1 Jun. 2023; J. Drinkwater, *The Changing Village* (Rotherham, 1981), 9.
3 Drinkwater, *The Changing Village*, 24.
4 'Nostalgia on Tuesday: Waves of Progress', *Yorkshire Post,* 15 Jan. 2019, www.yorkshirepost.co.uk/arts-and-culture/nostalgia-on-tuesday-waves-of-progress-157294, accessed 3 Jun. 2023. See, for example: Pilley, High Green, Treeton, Darfield, Royston, Thurnscoe, Goldthorpe, Wath upon Dearne and Cudworth in: Jones, *South Yorkshire Mining Villages,* 120–57.
5 W. Taylor, *South Yorkshire Pits* (Barnsley, 2012), 227; 'The New Dinnington Colliery', *Sheffield Daily Telegraph*, 5 Sep. 1904, 9.
6 Jones, *South Yorkshire Mining Villages,* 155.
7 Drinkwater, *The Changing Village*, 32.
8 Jones, *South Yorkshire Mining Villages*, 157.
9 See: 'Funeral of Mr. James England', *Sheffield Daily Telegraph*, 28 Dec. 1929, 5.

10 Dinnington Operatic Society, 'History of DOS', n.d., www.dinningtonoperatics.org/about-us/history-of-dos, accessed 1 Jun. 2023.
11 Ibid; 'Public Notices', *South Yorkshire Times,* 14 Oct. 1938, 3.
12 Dinnington Colliery Band, 'Our History', n.d., dinningtoncollieryband.co.uk/about, accessed 1 Jun. 2023.
13 'Wireless Telephony in a Yorkshire Pit', *Edinburgh Evening News*, 6 Sep. 1913, 4.
14 'Wireless Telephony at Dinnington', *Penistone, Stocksbridge and Hoyland Express*, 13 Sep. 1913, 3.
15 'Mining Education', *The Yorkshire Post,* 11 Oct. 1928, 4. This imposing red-brick building is now home to Rother Valley College.
16 *The Yorkshire Post,* 11 Oct. 1928, 4.
17 'Viscount Chelmsford at Wakefield', *Leeds Mercury*, 31 Jan. 1929, 5.
18 Taylor, *South Yorkshire Pits*, 229.
19 'Rotherham Harriers' Club', *Sheffield Daily Telegraph*, 29 Nov. 1887, 7.
20 '£13,800 Award for Miner', *Belfast Telegraph*, 20 Dec. 1956, 8.
21 '£17,600 Damages for Miner', *Daily Mirror*, 2 Jul. 1960, 3.
22 Ibid.
23 Ibid.
24 Taylor, *South Yorkshire Pits*, 229.
25 'A Night of Fire and Fury!', *Liverpool Echo*, 12 Nov. 1984, front page; '1,750 Join the Miners' Revolt', *Liverpool Echo*, 12 Nov. 1984, 2; 'Defiant Miners Spark Fury', *Aberdeen Evening Express*, 12 Nov. 1984, front page; 'Pit Fury as More Miners Go Back', *Reading Evening Post,* 13 Nov. 1984, front page.
26 J. Winterton and R. Winterton, *Coal, Crisis and Conflict: The 1984–85 Miners' Strike in Yorkshire* (Manchester, 1989), 201.
27 Ibid., 201–02.

28 In particular, 'hunger scabs' who returned to work in the last months of the strike received more empathy; see: Ibid., 200–01.

29 *Dinnington Digest*, newsletter, Oct. 1991, via: 'The End of an Era', Dinnington Heritage website, dinningtonheritage.weebly.com/the-end-of-an-era-1.html, accessed 13 Oct. 2023.

30 G. Wilbourne quoted in: *Dinnington Digest*, Oct 1991.

31 Hansard, HC Deb, 21 Oct. 1992, Vol. 212, Col. 471.

32 'Gay Vicar Says: "I'm Facing Death"', *Daily Mirror*, 1 Dec. 1994, 18.

33 *Simon's Cross*, dir. Charles Bruce, BBC North, 1995.

34 Simon's sister, Rosemary Bailey, wrote an account of her brother's experiences, in which she discussed some of the concerns raised about locals discovering Simon's diagnosis: R. Bailey, *Scarlet Ribbons: A Priest with AIDS* (London and New York, 1997), 78, 118.

35 'AIDS Vicar Dies', *Aberdeen Press and Journal*, 28 Nov. 1995, 5.

36 R. Bailey, 'A Parish Learns', *The Independent*, 15 Jan. 1995, www.independent.co.uk/arts-entertainment/a-parish-learns-1568069.html, accessed 25 Feb. 2024.

37 NUM Branch Secretary Granville Richardson quoted in: 'Nostalgia on Tuesday: The Price of Coal', *The Yorkshire Post*, 28 Feb. 2017, www.yorkshirepost.co.uk/whats-on/arts-and-entertainment/nostalgia-on-tuesday-the-price-of-coal-1781862, accessed 5 Jun. 2023.

38 Following the privatisation of British Coal in 1994, the RJB Mining company took control of most deep mines in the UK; see: BBC News, '"King Coal" Richard Budge, of RJB Mining, Dies Aged 69', 18 Jul. 2016, www.bbc.co.uk/news/uk-england-south-yorkshire-36825236, accessed 5 Jun. 2023.

39 *A Band for Britain*, BBC2, 2010.

40 Rotherham Metropolitan Borough Council, 'Dinnington Ward', n.d., www.rotherham.gov.uk/community-living/dinnington/2,

accessed 4 Jun. 2023; C. West, 'Dinnington Dance School and Florist's Left Gutted after Arson Attack', *Rotherham Advertiser*, 23 Apr. 2019, www.rotherhamadvertiser.co.uk/news/view,dinnington-dance-school-and-florists-left-gutted-after-arson-attack_31687.htm, accessed 5 Jun. 2023.

41 D. Smith, 'Foreword' in: Dinnington St John's Town Council, *Dinnington St John's Neighbourhood Plan 2016–2028 "From Tin Town to Great Town", A Vision for the Future of Our Community Delivered through the Implementation of a Dynamic Neighbourhood Plan*, Final Draft Referendum Version (Jan. 2021), 3–4, www.rotherham.gov.uk/downloads/file/775/01-neighbourhood-plan-draft-submission-version, accessed 5 Mar. 2024.

42 K. Hamilton, 'Town Traders Near Worksop Rally to Transform High Street after Missing Out on Levelling-Up Cash', *Worksop Guardian,* 24 Feb. 2023, www.worksopguardian.co.uk/news/people/town-traders-near-worksop-rally-to-transform-high-street-after-missing-out-on-levelling-up-cash-4040473, accessed 5 Jun. 2023; www.theyworkforyou.com/debates/?id=2023-03-21c.230.0, accessed 5 Mar. 2024.

43 G. Ford, 'I Grew Up in Forgotten South Yorkshire Town That's Got £12m Tory Cash to Spend but It All Feels Too Convenient', *Yorkshire Live*, 23 Mar. 2023, www.examinerlive.co.uk/news/news-opinion/grew-up-forgotten-south-yorkshire-26518146, accessed 6 Jun. 2023.

44 *Brassed Off*, dir. Mark Herman, 1996.

7. The Enemy Within

1 A. Travis, 'Battle of Orgreave: More Unreleased Police Files Uncovered', *Guardian*, 1 Mar. 2018, www.theguardian.com/politics/2018/mar/01/battle-of-orgreave-more-unreleased-police-files-uncovered, accessed 27 Sep. 2023. The exact number of police and pickets at Orgreave is unknown: in their article R. East, H. Power and P. A. Thomas give the higher figure of 8,000 police, see: 'The Death of Mass Picketing', *Journal of Law and Society*, 12/3 (1985), 305–19, 309; and Roger Geary gives the figure of 10,000 pickets in: *Policing Industrial Disputes: 1893 to 1985* (Cambridge, 1985), 140. The Orgreave Truth and Justice Campaign is still campaigning for an official government inquiry into the events of June 1984; see: Orgreave Truth and Justice Campaign, 'About', n.d., otjc.org.uk/about, accessed 26 Sep. 2023.

2 M. Pithers, 'The Battle of Orgreave', *Guardian*, 18 June 1984, www.theguardian.com/politics/1984/jun/18/past.features11, accessed 26 Sep. 2023.

3 A. Harding, '*Zulu* – the Film which Inspired UK and South Africa', *BBC News*, 10 Jun. 2014, www.bbc.co.uk/news/world-africa-27762901, accessed 26 Sep. 2023; D. P. O'Connor, 'Imperial Strategy and the Anglo-Zulu War of 1879', *The Historian*, 68/2 (2006), 285–304.

4 *Zulu, Theatrical Trailer* [online video], Paramount Pictures, 1964, uploaded 16 Jul. 2011, www.youtube.com/watch?v=JNV2M-WOgMM, accessed 5 Mar. 2024.

5 For an example of how the Zulus were termed 'savages' by the Victorian press, see: 'The Zulu Disaster', *The Graphic*, 15 Feb. 1879, 2.

6 Though Ormsby was not a miner himself, he organised support for the strike in County Durham.

7 A national strike was officially declared by the NUM on 12 March 1984.

8 Huw's experiences informed a later study of policing in the strike; see: M. Abdel-Rahim, *Strike Breaking in Essex: The Policing of Wivenhoe and the Essex Ports during the 1984 Miners' Strike* (London, 1985).

9 Geary, *Policing Industrial Disputes*, 122; the continuing legend of Saltley was evident in recent press coverage to mark the fiftieth anniversary of the action; see, for example: L. Elliot, 'Unions Don't Call the Shots Any More – But We'd All Be Better Off If They Did', *Guardian,* 10 Feb. 2022, www.theguardian.com/commentisfree/2022/feb/10/unions-do-not-call-shots-all-better-off-if--did, accessed 2 Mar. 2022; also: E. Ingram, '50 Years Since the Battle of Saltley Gate', *Tribune*, 5 Feb. 2022, tribunemag.co.uk/2022/02/battle-of-saltley-gate-1972-miners-strike-arthur-scargill-num, accessed 2 Mar. 2022.

10 K. Howells quoted in: M. Adeney and J. Lloyd, *The Miners' Strike, 1984–85: Loss Without Limit* (London, 1988), 113.

11 Economic Reconstruction Group, 'Final Report of the Nationalised Industries Police Group', PG/10/77/38, 8 July 1977, 24, source: Thatcher MSS (2/6/1/37), www.margaretthatcher.org/document/110795, accessed 5 Mar. 2024.

12 Ibid., 25.

13 J. Coulter, S. Miller and M. Walker, *A State of Siege, Politics and Policing of the Coalfields: Miners' Strike 1984* (London, 1984), 17; Geary, *Policing Industrial Disputes*, 128, 143; T. Bunyan, 'From Saltley to Orgreave via Brixton', *Journal of Law and Society,* 12/3 (1985), 293–303, 298.

14 Geary, *Policing Industrial Disputes*, 128. Tony Clement stated that he had 186 PSUs at Orgreave, each with an inspector, a sergeant and twenty constables, see: D. Conn, 'The Scandal of

Orgreave', *Guardian*, 18 May 2017, www.theguardian.com/politics/2017/may/18/scandal-of-orgreave-miners-strike-hillsborough-theresa-may, accessed 5 Mar. 2023.

15 See: IWM, 'How Modern Weapons Changed Combat in the First World War', n.d., www.iwm.org.uk/history/how-modern-weapons-changed-combat-in-the-first-world-war, accessed 10 Mar. 2023; Bunyan, 'From Saltley to Orgreave via Brixton', 293–303, 302.

16 M. Thatcher, 'Remarks on Orgreave Picketing', 30 May 1984, *Margaret Thatcher Foundation,* www.margaretthatcher.org/document/105691, accessed 5 Mar. 2024.

17 *Cleopatra*, dir. Joseph L. Mankiewicz, 1963.

18 See, for example, the diaries of Bruce Wilson and Arthur Wakefield: B. Elliot, ed., *Yorkshire's Flying Pickets in the 1984–85 Miners' Strike* (Barnsley, 2004); B. Elliot, ed., *The Miners' Strike Day by Day: The Illustrated Diary of Yorkshire Miner Arthur Wakefield* (Barnsley, 2002). Also: N. Strike, *Strike By Name: One Man's Part in the 1984–5 Miners' Strike* (London, 2009).

19 Conn, 'The Scandal of Orgreave'.

20 Orgreave Trial Transcripts, Sheffield Crown Court, 14 May 1985, 36, accessed via: Orgreave Truth and Justice website, otjc.org.uk/orgeave-trial-transcripts, accessed 5 Mar. 2024.

21 B. Wilson, '18th June', diary entry from the 18 Jun. 1984, 4–6.

22 Coulter, Miller and Walker, *A State of Siege*, 94.

23 Lesley Boulton interview, 1986, Sheffield City Archives, SY729/V5/1.

24 Ibid. The same Asda was later used as a location in the film *The Fully Monty*, dir. Peter Cattaneo, 1997; it has now been demolished.

25 *Labour Weekly*, 22 Jun. 1984, front page.

26 Lesley Boulton interview, 1986.

27 G. Shaw, 'What Happened Next . . .', *BBC Sheffield and South Yorkshire*, 2 Mar. 2009, www.bbc.co.uk/southyorkshire/content/articles/2009/03/02/lesley_boulton_orgreave_photo_feature.shtml, accessed 26 Sep. 2023.

28 A. Tempany, '"A Policeman Took a Full Swipe at My Head": Lesley Boulton at the Battle of Orgreave, 1984', *Guardian*, 16 Dec. 2016, www.theguardian.com/artanddesign/2016/dec/16/battle-orgreave-lesley-boulton-photograph, accessed 26 Sep. 2023.

29 R. Graef, *Talking Blues: The Police in Their Own Words* (London, 1989), 59–75.

30 Anonymous quote in: Graef, *Talking Blues*, 72.

31 One Metropolitan Police Sergeant alluded to a rape committed by two serving Met PCs during the miners' strike; see: Graef, *Talking Blues*, 71–72. For discussion of current problems within the Metropolitan Police, see, for example: M. Davis, 'Problems in Metropolitan Police "Not a Few Bad Apples", Chief Admits', *Independent*, 20 Apr. 2022, www.independent.co.uk/news/uk/metropolitan-police-cressida-dick-stephen-diana-johnson-mps-b2061495.html, accessed 17 Mar. 2023.

32 Anonymous quote in: Graef, *Talking Blues*, 61–62.

33 Ibid., 73.

34 C. Hart, 'Metaphor and Intertextuality in Media Framings of the (1984–1985) British Miners' Strike: A Multimodal Analysis', *Discourse and Communication*, 11/1 (2017), 3–30, 18.

35 Geary, *Policing Industrial Disputes*, 131.

36 M. Pithers, 'Blackest Day for Pit Strike Violence', *Guardian*, 19 Jun. 1984, front page.

37 Ibid.

38 See: E. Wade, 'The Miners and the Media: Themes in Newspaper Reporting', *Journal of Law and Society*, 12/3 (1985), 273–84.

39 *The Sun,* 15 May 1984, front page.

40 H. Arnold, 'The Truth', *Sun,* 19 Apr. 1989, front page.

41 P. Braund and A. Staniforth, 'Death Trap', *Daily Mirror,* 19 Jun. 1984, 4–5.

42 'The Real Assault Is on Democracy', *Daily Mail,* 19 Jun. 1984, 6.

43 See: P. Lazenby, 'Covering Coal in Yorkshire', in: G. Williams, ed., *Shafted: The Media, The Miners' Strike and the Aftermath* (London, 2009), 47–59, 50–51.

44 G. Peirce interviewed in: *The Battle for Orgreave* [online video], dir. Yvette Vanson, 1985, www.yvettevanson.com/the-battle-for-orgreave.html, accessed 5 Mar. 2024.

45 The exact number of those killed is disputed, ranging from eleven to eighteen people.

46 *The Battle for Orgreave*, dir. Yvette Vanson, 1985.

47 See: Conn, 'The Scandal of Orgreave'.

48 Several miners had the good fortune to be represented by Michael Mansfield QC, a barrister with a formidable record in human rights litigation, which would later include representing the family of Stephen Lawrence, members of the Birmingham Six and victims of the Hillsborough disaster.

49 Orgreave Trial Transcripts, Sheffield Crown Court, 14 May 1985, via Orgreave Truth and Justice website, otjc.org.uk/orgeave-trial-transcripts, accessed 5 Mar. 2024.

50 D. Rose, 'Orgreave Police Bungled – Secret File', *Observer,* 23 Jun. 1991, 3.

51 *We Are Waverley – Autumn 2020 – A Project by Harworth* [online video], Harworth Group plc, 2020, www.youtube.com/watch?v=nslvHlXWA3Y, accessed 10 Mar. 2023.

52 S. Swire, *Diary of an MP's Wife: Inside and Outside Power* (London, 2020), 265.

8. The Rescuer

1 *Our Friends in the North,* dir. Simon Cellan-Jones, BBC2, 11 Mar. 1996.
2 C. Phillips, 'The Black Pompeii', *Hull Daily Mail,* 22 Oct. 1966, 5.
3 'The Long Agony at Lofthouse', *Daily Mirror,* 27 Mar. 1973, 2.
4 BBC News, 'Rescuers Recall Missing Lofthouse Colliery Miners', 21 Mar. 2013, www.bbc.co.uk/news/uk-england-leeds-21863448, accessed 14 Feb. 2023.
5 A. J. Cronin, *The Stars Look Down* (London, 1935).
6 See: Coal Mines Act, 1911, 1 & 2 Geo. 5. Ch. 50, available at: www.dmm.org.uk/books/cma11-00.htm, accessed 27 Feb. 2024.
7 See: M. Smith, '"We Thought There Was No Way Out." The Last Survivor of Scotland's Greatest Mines Rescue', *Herald,* 29 Aug. 2020, www.heraldscotland.com/news/18676856.we-thought-no-way-out-last-survivor-scotlands-greatest-mines-rescue, accessed 16 Jan. 2024.
8 *The Brave Don't Cry,* dir. Philip Leacock, 1952.
9 *Sheffield Daily Telegraph,* 20 Jun. 1902, 4.
10 'Lancashire Mines New Rescue Station', *Blackburn Times,* 25 Nov. 1933, 5.
11 'Mines Rescue Station', *Liverpool Echo,* 18 Nov. 1933, 16.
12 'Pit Rescue Workers' Bravery', *Liverpool Daily Post,* 8 Feb. 1950, 5.
13 Ibid.
14 The Casey Group Ltd, *Orchard House,* brochure, n.d., casey.myzen.co.uk/images/Orchard_House/Brochure_Pages_web.pdf, accessed 25 Sep. 2023.
15 R. Silverwood, 'Pits Have Gone, But There's Still a Role for Mansfield's Mines Rescue Service', *The Chad,* 24 May 2021,

www.chad.co.uk/news/people/pits-have-gone-but-theres-still-a-role-for-mansfields-mines-rescue-service-3248517, accessed 27 Feb. 2024.

16 *Mines Rescue Station* [online video], British Pathé, 1952, uploaded 13 Apr. 2014, www.youtube.com/watch?v=ddVpVU9KY9Q, accessed 12 Oct. 2023.

17 L. Houghton, 'In Memory of Nicola: Recalling the Devastating Tactics Used to Break the Miners' Strike', *Yorkshire Bylines*, 6 Mar. 2022, yorkshirebylines.co.uk/region/in-memory-of-nicola-recalling-the-devastating-tactics-used-to-break-the-miners-strike, accessed 16 Jan. 2024.

18 Allerton Bywater Parish Council, 'Coal Mining in Allerton Bywater', n.d., www.allertonbywaterparishcouncil.co.uk/history/allerton-bywater-colliery, accessed 27 Feb. 2024.

19 P. Hetherington, 'Millennium Village Put on Hold', *Guardian* online, 20 Aug. 2002, www.theguardian.com/uk/2002/aug/20/politics.communities, accessed 25 Sep. 2023.

20 'Coal Not Dole' was a popular slogan used by striking miners and their supporters during the 1984–85 strike; see reference to Kay Sutcliffe's poem in Chapter 11.

21 Hansard, HC Deb, 13 Jan. 1999, Vol. 323, Col. 416.

22 *The Full Monty*, dir. Peter Cattaneo, 1997.

9. Fathers, Sons and Picket Lines

1 A term used to describe the appearance of miners who struggled to remove the coal dust from around their eyes in the pithead baths. Some men remembered intentionally leaving these traces of the pit on their faces as young miners, as a signifier of their masculinity above ground.

2 C. Matthews and C. Hartwell, *Model Villages of the Nottinghamshire Coalfield* (Moorgreen, 2022), 25.

3 *Kes,* dir. Ken Loach, 1969.

4 Nottinghamshire County Council, 'History of Bestwood', n.d., www.nottinghamshire.gov.uk/culture-leisure/country-parks/history-of-bestwood, accessed 13 Jun. 2023.

5 'Bestwood's Lucky Break', *COAL,* Dec. 1948, 29.

6 Located just outside of Birmingham, Longbridge's so-called shadow factory had given wings to the Hurricanes and Lancasters that policed the skies above Britain during the Second World War; see: J. Griffin, 'Special Report: How Longbridge Defied the Nazis to Help Britain Win World War Two', *Birmingham Live,* 24 Sep. 2011, www.birminghammail.co.uk/news/local-news/special-report-how-longbridge-defied-161993, accessed 9 Jun. 2023.

7 Historian Norma Gregory has done much to highlight the role of black miners in the British mining industry; see: Black Miners Museum, blackcoalminers.com.

8 In an article which appeared in the radical men's magazine *Achilles Heel* in 1982, miner Kevin Devaney recalled using humour 'to keep an emotional situation in control', when he and a colleague carried a stretcher out of the pit, see: K. Devaney, 'Mining – A World Apart', in: V. J. Seidler, ed., *The Achilles Heel Reader: Men, Sexual Politics and Socialism* (London, 1991), 151–60, 157.

9 P. Ray, 'Sportsmen's Pit', *COAL,* Nov. 1958, 9.

10 N. R. Smith quoted in: Ray, 'Sportsmen's Pit'.

11 'It's a Good Future Now Mate', *Coal News,* 127, HQ & Kent edn, Jan. 1972, 4.

12 As Tony explained, this was a patented horizontal bunker mounted on rails, used to collect coal if there was a problem outbye and the belts were not running.

13 '£90,000 Miners' Welfare Centre Opens at Hucknall Today', *Nottingham Guardian*, 25 May 1963, 6.

14 '£90,000 Centre Is Opened for Hucknall Miners', *Nottingham Evening News*, 27 May 1963, 7.

15 *Nottingham Evening Post,* 23 Feb. 1972, cover.

16 Figures taken from: H. Paterson, *Look Back in Anger: The Miners' Strike in Nottinghamshire 30 Years On* (Nottingham, 2014), 11.

17 'Stoppage at Linby Colliery', *Hucknall Star and Advertiser,* 30 Mar. 1900, 8.

18 See, for example: J. Owens, 'Introduction' in: J. Owens, ed., *Miners 1984–1994: A Decade of Endurance* (Edinburgh, 1994), 6–7; Paterson, *Look Back in Anger,* 87–88.

19 See: A. J. Richards, *Miners on Strike: Class Solidarity and Division in Britain* (Oxford, 1996), 42, 180; J. Winterton and R. Winterton, *Coal, Crisis and Conflict: The 1984–85 Miners' Strike in Yorkshire* (Manchester, 1989), 75–77; P. Gibbon, 'Analysing the British Miners' Strike of 1984–5', *Economy and Society,* 17/2 (1988),139–94, 170–76; J. Phillips, 'The Meanings of Coal Community in Britain Since 1947', *Contemporary British History,* 32/1 (2018), 39–59, 47–48; Paterson, *Look Back in Anger,* 56.

20 *Spectator,* 14 Apr. 1984, 5; Richards, *Miners on Strike,* 44, 54; Paterson, *Look Back in Anger,* 19–20. During the General Strike in 1926, George Spencer, a Labour MP and ex-President of the Nottinghamshire Miners' Association, led a revolt and formed an alternative miners' union in Nottinghamshire, which was joined by the majority of Nottinghamshire's miners. It was over a decade before the Nottinghamshire Miners' Industrial Union, or 'Spencer Union', was brought into the Mineworkers Federation of Great Britain; see: D. Gilbert, 'The Landscape of Spencerism: Mining Politics in the Nottinghamshire Coalfield, 1910–1947', in: A. Campbell, N. Fishman and

D. Howell, eds, *Miners, Unions and Politics, 1910–47* (Aldershot, 1996), 175–98.

21 For a discussion of the formation of the Union of Democratic Mineworkers, see: Winterton and Winterton, *Coal, Crisis and Conflict*, 226–35.

22 Ibid, 70; H. Beynon, 'Introduction", in: H. Beynon, ed., *Digging Deeper: Issues in the Miners' Strike* (London, 1985), 1–26, 6–7.

23 Winterton and Winterton, *Coal, Crisis and Conflict*, 73.

24 See: 'Radio Arthur – Nottingham', The Pirate Archive, n.d., www.thepiratearchive.net/arthur, accessed 13 Oct. 2023.

25 R. Ratcliffe, 'Striking Miners Blot Out Radio Trent for "Radio Free Arthur"', *Sunday Times*, 25 Nov. 1984.

26 'Hunt On for Pirate Radio Men', *Nottinghamshire Free Press*, 31 Aug. 1984.

27 'Industry Gloom for Hucknall', *Nottingham Recorder*, 3 Dec. 1987, 3.

28 'Historic Engine Streams Back into Action', *Nottingham Evening Post,* 11 May 1996, 15.

29 As Labour Party politician Peter Hain acknowledged in his memoir, during the strike Nottingham Forest's manager Brian Clough made the first donation to the Miners' Families Christmas Appeal in December 1984 to support strikers. See: P. Hain, *Outside In* (London, 2012), 233.

30 See: J. Emery, 'After Coal: Affective-Temporal Processes of Belonging and Alienation in the Deindustrializing Nottinghamshire Coalfield, UK', *Frontiers in Sociology*, 5/28 (2020), 1–16, 11, doi:10.3389/fsoc.2020.00038; J. Emery, '"That Once Romantic Now Utterly Disheartening (Former) Colliery Town": The Affective Politics of Heritage, Memory, Place and Regeneration in Mansfield, UK', *Journal of Urban Cultural Studies,* 6/2 (2019), 219–40, repository copy, eprints.whiterose.ac.uk/156675, accessed 5 Mar. 2024; G. Nanrah, 'A Guide to the Memorials

Dedicated to the History of Coal Mining across Nottinghamshire', *Nottingham Post,* 27 Aug. 2020, www.nottinghampost.com/news/history/gallery/guide-memorials-dedicated-history-coal-4458318, accessed 26 Sep. 2023.

31 P. Cox, 'Memorial Bench Unveiled for Striking Miner Who Died at Ollerton Colliery', *Chad* online, 7 Mar. 2023, www.chad.co.uk/news/people/memorial-bench-unveiled-for-striking-miner-who-died-at-ollerton-colliery-4053542, accessed 13 Jun. 2023.

10. Man of the People

1 G. Hendrie, *The Parish of Dalmellington, Its History, Antiquities and Objects of Interest* (Dalmellington,1889), 26–27, quoted in: East Ayrshire Council, *Dalmellington, East Ayrshire, Outline Chronology,* n.d., 22, www.east-ayrshire.gov.uk/Resources/PDF/D/Dalmellington-Chronology.pdf, accessed 5 Mar. 2024.

2 East Ayrshire Council, *Dalmellington.*

3 J. Strawhorn and W. Boyd, *Ayrshire: The Third Statistical Account of Scotland* (Edinburgh, 1951), 736.

4 J. McPhail, 'Benwhat – Random Reflections', in: D. L. Reid, *The Last Miners of Ayrshire's Doon Valley* (Beith, 2016), 73–78, 75.

5 Strawhorn and Boyd, *Ayrshire,* 738.

6 Ibid.

7 Ibid., 739.

8 Ibid., 736–37.

9 Ibid., 739; D. L. Reid, *The Last Miners of Ayrshire's Doon Valley* (Beith, 2016), 25–26.

10 Strawhorn and Boyd, *Ayrshire,* 739.

11 A. Moffat, *My Life with the Miners* (London, 1965), 10.

12 *Mining Review 2nd Year No. 11,* dir. Peter Pickering, 1949.

13 Alfred Hayes's poem about the Swedish-American Labour activist Joe Hill, who was executed by a firing squad in Utah in 1915, was set to music by Earl Robinson in 1936. Robeson's rendition of the song has since become a popular choice amongst Labour politicians appearing on BBC Radio 4's *Desert Island Discs*; see: M. Weaver and G. Arnett, 'Will Theresa May Toe Party Line on Desert Island Discs?', *Guardian*, 21 Nov. 2014, www.theguardian.com/tv-and-radio/2014/nov/21/theresa-may-desert-island-discs, accessed 2 Oct. 2023.

14 The Tower Mine was closed by the Coal Board in 1964.

15 'National Coal Board, West Ayr Area Progress Report', *Irvine Herald,* 25 Jan. 1963, 4; 'Local Machines Boost Their Output', *The Wishaw Press and Advertiser,* 18 Dec. 1964, 15.

16 See: Canmore National Record of the Historic Environment, 'Killoch Colliery', n.d., canmore.org.uk/site/42745/killoch-colliery, accessed 18 Jul. 2023.

17 W. Ashworth, *The History of the British Coal Industry*, Vol. 5, *1946–1982: The Nationalized Industry* (Oxford, 1986), 261–62.

18 Ibid.

19 Incidentally, the spelling of Humphrey Davy Road deviates from his actual name which was 'Humphry Davy'.

20 Hansard, HC, 12 Dec. 1962, Electricity (Borrowing Powers) (Scotland) Bill, Vol. 669, Col. 512.

21 Ibid.

22 L. Huckfield quoted in: 'Coal Board One of Worst Landlords, Says MP', *Coventry Evening Telegraph*, 25 Jul. 1967, 11; 'NCB Investigates Complaints by Bedworth Tenants', *Coventry Evening Telegraph*, 15 May 1967, 7.

23 'Coal Board One of Worst Landlords', *Coventry Evening Telegraph.*

24 'Sympathetic Ear for Tenants', *Coventry Evening Telegraph*, 17 Aug. 1967, 17.

25 Ibid.

26 Ibid.

27 'NCB Complaints Caravan Plan', *Coventry Evening Telegraph*, 18 Nov. 1967, 10.

28 'Lord Robens Asked to Open Bedworth Centre', *Coventry Evening Telegraph*, 1 Mar. 1968, 25.

29 'New Amenity Targets by NCB Tenants', *Coventry Evening Telegraph*, 12 Feb. 1968, 12.

30 'NCB Tapping New Seams for Recruits', *Coventry Evening Telegraph*, 12 Feb. 1971, 23.

31 'Auld Lang Syne' is a traditional Scottish folk song. The lyrics are attributed to Robert Burns, though the composer is unknown. It is traditionally sung at midnight on Hogmanay (New Year's Eve).

32 'A Rehabilitation Centre for the Casualties in the "Battle for Coal"', *Illustrated London News*, 30 Aug. 1947, 238–39.

33 The solidarity Londoners showed the miners in 1972 was to continue in the strikes of 1974 and 1984–85; see: D. Kelliher, *Making Cultures of Solidarity: London and the 1984–5 Miners' Strike* (Abingdon, 2021), 24–25.

34 'If Somebody Put a Light to This Lot . . .', *Sunday Mirror*, 1 Nov. 1970, 17.

35 C. Campbell, 'Pit Pickets Are Facing Big Brother', *Coventry Evening Telegraph*, 23 Mar. 1984, 7.

36 'Miners Spat at "Wrong" Band', *Bedworth Echo*, 21 Jun. 1984, front page.

37 I. Chadband, 'Mine Jobs Pledge', *Coventry Evening Telegraph*, 22 Aug. 1984, 13; T. Quirke, 'On Dawn Patrol with the Angry Men of Coal', *Birmingham Mail*, 28 Mar. 1984, 6.

38 D. Pearce quoted in: Quirke, 'On Dawn Patrol with the Angry Men of Coal'.

39 'Outbye' was a term used to denote working away from the coalface, as opposed to working 'inbye', towards the coalface.

40 'It's a Record', *Aberdeen Press and Journal*, 3 Jul. 1985, 6.
41 'Breakaway Pit Extends Battle', *Birmingham Mail*, 6 Nov. 1985, 9.
42 M. Taylor, 'Daw Mill Colliery Closure Marks End of an Era for 650 Miners', *Guardian*, 7 Mar. 2013, www.theguardian.com/business/2013/mar/07/daw-mill-colliery-closure-650-miners, accessed 18 Jul. 2023.
43 BBC News, 'Daw Mill: Hundreds of Jobs Go at Fire-Hit Mine', 7 Mar. 2013, www.bbc.co.uk/news/uk-england-coventry-warwickshire-21696875, accessed 18 Jul. 2023; 'Daw Mill Coal Mine Fire Extinguished', 15 May 2013, www.bbc.co.uk/news/uk-england-coventry-warwickshire-22547678, accessed 18 Jul. 2023.
44 J. Ellis, 'Pupils' Safety Awards', *Heartland Evening News*, 6 Jun. 1996, 5; 'Furry Friends at Bramcote Barracks', *Heartland Evening News*, 18 Jun. 1996, 8; 'Christmas Lights Set for the Big Switch On', *Heartland Evening News*, 18 Nov. 1996, 11.
45 J. Linstead, 'Dream Comes True for Drugs Battle', *Heartland Evening News*, 4 Oct. 1996, 3.
46 'Mick Boost for Mayor', *Heartland Evening News*, 14 May 1997, 15; K. Hambridge, 'Dream is a Reality', *Heartland Evening News*, 26 Feb. 1997, 3.
47 Linstead, 'Dream Comes True for Drugs Battle'; Hambridge, 'Dream is a Reality'.
48 Hambridge, 'Dream is a Reality'.
49 Ibid.
50 J. Linstead, 'Back on the Road!', *Heartland Evening News*, 11 March 1998, front page.
51 Quoted in: Linstead, 'Back on the Road!'.
52 'Nuneaton's Mobile Advice Service for Children Faces Axe', *Coventry Live*, 22 Oct. 2009, www.coventrytelegraph.net/news/coventry-news/nuneatons-mobile-advice-service-children-3075315, accessed 18 Jul. 2023.

53 C. Harrison, 'Nuneaton and Bedworth Has Highest Booze and Drug Referrals in Warwickshire – Including Children', *Coventry Live*, 16 Apr. 2023, www.coventrytelegraph.net/news/local-news/nuneaton-bedworth-highest-booze-drug-26667599, accessed 17 Jul. 2023.

54 J. Linstead, 'John Glass Reflects on His Mayoral Year', *Heartland Evening News*, 27 May 1997, 10.

55 There is a 'Blue Labour' campaign group, established by Maurice Glasman in 2010, who describe their socialism as 'both radical and conservative'; see: www.bluelabour.org/about-us, accessed 1 Mar. 2024.

56 R. Burns, 'A Man's a Man for A' That' (1795).

11. The Men of Kent

1 R. Williams, *People of the Black Mountains 1: The Beginning* (London, 1989); R. Williams, *People of the Black Mountains 2: The Eggs of the Eagle* (London, 1990); R. Llewellyn, *How Green Was My Valley* (London, 1939).

2 See, for example: D. Hornsby, 'A New Dialect for a New Village: Evidence of Koinéization in East Kent', in: L. Wright, ed., *Southern English Varieties Then and Now* (Berlin and Boston, 2018), 74–109.

3 L. P. Abercrombie, 'The Kent Coalfields', *Journal of the Royal Society of Arts*, 79/4091 (1931), 504–19, 505.

4 'Miner's Death in Snowdown Colliery', *Dover Express and East Kent News*, 1 Jun. 1934, 19.

5 Ibid.

6 Ibid.

7 Ibid.

8 See, for example, adverts for 'Flats to Let or Wanted', *Dover Express and East Kent News,* 20 May 1932, front page.

9 H. Keenan, 'No Miners Need Apply', *Dover Express and East Kent News,* 20 Nov. 1931, 12.

10 Abercrombie, 'The Kent Coalfields', 506.

11 'Kent's First Colliery Town', *Kentish Express and Ashford News,* 12 Nov. 1927, 7.

12 'Paradise for Miners', *Westminster Gazette,* 21 Feb. 1927, 5.

13 'The Development of East Kent', *Dover Express and East Kent News,* 25 May 1928, 7; 'The Lesson of Aylesham', *Dover Express and East Kent News,* 23 May 1930, 7.

14 See: V. L. Hughes, 'A Social Survey of the East Kent Coalfield', PhD Thesis (London School of Economics and Political Science, 1934), etheses.lse.ac.uk/4030, 200—01, 206.

15 'Aylesham's Recreation Ground', *Dover Express and East Kent News,* 6 Jun. 1930, 4.

16 'Would Mayor's Gold Chain Be Safe at Aylesham?', *Dover Express and East Kent News,* 15 Aug. 1930, 12.

17 See: Hughes, 'A Social Survey of the East Kent Coalfield', 227–28.

18 'Miner and Cabbages', *Dover Express and East Kent News,* 16 May 1930, 9; 'Miners' Broccoli Raid', *Dover Express and East Kent News,* 5 May 1933, 9.

19 A. K. Mowll quoted in: 'Poaching Miners', *Dover Express and East Kent News,* 17 Jan. 1930, 9.

20 Under the scheme, 10 per cent of men aged between eighteen and twenty-five were conscripted to serve in Britain's coal mines as opposed to the armed forces, with their fate determined by an anonymous ballot. Other men, the 'optants', volunteered to serve in the mines as opposed to the armed forces.

21 See, for example, David Day's memoir of his experiences as a Bevin Boy at Littleton Colliery in Cannock Chase, Staffordshire:

D. Day, *The Bevin Boy* (Kineton, 1975); also: D. Day, 'Reluctant Boys from the Black Stuff: Fifty Years Ago, Bevin Boys Were Born. David Day Looks Back on Dark Days as a Wartime Pit Conscript', *Independent*, 31 Dec. 1993, www.independent.co.uk/voices/reluctant-boys-from-the-black-stuff-fifty-years-ago-bevin-boys-were-born-david-day-looks-back-on-dark-days-as-a-wartime-pit-conscript-1470090.html, accessed 3 Oct. 2023.

22 *Bevin Boys* [online video], British Pathé, 1945, www.british-pathe.com/asset/78293. Accessed 3 Oct. 2023.

23 Ibid.

24 A. Shaffer, *So What Did You Expect? A Memoir* (London, 2001), 15–16.

25 See, for example: 'Transcript of interview with Rev. Ivor H., conducted at his home on 2 Oct. 2002 by Ann Kneif', in: M. A. Kneif, 'Directed to the Mines: The Bevin Boys, 1943 to 1948', PhD Thesis (University of Kent, 2005), uk.bl.ethos.756105, accessed 5 Mar. 2024; also: 'Ninian Winder "Ian" McInnes Oral History', 2 Feb. 2000, IWM, 20061, www.iwm.org.uk/collections/item/object/80018815, accessed 13 Oct. 2023.

26 M. Pitt, *The World on Our Backs: The Kent Miners and the 1972 Miners' Strike* (London, 1979), 17.

27 Ibid., 19.

28 See: 'Coal Not Dole', Mainly Norfolk: English Folk and Other Good Music, n.d., mainlynorfolk.info/watersons/songs/coalnotdole.html, accessed 12 Oct. 2023.

29 Chislet Colliery had closed in 1969, with most of its workforce transferred to the three remaining Kent pits: Betteshanger, Snowdown, and Tilmanstone.

30 'Boos and Jeers for Pit Wives', *Leicester Mercury*, 26 Mar. 1984, 5.

31 See: M. Plummer, 'Miners Started Picketing the Dock Gates at Wivenhoe in 1984', *Daily Gazette*, 12 Mar. 2021, www.

gazette-news.co.uk/news/19153479.north-essex-became-focal-point-miners-started-picketing-dock-gates-wivenhoe, accessed 3 Mar. 2024.

32 *Name changed to preserve anonymity.

33 P. Wintour, 'Coalfields Split on Return', *Guardian*, 2 Mar. 1985, 30; M. Weaver, 'Kent Miners Expected to Go Back on Monday', *Daily Telegraph*, 9 Mar. 1985, 1, 36. The number of miners sacked disproportionately impacted Scotland, where 206 miners were dismissed out of 15,000 men on strike, versus 800 dismissed out of 192,000 strikers in England and Wales. As a result of the Miners' Strike (Pardons) (Scotland) Act 2022, miners convicted of certain offences committed during the strike were pardoned; see: J. Phillips, 'Strategic Injustice and the 1984–85 Miners' Strike in Scotland', *Industrial Law Journal*, 52/2 (2023), 283–311, 292, doi.org/10.1093/indlaw/dwac017. To date, miners in England and Wales have received no such pardon.

34 'Miners Accept Pit Closedown', *Dover Express*, 23 Oct. 1987, 11.

35 P. Wilson quoted in: '"The Lads Have Been Misled"', *Dover Express*, 23 Oct. 1987, 11.

36 Anon., '"Bitter and Angry", It's Your Opinion', *East Kent Mercury*, 21 Sep. 1989, 8.

37 D. Sneller quoted in: J. Harbidge, 'Savage Blow', *Dover Express*, 25 Aug. 1989, 5.

38 On 6 March 1987, *Herald of Free Enterprise*, a car ferry sailing from the Belgian port of Zeebrugge to Dover capsized killing 193 people, many of whom lived in East Kent. On 22 September 1989, the IRA detonated a bomb at the Royal Marines School of Music in Deal Barracks, killing eleven marines and injuring a further twenty-one.

39 G. Lings quoted in: 'Let Flowers Grow into Friendships', *East Kent Mercury*, 28 Sep. 1989, 24.

40 A. Onions, 'Shameful Scuttling', Letters, *Dover Express*, 2 Aug. 1991, 2.

41 S. Lennon, 'Aylesham, between Canterbury and Dover, Has Become "Village of Strangers" with So Many New-Builds, Say Residents', *Kent Online*, 20 Apr. 2023, www.kentonline.co.uk/dover/news/there-are-so-many-new-builds-its-become-a-village-of-str-285630, accessed 3 Oct. 2023.

42 K. Sutcliffe, 'Coal Not Dole' (1984).

12. The Price of Coal

1 G. Orwell, *The Road to Wigan Pier* (London, 2001), 32.

2 See: C. Holdsworth, 'Dr John Thomas Arlidge and Victorian Occupational Medicine', *Medical History*, 42 (1998), 458–75, 468; A. Meiklejohn, 'History of Lung Diseases of Coal Miners in Great Britain: Part III, 1920–1952', *British Journal of Industrial Medicine,* 9/3 (1952), 208–20, 208–09; A. L. Cochrane, 'Tuberculosis and Coalworkers' Pneumoconiosis', *British Journal of Tuberculosis and Diseases of the Chest*, 48/4 (1954), 274–85; J. E. Martin, 'Coal Miners' Pneumoconiosis', *American Journal of Public Health*, 44/5 (1954), 581–91.

3 See: H. Francis and D. Smith, *The Fed: A History of the South Wales Miners in the Twentieth Century* (London, 1981), 439.

4 A description used by Charles Fletcher, Director of the Pneumoconiosis Research Unit, see: C. Fletcher, 'Fighting the "Modern Black Death"', *The Listener*, 28 Sep. 1950, 407–08.

5 'Deterrent to the Young', *Thanet Advertiser and Echo,* 26 Mar. 1946, front page.

6 See: J. E. Cotes, 'The Medical Research Council Pneumoconiosis Research Unit, 1945–1985: A Short History and Tribute', *Occupational Medicine,* 50/6 (2000), 440–49.

7 'Scientists Fight Against Dust', *COAL*, Jul. 1947, 5–7.

8 See: Cotes, 'The Medical Research Council Pneumoconiosis Research Unit', 441–44. During the 1950s, mass radiography work was also conducted by the Industrial Health Survey Team at King's College Newcastle in partnership with the Durham Regional Hospital Board, to investigate the prevalence of pneumoconiosis amongst miners in the region; see: W. R. Garside, *The Durham Miners, 1919–1960* (London, 1971), 480.

9 'Scientists Fight against Dust', *COAL*, July 1947, 7.

10 'Miners' Dust Disease Is Being Overcome', *Western Mail,* 25 Sep. 1952, 5.

11 Francis and Smith, *The Fed*, 439. Over the years, various theories have been put forward as to why there was a high incidence of pneumoconiosis amongst the miners of South Wales, including prolonged exposure to coal dust due to the low average age of workers starting at the coalface in the area's pits; the length of time these miners had spent in the industry as a result of few local alternatives, and the mine conditions, which were often old, deep and dry. The high rate of pneumoconiosis amongst workers in the anthracite pits in the West of the region led researchers to query whether the 'rank' of coal had a bearing on the problem, with anthracite having a higher carbonaceous content compared to steam coal and bituminous coal. However, it was later found that the incidence of pneumoconiosis correlated with miners' exposure to dust, which was particularly high when using coal-cutting machinery, and this had been introduced earlier in the anthracite mines. Likewise, it was argued that as anthracite mines

had a lower risk of explosion, they were not as well ventilated. See discussion in: A. R. Ness, L. A. Reynolds and E. M. Tansey, eds, *Population-Based Research in South Wales: The MRC Pneumoconiosis Research Unit and the MRC Epidemiology Unit*, Wellcome Witnesses to Twentieth Century Medicine, Vol. 13 (2002), 7–8, 16; also: N. Woodward, 'Why Did South Wales Miners Have High Mortality? Evidence from the Mid-Twentieth Century', *Welsh History Review/Cylchgrawn Hanes Cymru,* 20/1 (2000), 116–42, 126–28.

12 See: 'Miners to March Through Cardiff', *Western Mail,* 16 Sep. 1953, 5; also: 'Miners Acclaim Industrial Action Threats', *Western Mail,* 19 Oct. 1953, 3.

13 Back in 1935, miners of the Great Mountain Lodge in Wales had raised concerns over the amount of dust at the pitheads of some collieries, which they felt posed a significant danger to the health not only of miners but also of local residents; see: 'Alleged Dust at Pit-Head', *Western Mail,* 24 Jul. 1935, 6.

14 'Miners Acclaim Industrial Action Threats', *Western Mail,* 19 Oct. 1953, 3.

15 Fatal fires occurred at Whitehaven 'William' Colliery, Cumberland, in 1947; at Creswell Colliery, Derbyshire, in 1950; at Auchengeich Colliery, Lanarkshire, in 1959; and at Michael Colliery, Fife, in 1967.

16 National Coal Board, *How to Use Your Self-Rescuer,* pamphlet (London and Maidstone, 1972), accessed via: 'Self-Rescuer', Mining Heritage website, miningheritage.co.uk/self-rescuer, accessed 13 Oct. 2023.

17 W. Ashworth, *The History of the British Coal Industry,* Vol. 5, *1946–1982: The Nationalized Industry* (Oxford, 1986), 561.

18 Miners' nystagmus, believed to be caused by poor lighting underground, caused miners' eyes to oscillate and led to photophobia, headaches, insomnia and depression. See: S. W.

Fisher, 'Medical Aspects of Coal-Mining', *Proceedings of the Royal Society of Medicine*, 38/2 (1944), 59–64, 61. In 1929, 9,838 cases of nystagmus were recorded amongst British miners; see: W. J. Roche, 'An Investigation of Miners' Nystagmus', *British Journal of Ophthalmology*, 15/4 (1931), 211–44, 211. In 1947, the Coal Mines Act, Coal Mines (Lighting) General Regulations improved standards of illumination underground; see: Garside, *The Durham Miners*, 479.

19 'Beat' conditions included subcutaneous cellulitis of the hand (beat hand); subcutaneous cellulitis or acute bursitis arising at or about the knee (beat knee) or elbow (beat elbow), and inflammation of the synovial lining of the wrist joint and tendon sheaths. See: Fisher, 'Medical Aspects of Coal-Mining', 61.

20 See: A. McIvor and R. Johnston, *Miners' Lung: A History of Dust Disease in British Coal Mining* (Abingdon, 2016), 244.

21 Ibid.

22 See: Garside, *The Durham Miners*, 477; also: McIvor and Johnston, *Miners' Lung*, 167–76.

23 B. L. Coombes, 'Terrible Toll Exacted by Dust Disease', *Porthcawl Guardian*, 13 Apr. 1951, 4.

24 Ibid.

25 McIvor and Johnston, *Miners' Lung*, 312.

26 D. Douglas, 'Production and Safety', Postbag, *Coal News*, 174, S. Yorks. and all edns, Jan. 1976, 11. *Coal News* misspelled Douglass, as 'Douglas'.

27 J. Collinson quoted in: 'Production and Safety'.

28 McIvor and Johnston, *Miners' Lung*, 245.

29 See also: E. Gibbs, *Coal Country: The Meaning and Memory of Deindustrialization in Postwar Scotland* (London, 2021), 174.

30 'Inquest into Miner's Death', *East Kent Mercury*, 13 Apr. 1989, 6.

31 See, for example, National Union of Mineworkers advert in: *Thanet Times*, 23 Feb. 1971, 10.

32 Francis and Smith, *The Fed*, 479.

33 'Killer Pit Dust Men Rush for Cash Claims', *Newcastle Evening Chronicle*, 15 Jul. 1974, 5.

34 'Deterrent to the Young', *Thanet Advertiser and Echo,* 26 Mar. 1946, front page; 'Pneumoconiosis Was Cause of Death', *South Wales Gazette*, 18 Feb. 1955, 2; 'Pneumoconiosis Killed Ex-Miner', *Leicester Evening Mail*, 12 Jan. 1961, 6; 'Miner Died from Pneumoconiosis', *Buckinghamshire Examiner*, 3 Sep. 1965, 2; 'Miner Had "The Dust"', *Rugeley Times*, 7 Dec. 1974, 5; 'Disease Death', *Staffordshire Sentinel*, 4 May 1990, 9; 'Disease Death', *Staffordshire Sentinel*, 16 Jun. 1990, 5; 'Ex-Coal Miner – Inquest', *Nottingham Evening Post*, 1 Mar. 1996, 5; 'Inquest Verdict', *Carmarthen Journal*, 5 May 1999, 13; 'Coal Miner's Disease Death', *Bury Free Press*, 23 Jul. 1999, 25.

35 See, for example: P. Linford, 'Suffering Ex-Miners Refused All Benefits', *South Wales Echo*, 13 Jul. 1994, 6–7.

36 Ibid.

37 See, for example: P. Linford, '"Dust Killed Dad after All-Clear"', *South Wales Echo*, 15 Jul. 1994, 10; H. Ward, 'Miners Miss Out on Benefits', *Nottingham Evening Post*, 9 Jan. 1996, 10.

38 J. Flinn, 'MPs Back Pit Payout Call', *Newcastle Journal*, 25 Nov. 1994, 17.

39 Health and Safety Executive, *Silicosis and Coal Workers' Pneumoconiosis Statistics in Great Britain, 2023* (22 November 2023), 4, www.hse.gov.uk/statistics/assets/docs/pneumoconiosis-and-silicosis.pdf.

40 Between 2013 and 2021, over 1,000 men died from coal-related lung disease in England, Scotland and Wales. Annual deaths from non-asbestosis pneumoconiosis remained relatively constant over the decade leading up to 2019, with an average of around 130 deaths per year. There were 63 deaths in 2021 and 73 in 2020, with figures possibly affected by the

coronavirus pandemic. See: HSE, *Silicosis and Coal Workers' Pneumoconiosis Statistics in Great Britain, 2023*, 5; HSE, 'Table DCO1: Annual Deaths due to Occupationally Related Lung Disease, Other Than Mesothelioma and Asbestosis in Great Britain, 1993–2021', data table, (23 Nov. 2022), www.hse.gov.uk/statistics/tables/index.htm, accessed 5 Mar. 2024.

41 Accompanying notes in: A. L. Lloyd, ed., *Come All Ye Bold Miners: Ballads & Songs of the Coalfields* (London, 1978), 349.

42 See: J. Ghedi, 'Ah Cud Hew,' *In the Furrows of Common Place*, [CD], UK, Basin Rock, B08GLWD2CF, 2021.

43 Jack Drum Arts, 'Who We Are', n.d., www.jackdrum.co.uk/whoweare, accessed 4 Oct. 2023.

44 E. Pickford, 'Ah Cud Hew' (*c.* 1971).

13. Fight Like Hell for the Living

1 R. MacNeil, 'Working Man', *Part of the Mystery* [LP], Canada, Big Pond Records, 1981.

2 'Gresford' or 'The Miners' Hymn' was written by miner turned composer Robert Saint in memory of the disaster that took place at Gresford Colliery near Wrexham, North East Wales, in September 1934, when 266 miners were killed in an underground explosion and fire. The hymn is played each year at the Durham Miners' Gala as well as at other mining events across the country. The 'Concierto de Aranjuez' composed by Joaquín Rodrigo in 1939, appears in the 1996 film *Brassed Off*, in which the miners refer to it as the 'Concierto de Orange Juice'.

3 See: A Ramsay, 'On Brass Bands and Brexit; Culture and Cuts: The Case of Shirebrook', *Open Democracy*, 15 Aug. 2017, www.

opendemocracy.net/en/opendemocracyuk/on-brass-bands-and-brexit-culture-and-culture-war-case-of-shirebrook, accessed 6 Oct. 2023.

4 See: 'Former Mining Communities "Still Scarred by Past"', *BBC News*, 16 Oct. 2019, www.bbc.co.uk/news/uk-england-50069336, accessed 15 Oct. 2023; C. Beatty, S. Fothergill and T. Gore, *The State of the Coalfields 2019: Economic and Social Conditions in the Former Coalfields of England, Scotland and Wales* (Jul. 2019), Coalfields Regeneration Trust, www.coalfields-regen.org.uk/wp-content/uploads/2019/10/The-State-of-the-Coalfields-2019.pdf. For examples of drug use and social deprivation in the former coalfields, see: Hansard, HC Deb, 2 Jul. 1999, Vol. 334, Col. 592; M. Wainwright, 'Ex-Coalfields Ravaged by Heroin Use', *Guardian*, 18 Oct. 2002, www.theguardian.com/society/2002/oct/18/drugsandalcohol.politics, accessed 2 Mar. 2023; M. Wainwright, 'Former Pit Towns Say No to Drug Addiction', *Guardian*, 12 Jul. 2004, www.theguardian.com/society/2004/jul/12/drugsandalcohol.drugs, accessed 2 Mar. 2023; 'Heroin Usage "Twice in Valleys"', *BBC News*, 31 Aug. 2007, news.bbc.co.uk/1/hi/wales/6971048.stm, accessed 2 Mar. 2023. For a study of political apathy in the former coalfields, see: M. Abreu and C. Jones, 'The Shadow of the Pithead. Understanding Social and Political Attitudes in Former Coal Mining Communities in the UK', *Applied Geography*, 131 (2021), doi.org/10.1016/j.apgeog.2021.102448. In 2022, 2021 and 2020, the highest suicide rate was in the North East of England, and in 2019 it was in Yorkshire and The Humber. Around three quarters of suicides were males. See: Office for National Statistics, 'Suicides in England and Wales: 2022 Registrations', Statistical Bulletin, 19 Dec. 2023, www.ons.gov.uk/peoplepopulationandcommu

nity/birthsdeathsandmarriages/deaths/bulletins/suicidesintheunitedkingdom/2022registrations.

5 G. Faulconbridge, K. MacLellan, '"I'll Make Britain Great Again", PM Johnson Says, Echoing Trump', *Reuters,* 25 Jul. 2019, www.reuters.com/article/us-britain-eu-idUSKCN1UK0OG, accessed 15 Oct. 2023. For a discussion of coalfield voting in the Brexit referendum of 2016 and the general election of 2019, see: Chapter 15: 'The People Speak Out', in: H. Beynon and R. Hudson, *The Shadow of the Mine: Coal and the End of Industrial Britain* (London, 2021), 315–33.

6 See: E. J. Gorn, 'The History of Mother Jones', *Mother Jones* (May/June 2001), www.motherjones.com/about/history/, accessed 6 Mar. 2024.

7 D. Thomas, 'Do Not Go Gentle into That Good Night' (1951)

Illustration Credits

5	©Amgueddfa Cymru – Museum Wales.
6	Image by author.
31	© The Francis Frith Collection.
40	Courtesy of Beamish Museum.
41	Courtesy of Beamish Museum.
56	Photo taken by Jack Brown of Burnopfield. Courtesy of Beamish Museum.
72	Courtesy of Durham Bannermakers.
76	Courtesy of the National Coal Mining Museum for England.
77	Image by author.
92	Courtesy of The Coventry Evening Telegraph/ Reach plc.
94	Courtesy of Fiona Matthewson/Art UK.
98	Private collection.
106	Image by author.
107	Image by author.
114	Courtesy of Out Of The Blue Artifacts.com.
116	© Patrick Ward. Courtesy of the National Coal Mining Museum for England.
124	Courtesy of Stoke Sentinel/Reach plc.
145	Image by author.
150	Private collection.
159	© Martin Jenkinson Image Library. All rights reserved. DACS/Artimage 2024.
168	© John Harris/reportdigital.co.uk.

172 © Martin Mayer/reportdigital.co.uk
202 Image by author.
203 Image by author.
204 Courtesy of Brian Morley and the Nottinghamshire Mining Museum.
211 Courtesy of The National Archives.
236 © Homer Sykes / Alamy Stock Photo.
244 Courtesy of Medway Urban Explorer.
247 Image by author.
249 Image by author.
254 Courtesy of Glamorgan Archives.
268 © Vivien Kent / Alamy Stock Photo.
272 Image by author.